T0324275

INTRODUCTION TO EVOLUTIONARY INFORMATICS

INTRODUCTION TO
EVOLUTIONARY
INFORMATICS

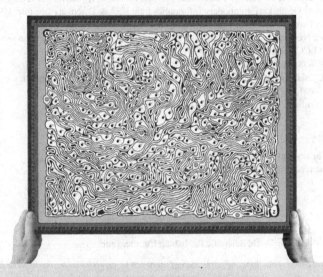

Robert J Marks II
Baylor University, USA

William A Dembski
Evolutionary Informatics Lab, USA

Winston Ewert
Evolutionary Informatics Lab, USA

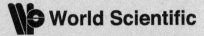
World Scientific

NEW JERSEY · LONDON · SINGAPORE · BEIJING · SHANGHAI · HONG KONG · TAIPEI · CHENNAI · TOKYO

Published by

World Scientific Publishing Co. Pte. Ltd.
5 Toh Tuck Link, Singapore 596224
USA office: 27 Warren Street, Suite 401-402, Hackensack, NJ 07601
UK office: 57 Shelton Street, Covent Garden, London WC2H 9HE

Library of Congress Cataloging-in-Publication Data
Names: Marks, Robert J., II (Robert Jackson), 1950– author. |
    Dembski, William A., 1960– author. | Ewert, Winston, author.
Title: Introduction to evolutionary informatics / Robert J. Marks II (Baylor University, USA),
    William A. Dembski (Evolutionary Informatics Lab, USA & Discovery Institute, USA) &
    Winston Ewert (Evolutionary Informatics Lab, USA).
Description: New Jersey : World Scientific, 2016. | Includes bibliographical references and index.
Identifiers: LCCN 2016014235| ISBN 9789813142138 (hc : alk. paper) |
    ISBN 9789813142145 (pbk : alk. paper)
Subjects: LCSH: Evolutionary computation. | Information technology--Mathematics.
Classification: LCC TA347.E96 M37 2016 | DDC 006.3/823--dc23
LC record available at https://lccn.loc.gov/2016014235

British Library Cataloguing-in-Publication Data
A catalogue record for this book is available from the British Library.

Desk Editor: Suraj Kumar

Typeset by Stallion Press
Email: enquiries@stallionpress.com

Printed in Singapore

CONTENTS

PREFACE

"My theory of evolution is that Darwin was adopted"

Steven Wright

Science has made great strides in modeling space, time, mass, and energy but has done little to definitively model the obvious meaningful information ubiquitous in our universe. Today, information theory is used to measure the storage capacity of a Blu-ray disc or for describing the bandwidth of a Wi-Fi connection. Yet the difficulty associated with the *design* of the Blu-ray contents and the *meaning* of data transmitted across the Wi-Fi connection are not addressed. New results in information theory now allow meaning and design difficulty to be measured. Explaining the foundation of this exciting theory at an accessible level is our goal in *Introduction to Evolutionary Informatics*.

Evolutionary models to date point strongly to the necessity of design. Indeed, all current models of evolution require information from an external designer in order to work. All current evolutionary models simply do not work without tapping into an external information source.

Foundation

This monograph's contents stem from the seminal works of one of your humble co-authors, William A. Dembski,[1] and subsequent edited volumes.[2] The authors have penned numerous papers and book chapters that contain the foundational development of material for this monograph.[3] Links to many of these papers are available on our website EvoInfo.org. In certain places in this monograph we have lifted prose and figures from some of these papers, in some cases verbatim. We have attempted in all cases to make specific reference, but might have missed some.

As witnessed by this body of work, the material in this monograph stands on firm ground. Peer-reviewed papers, though, are written at a level where only dedicated nerds can understand them. This monograph serves two purposes. The first is explanation of evolutionary informatics at a level accessible to the well-informed reader. Secondly we believe *a la* Romans 1:20 and like verses that the implications of this work in the apologetics of perception of meaning are profound.

The Math Herein and the † Symbol

Although we have attempted to minimize the mathematics in this book, its use in some areas is necessary. In such cases, we have isolated the math and give as clear an explanation of the underlying reasoning as possible. The math material can be understood with rudimentary knowledge of

- simple logarithms,
- elementary probability,
- elementary concepts in statistics such as averages (or sample means) being estimates of distribution means,
- numbers represented in binary (base 2), and
- simple Boolean logic operations such as AND, OR, NOT, NAND, NOR, XOR, etc.

To aid those who wish to read the book more quickly or who are not interested in mathematical details, sections marked with a dagger (†) can be skipped. Some mathematical details are also relegated to footnotes and are also marked with a dagger.

Footnotes and Endnotes

Generally notes at the end of the chapters are references whereas footnotes contain elaboration on the chapter story. For fast or casual reading, the footnotes can be skipped.

Chapter Summaries

Chapter 1: Introduction

Summary: Rather than placing a theory or ideology on the throne like a Queen as scientists and philosophers often do, engineers make the Queen come down from the throne and scrub the floor. And if she doesn't work, she is fired.

Scientists once thought evolution models running on fast computers would someday confirm evolution. The opposite has happened. Prophets of computer-based demonstration of undirected evolution failed to take into account Borel's law and the Conservation of Information. Borel's law dictates that events described by a sufficiently small probability are impossible events. For example, there is a small probability that you will experience quantum tunneling through the chair in which you sit. The probability is so small, however, that we can categorize the event as impossible.

Chapter 2:   Information: What is It?

Summary: Information is neither matter nor energy. It stands as an independent component of nature.

The term information is typically not well defined, whether used in casual conversation or in a journal article. Shannon information theory is perhaps the best-known mathematical model of information. Shannon noted the obvious: His model of information is narrow and not applicable to the broad range of possible definitions of information.

Kolmogorov–Chaitin–Solomonov (KCS) information theory, also known as algorithmic information theory, is another popular information model. However, both the Shannon and KCS models fail to model information in the sense of measuring the meaning or the design difficulty associated with an object.

Chapter 3:   Design Search in Evolution and the Requirement
of Intelligence

Summary: Engineering design is invariably an iterative search guided by the domain expertise of the designer. WD-40 took 40 trials to design and Formula 409 required 409 tries. That's how these products got the numerical part of their names.

The anatomy of a search is illustrated by a chef's design of a good pancake recipe. The important components of design are identified, including the role of domain expertise and the curse of dimensionality that can quickly make uninformed designs impossible.

Analysis of NASA's design of an antenna using evolutionary search shows that the design domain expertise in evolutionary design is rich and the search problem was not that difficult.

Trade-offs are necessary in design. Designing a car that is both inexpensive and safe requires one criterion to be balanced against the other. Cheap cars aren't safe and safe cars aren't cheap. More than not, global optimality necessitates component suboptimality. Ill-informed critical claims of suboptimal design in biological systems is clarified with a discussion of the trade-offs inherent in any multi-objective design.

Chapter 4: Determinism in Randomness

Summary: It may sound like an oxymoron, but there are elements of determinism in randomness. If, for example, a fair coin is repeatedly flipped thousands of times, the proportion of heads will always approach the deterministic value of one half. In a similar manner, many programs purporting to demonstrate Darwinian evolution are invariably written to converge to a specific deterministic outcome most of the time. As with the steel ball in a pinball machine, different paths can be taken in every trial, but the steel ball always ends up going down the little hole underneath the flippers.

Bernoulli's Principle of Insufficient Reason (PrOIR), although fancy sounding, simply says that the chance of winning a lottery with 1000 tickets sold is one chance in 1000 if you have purchased only one ticket. Equal probability is assigned to every possible outcome in the drawing. Bernoulli's PrOIR is used in the modeling of random blind search.

Basener's ceiling imposes a severe restriction on any evolutionary process. It demands that any evolutionary computer search will reach a point where further improvement is not possible. It is common sense that an evolutionary program written to design an antenna will not continue to evolve to the point where, for example, the program learns to play chess. The theory behind this limitation of evolutionary processes is firmly established by Basener's ceiling.

Chapter 5: Conservation of Information in Computer Search

Summary: We now have the tools needed to present the Law of Conservation of Information as illustrated by the No Free Lunch Theorem. The No Free Lunch theorem dictates that, when seeking to iteratively design an object, one procedure is as good on the average as any other procedure if the designer has absolutely no domain expertise. The No Free Lunch Theorem published in 1997 by Wolpert and Macready raised the eyebrows of the machine intelligence community who often placed one search algorithm against another to see which was best. The results of that competition, it turns out, said nothing about the effectiveness of one search algorithm over another. It only said that one search algorithm was better on the problem being examined. The performance ranking was not necessarily valid for other problems.

The No Free Lunch Theorem was also the inspiration behind Bill Dembski's book with a similar title.

If no domain expertise is available, we expect a random search to work as well as any other. The problem is that random searches quickly exhaust the probabilistic resources in the universe. Even the probability resources of a multiverse are insufficient to generate the table of contents for the first chapter of this book by blind chance. Design requires intelligence.

An evolutionary search can be made better than average by the use of domain expertise. Fewer iterations are required to achieve a successful design. Active information measures the degree to which domain expertise helps in a search. Active information is illustrated by easily understood examples such as the Cracker Barrel puzzle and the game show Let's Make a Deal.

The No Free Lunch Theorem has been claimed to be violated by the so-called process of coevolution. We straightforwardly show that this is not the case.

Lastly we broach the topic of a search-for-a-search. If all search procedures work the same on average, could we not have the computer search for a good search that works better than average? The answer turns out to be an emphatic NO! A search-for-a-search is shown to be exponentially more difficult than the search itself.

Chapter 6: Analysis of Some Biologically Motivated Evolutionary Models

Summary: There are a number of computer programs that purport to demonstrate undirected Darwinian evolution. The most celebrated is the Avida evolution program whose performance was touted by evolution proponents at the 2004–2005 Kitzmiller versus Dover Area School District trial. This trial examined the appropriateness of teaching intelligent design. Conservation of information, discovered and published five years later, soundly discredits Avida.

Since Avida is attempting to solve a moderately hard problem, the writer of the program must have infused domain expertise into the code. We identify the sources and measure the resulting infused active information. Avida is shown to contain a lot of clutter used to slow down its performance. When the clutter is removed the program converges to the solution more quickly.

Another evolutionary program discredited through the identification and measurement of active information is dubbed EV.

Once a source of knowledge is identified in an evolutionary program, active information can be mined in different ways by using other search programs. For both Avida and EV, alternative search programs are shown to generate the same results as the evolutionary search. The computational burden of the evolutionary approach in both cases is significantly higher.

On EvoInfo.org, we have developed online GUIs (graphical user interfaces) to illustrate the performance of both Avida and EV. There is also a GUI that allows experimental exploration of Richard Dawkins's famous Weasel search algorithm. The performance and use of these GUIs is sufficiently explained so that the reader, if so motivated, can go online and try the experiment themselves.

Lastly, a model proposed by Gregory Chaitin (the C in KCS) in his 2013 book *Proving Darwin: Making Biology Mathematical* is analyzed. Chaitin's model, built in the beautiful and surrealistic world of algorithmic information theory, is shown to be overflowing with active information. Like other computer programs written to demonstrate undirected Darwinian evolution, it works only because it was designed to work.

Chapter 7:   Measuring Meaning: Algorithmic Specified Complexity

Summary: Specified complexity has been proposed in the intelligent design literature as a method of assessing the degree to which an object is designed or has meaning. Algorithmic specified complexity (ASC) measures this property in bits.

Algorithmic specified complexity assumes that meaning is based on context. A picture of my family has more meaning to me than to someone who has never met my family. A page of kanji characters has more meaning to a Japanese reader than to someone who doesn't know Japanese.

Winning hands in the game of poker is an example. For a deck of 52 distinct cards, there are 2,869,682 possible five card hands. Some hands, like a royal flush, are more meaningful than others, e.g. a pair of twos. We show that the ASC of a royal flush is a hefty 16 bits whereas that of a hand with one pair is zero.

Another illustrative example deals with snowflakes. Although a single individual snowflake displays a high degree of complexity, high complexity events happen all the time. We show that the ASC of two different snowflakes is near zero. But two identical snowflakes have very large ASC.

Lastly, the ASC of objects in Conway's cellular automata Game of Life is calculated. Invented in 1970, interest in the Game of Life continues to grow. Today there are online user groups where intricate and complicated objects are constructed using Conway's four simple rules. As expected, large complex objects are assigned high values of ASC whereas simple objects that have a high chance of being produced randomly have low values of ASC.

Chapter 8:   Intelligent Design & Artificial Intelligence

The fields of *artificial intelligence* (AI) and *intelligent* design (ID) share a variation of the word "intelligent." There is a deeper relationship. Strong AI using computers has been largely dethroned. Roger Penrose argues convincingly that human intelligence will never be achieved by a Turing machine (i.e. a computer). His argument, backed by the astonishing incompleteness theorem of Kurt Gödel, is based on the inability of computers to be creative beyond what they are told.

We see the same thing in models that purport to demonstrate Darwinian evolution. Again and again, such models have been shown to work only because the programmer has infused information into the process. And, of course, these models of Darwinian evolution are run on a Turing machine.

Darwinian evolution cannot create information. Neither can a computer. For humans, Penrose believes the answer might lie in quantum phenomena resident in our neurons. Alternatively, in both AI and ID, creation of information can be explained by externally applied intelligence.

Notes

1. William A. Dembski, *The Design Inference: Eliminating Chance through Small Probabilities* (Cambridge University Press, 1998).
   William A. Dembski, *Intelligent Design: The Bridge between Science and Theology* (InterVarsity Press, Downer's Grove, Illinois, 1999).
   William A. Dembski, *No Free Lunch: Why Specified Complexity Cannot Be Purchased without Intelligence* (Rowman & Littlefield, Lanham, Md, 2002).
   William A. Dembski, *Being as Communion: A Metaphysics of Information* (Ashgate Publishing Ltd., 2014).
2. Bruce Gordon and William Dembski, editors, *The Nature of Nature* (Wilmington, Del, 2011).
   R.J. Marks II, M.J. Behe, W.A. Dembski, B.L. Gordon, J.C. Sanford, editors, *Biological Information — New Perspectives* (Cornell University, World Scientific, Singapore, 2013).
3. William A. Dembski and Robert J. Marks II, "Conservation of Information in Search: Measuring the Cost of Success." *IEEE Transactions on Systems, Man and Cybernetics A, Systems and Humans*, vol. 39, #5, September 2009, pp. 1051–1061.
   William A. Dembski and R.J. Marks II, "Bernoulli's Principle of Insufficient Reason and Conservation of Information in Computer Search." *Proceedings of the 2009 IEEE International Conference on Systems, Man, and Cybernetics.* San Antonio, TX, USA — October 2009, pp. 2647–2652.
   Winston Ewert, William A. Dembski and R.J. Marks II, "Evolutionary Synthesis of Nand Logic: Dissecting a Digital Organism." *Proceedings of the 2009 IEEE International Conference on Systems, Man, and Cybernetics.* San Antonio, TX, USA — October 2009, pp. 3047–3053.
   Winston Ewert, George Montañez, William A. Dembski, Robert J. Marks II, "Efficient Per Query Information Extraction from a Hamming Oracle." *Proceedings of the 42nd Meeting of the Southeastern Symposium on System Theory.* IEEE, University of Texas at Tyler, March 7–9, 2010, pp. 290–229.
   William A. Dembski and Robert J. Marks II, "The Search for a Search: Measuring the Information Cost of Higher Level Search." *J Adv Comput Intell Intelligent Inf*, 14(5), pp. 475–486 (2010).

George Montañez, Winston Ewert, William A. Dembski, and Robert J. Marks II, "Vivisection of the ev Computer Organism: Identifying Sources of Active Information." *Bio-Complexity*, 2010(3), pp. 1–6 (December 2010).

William A. Dembski and Robert J. Marks II, "Life's Conservation Law: Why Darwinian Evolution Cannot Create Biological Information." In Bruce Gordon and William Dembski, eds., *The Nature of Nature* (ISI Books, Wilmington, Del., 2011), pp. 360–399.

Winston Ewert, William A. Dembski, and Robert J. Marks II, "Climbing the Steiner Tree—Sources of Active Information in a Genetic Algorithm for Solving the Euclidean Steiner Tree Problem." *Bio-Complexity*, 2012(1), pp. 1–14 (April, 2012).

Winston Ewert, William A. Dembski, Ann K. Gauger, and Robert J. Marks II, "Time and Information in Evolution." *Bio-Complexity*, 2012(4) 7 pages. doi:10.5048/BIO-C.2012.4.

Winston Ewert, William A. Dembski and Robert J. Marks II, "On the Improbability of Algorithmically Specified Complexity." *Proceedings of the 2013 IEEE 45th Southeastern Symposium on Systems Theory (SSST)*, Baylor University, March 11, 2013, pp. 68–70,

Jon Roach, Winston Ewert, Robert J. Marks II and Benjamin B. Thompson, "Unexpected Emergent Behaviors from Elementary Swarms." *Proceedings of the 2013 IEEE 45th Southeastern Symposium on Systems Theory (SSST)*, Baylor University, March 11, 2013, pp. 41–50.

Winston Ewert, William A. Dembski and Robert J. Marks II, "Conservation of Information in Relative Search Performance." *Proceedings of the 2013 IEEE 45th Southeastern Symposium on Systems Theory (SSST)*, Baylor University, March 11, 2013, pp. 41–50.

Albert R. Yu, Benjamin B. Thompson, and Robert J. Marks II, "Competitive evolution of tactical multiswarm dynamics." *IEEE Transactions on Systems, Man and Cybernetics: Systems*, 43(3), pp. 563–569 (May 2013).

Robert J. Marks II, "Information Theory & Biology: Introductory Comments." In *Biological Information — New Perspectives*, edited by R.J. Marks II, M.J. Behe, W.A. Dembski, B.L. Gordon, and J.C. Sanford (World Scientific, Singapore, 2013) pp. 1–10.

William A. Dembski, Winston Ewert, Robert J. Marks II, "A General Theory of Information Cost Incurred by Successful Search." In *Biological Information — New Perspectives*, edited by R.J. Marks II, M.J. Behe, W.A. Dembski, B.L. Gordon, and J.C. Sanford (World Scientific, Singapore, 2013) pp. 26–63.

W. Ewert, William A. Dembski, and Robert J. Marks II, "Tierra: The Character of Adaptation." In *Biological Information — New Perspectives*, edited by

R.J. Marks II, M.J. Behe, W.A. Dembski, B.L. Gordon, and J.C. Sanford (World Scientific, Singapore, 2013) pp. 105–138.

G. Montañez, Robert J. Marks II, Jorge Fernandez, and John C. Sanford, "Multiple Overlapping Genetic Codes Profoundly Reduce the Probability of Beneficial Mutation." In *Biological Information — New Perspectives*, edited by R.J. Marks II, M.J. Behe, W.A. Dembski, B.L. Gordon, and J.C. Sanford (World Scientific, Singapore, 2013), pp. 139–167.

W. Ewert, William A. Dembski, and Robert J. Marks II, "Algorithmic specified complexity." In *Engineering and the Ultimate: An Interdisciplinary Investigation of Order and Design in Nature and Craft*, edited by J. Bartlett, D. Halsmer, and M. Hall (Blyth Institute Press, 2014), pp. 131–149.

W. Ewert, Robert J. Marks II, Benjamin B. Thompson, and Al. Yu, "Evolutionary inversion of swarm emergence using disjunctive combs control." *IEEE Transactions on Systems, Man and Cybernetics: Systems*, 43(5), pp. 1063–1076 (September 2013).

W. Ewert, William A. Dembski, and Robert J. Marks II, "Algorithmic Specified Complexity in the Game of Life." *IEEE Transactions on Systems, Man and Cybernetics: Systems*, 45(4), pp. 584–594 (April 2015).

W. Ewert, William A. Dembski, and Robert J. Marks II, "Measuring meaningful information in images: algorithmic specified complexity." IET Computer Vision (2015). DOI: 10.1049/iet-cvi.2014.0141.

ABOUT THE AUTHORS

 **Robert J. Marks II** is Distinguished Professor of Engineering in the Department of Engineering at Baylor University, USA. Marks is Fellow of both IEEE and The Optical Society of America. His consulting activities include Microsoft Corporation, DARPA, and Boeing Computer Services. His contributions include the Zhao-Atlas-Marks (ZAM) time-frequency distribution in the field of signal processing, and the Cheung–Marks theorem in Shannon sampling theory. He is listed as one of the "The 50 Most Influential Scientists in the World Today" By TheBestSchools.org. (2014).

Marks's research has been funded by organizations such as the National Science Foundation, General Electric, Southern California Edison, the Air Force Office of Scientific Research, the Office of Naval Research, the United States Naval Research Laboratory, the Whitaker Foundation, Boeing Defense, the National Institutes of Health, the Jet Propulsion Lab, the Army Research Office, and NASA. His Books include *Handbook of Fourier Analysis and Its Applications* (Oxford University Press), *Introduction to Shannon Sampling and Interpolation Theory* (Springer Verlag), and *Neural Smithing: Supervised Learning in Feedforward Artificial Neural Networks* (MIT Press) with Russ Reed. Marks has edited/co-edited five other volumes in fields such as power engineering, neural networks, and fuzzy logic. He was instrumental in defining the discipline of Computational intelligence (CI) and is a coeditor of the first book using CI in the title: *Computational*

Intelligence: Imitating Life (IEEE Press, 1994). His authored/coauthored book chapters include nine papers reprinted in collections of classic papers. Other book chapters include contributions to Michael Arbib's *The Handbook of Brain Theory and Neural Networks* (MIT Press, 1996), and Michael Licona *et al.*'s *Evidence for God* (Baker Books, 2010). Marks served for 17 years as the faculty advisor for Campus Crusade for Christ at the University of Washington, Seattle. His Erdős-Bacon is five.

William A. Dembski is Senior Research Scientist at the Evolutionary Informatics Lab in McGregor, Texas; and also an entrepreneur developing educational websites and software. He holds a B.A. in psychology, M.S. in statistics, Ph.D. in philosophy, and a Ph.D. in mathematics (awarded in 1988 by the University of Chicago, Chicago, Illinois, USA), and an M.Div. degree from Princeton Theological Seminary (1996, New Jersey, USA). Dembski's work experience includes being an Associate Research Professor with the Conceptual Foundations of Science, Baylor University, Waco, Texas, USA; where he also headed the first intelligent design think-tank at a major research university: The Michael Polanyi Center. He has taught at Northwestern University, Evanston, Illinois, USA; the University of Notre Dame, Notre Dame, Indiana, USA; and the University of Dallas, Irving, Texas, USA. He has done postdoctoral work in mathematics with the Massachusetts Institute of Technology, Cambridge, USA; in physics with the University of Chicago, USA; and in computer science with Princeton University, Princeton, New Jersey, USA. He is a Mathematician and Philosopher. He has held National Science Foundation graduate and postdoctoral fellowships, and has published articles in mathematics, engineering, philosophy, and theology journals and is the author/editor of more than twenty books. In *The Design Inference: Eliminating Chance Through Small Probabilities* (Cambridge University Press, 1998), he examined the design argument in a post-Darwinian context and analyzed the connections linking chance, probability, and intelligent causation. The sequel to *The Design Inference* critiques Darwinian and other naturalistic accounts of evolution; it is titled *No Free Lunch: Why Specified Complexity Cannot Be Purchased Without Intelligence* (Rowman & Littlefield, 2002). He has edited several influential anthologies, including *Uncommon Dissent: Intellectuals Who Find Darwinism Unconvincing* (ISI, 2004) and *Debating Design: From Darwin to DNA* (Cambridge University Press, 2004, coedited with M. Ruse). His newest book is *Being as Communion: A Metaphysics of Information* (Ashgate Pub. Co., 2014). His area of interest in intelligent design has grown in the wider culture; he has assumed the role of public intellectual. In addition to lecturing around the world at colleges and universities, he has been interviewed extensively on radio and television. His work has been cited in numerous newspaper and magazine articles, including three front-page stories in *The New York Times* as well as the August 15, 2005 *Time Magazine* cover story on intelligent design. He has appeared on the BBC, NPR (*Diane Rehm*, etc.), PBS (*Inside the Law* with Jack Ford and *Uncommon Knowledge* with Peter Robinson), CSPAN2, CNN, Fox News, ABC Nightline, and the *Daily Show* with Jon Stewart.

Winston Ewert is currently a Software Engineer in Vancouver, Canada. He is a Senior Research Scientist at the Evolutionary Informatics Lab. Ewert holds a Ph.D. from Baylor University, Waco, Texas, USA. He has written a number of papers relating to search, information, and complexity including studies of computer models purporting to describe Darwinian evolution and developing information theoretic models to measure specified complexity. Dr. Ewert is a frequent contributor to EvolutionNews.org.

1

INTRODUCTION

"The honor of mathematics requires us to come up with a mathematical theory of evolution and either prove that Darwin was wrong or right!"

Gregory Chaitin[1]

In order to establish solid credibility, a science should be backed by mathematics and models. Even some soft sciences, such as finance, offer compelling mathematical and computer models that win Nobel prizes. The purpose of *evolutionary informatics* is to scrutinize the mathematics and models underlying evolution and the science of design.

There is a recognized difference between models and reality. A mantra popular with engineers is: "In theory, theory and reality are the same. In reality they are not." Models in physics have been shown to display incredible experimental agreement with theory. But what of Darwinian evolution? There have been numerous models proposed for Darwinian evolution. Some are examined in this monograph. Each, however, is intelligently designed and the degree to which they are designed can be measured, in bits, using *active information*. If these models do indeed capture the Darwinian process, then we must conclude that evolution is guided by an intelligence. Without the application of this intelligence, the evolutionary models simply do not work. The computational resources of our universe and, indeed, the current model of the multiverse proposed by string theory are insufficient to allow the small probabilities of evolution by pure chance. The participation of a designer is mandatory.

Our work was initially motivated by attempts of others to describe Darwinian evolution by computer simulation or mathematical models.[2] The authors of these papers purport that their work relates to biological evolution. We show repeatedly that the proposed models all require inclusion of significant knowledge about the problem being solved. If a goal of a model is specified in advance, that's not Darwinian evolution: it's intelligent design. So ironically, these models of evolution purported to demonstrate Darwinian evolution necessitate an intelligent designer. The programmer's contribution to success, dubbed *active information*, is measured in bits.

Mount Rushmore's carved busts of United States presidents indicate design when compared to, say, Mount Fuji. The Search for Extraterrestrial Intelligence (SETI) assumes that signals received from space containing intelligence can be detected. A model to measure meaningful information from observations is the topic of Chapter 7.

1.1   The Queen of Scientists & Engineers

Engineers don't brag enough. Scientists did not put man on the moon. Engineers did. Scientists are not responsible for the Internet. Engineers are. The latest medical breakthrough is most likely the work of an engineer, not a scientist or a medical doctor. And from whose viewpoint is it better to address intelligent design? Engineers design things.

The engineer's job is to understand science and mathematics, apply this understanding to reality, and make things work.

There are fundamental philosophical differences between engineers and scientists. Scientists are generally more interested in simply understanding nature. They formulate models, often beautiful and powerful models, and scrutinize them. Once vetted by the acceptance of most, the models are placed on a throne like a queen where they are worshiped. It often takes a major coup to overthrow a scientist's ensconced dogma. Engineers, on the other hand, make the queen come down from the throne and scrub the floor. If she works, we use her talents. And if she doesn't work, we fire her.

The story of the queen describes this monograph. We analyze the computer models of evolution offered by scientists and conclude they work only because the programmers designed them to work. There is no creation of information or spontaneous increase in meaningful complexity. The law of conservation of information precludes it. We are able to examine the proposed computer models, identify the source of active information, and show that the evolutionary process, although successful, is a poor way to use available resources. Since the proposed models do not display characteristics of undirected Darwinian search, the reigning queen of undirected Darwinian evolution must be given a pink slip.

1.2 Science and Models

Science requires explanative models. Darwinian evolution, using the repeated processes of mutation and survival of the fittest, looks on the surface to be a science well positioned for modeling using probabilistically based simulation.

Repeatedly observable laws, such as Newton's law of motion or the laws of thermodynamics, can be confirmed by repeating experiments again and again. Such laws are said to be formed by the application of *inductive inference*. Non-repeatable phenomena cannot be modeled this way. The theory of the creation of the universe from the Big Bang is an example. In such cases, *abductive inference* or *inference to the best explanation* is used to establish laws. Abductive inference has certainly not been a hindrance in forming a rich theoretical explanation of the Big Bang or the science of geology.

The entirety of Darwinian evolution theory over eons of life on earth cannot be repeated in the laboratory. We have, though, some supportive repeatable science to help. Dogs and horses can be bred, bacteria strains lose their vulnerability to antibiotics and the beaks of finches vary in accordance with food sources on the Galapagos Islands. Cannot we extrapolate a viable model of evolution from these phenomena? Those who support Darwinian evolution say yes. Mathematically, though, extrapolation models of temporal processes can be useless. Small perturbations in observations can result in wildly varying extrapolation results.[a,3] Chapter 6 contains a discussion of published models whose proponents feel they have a successful model of Darwinian evolution. They have not. At best, they have

---

[a]† Example characteristics of extrapolation and forecasting include ill-conditioned and ill-posed processes. An ill-conditioned process is one in which small changes in the observed data can result in enormous variations in extrapolation. An ill-posed process is the extreme of this. No matter how little the known portion of the process is perturbed, the variation in the extrapolation error becomes unknowable in the sense that it cannot be bounded.

guided the goal-seeking breeding of a thoroughbred horse from available stock.

1.2.1   *Computer models*

The invention of the computer in the mid-20th century gave rise to expectations in the science of evolution. It was hoped the evolutionary process could, for the first time, be modeled and demonstrated by a computer program. Evolutionary computation was founded on the assumption that, unlike glacially slow biological wetware, the speed of a computer would allow sufficient generations to conclusively demonstrate Darwinian evolution. In 1962, Nils Barricelli wrote[4]

> "The Darwinian idea that evolution takes place by random hereditary changes and selection has from the beginning been handicapped by the fact that no proper test has been found to decide whether such evolution was possible and how it would develop under controlled conditions."

In the mid-1960s J. L. Crosby[5] looked to the computer of the future as a remedy for this condition.

> "In general, it is usually impossible or impracticable to test hypotheses about evolution in a particular species by the deliberate setting up of controlled experiments with living organisms of that species. We can attempt to partially to get around this difficulty by constructing [computer] models representing the evolutionary system we wish to study, and use these to test at least the theoretical validity of our ideas."

1.2.2   *The improbable and the impossible*

Contrary to expectation, computer science research has revealed numerous problems for a model of evolution without an intelligent designer. The principle of conservation of information shows that evolutionary processes on average are incapable of generating information. Rather, they are restricted to extracting information from a source of knowledge. The success of any evolutionary process is not due to any magic in the process itself, but rather to the creative knowledge available to that process. Computer simulation of evolution has demonstrated that information sources are created by programmers exploiting their knowledge of problem spaces, a process with no analog in a non-teleological world.

Evolutionary models are stochastic, so one might argue "Sure, it's not probable. But it's possible!" This is right in the sense that all probable things are possible but not all possible things are probable or, in the contrapositive sense, everything impossible is improbable but improbable events need not be impossible. But, like many contrasts, there comes a point where the improbable and impossible blur together and, within the resources of our finite universe (or even the hypothesized multiverse), an event can be so improbable as to be accurately labeled as impossible. This proposition is commonly referred to as Borel's Law.[6] When I stand, is it possible part of my foot will experience quantum tunneling through the floor? Yes. But the event is so improbable that I can stand and sit every picosecond since the creation of the universe and my toes will never experience quantum tunneling. We argue that this technically possible event is, indeed, impossible in practice. Here's another example. Suppose I randomly choose a billion atoms in the known universe and, without consulting me, you choose a billion. In the strictest of senses, it is possible that the billion atoms you choose are the same as mine. But the probability of matching atoms is so small we could both choose atoms over and over for trillions of years and there would be no chance our billion atoms would exactly match. A successful matching is impossible with the probability resources available in our universe—or even the largest multiverse predicted by string theorists.

Could the biology we observe today have been created by undirected Darwinian evolution? There may be a minuscule probability but, like the examples of quantum tunneling and atom choosing, the development is impossible. Evolutionary informatics shows the observed universe (or a multiverse) is not large enough nor old enough to allow it.

Notes

1. G.J. Chaitin, *Proving Darwin: Making Biology Mathematical* (Pantheon, 2012).
2. H.S. Wilf and W.J. Ewens, "There's plenty of time for evolution." *P Natl Acad Sci*, 107, pp. 22454–22456 (2010).

   R.E. Lenski, C. Ofria, R.T. Pennock and C. Adami, "The evolutionary origin of complex features." *Nature*, 423, pp. 139–144 (2003).

   T.D. Schneider, "Evolution of biological information." *Nucleic Acids Res*, 28, pp. 2794–2799 (2000).

R. Dawkins, *The Blind Watchmaker: Why the Evidence of Evolution Reveals a Universe Without Design* (Norton, New York, 1996).

D. Thomas, "War of the Weasels: An evolutionary algorithm beats intelligent design." *Skeptical Inquirer*, 43, pp. 42–46 (2010).

G.J. Chaitin, *Proving Darwin: Making Biology Mathematical* (Pantheon, 2012).

3. R.J. Marks II, *Handbook of Fourier Analysis and its Applications* (Oxford University Press, 2008).

R.J. Marks II, "Gerchberg's extrapolation algorithm in two dimensions." *Appl Opt*, 20, pp. 1815–1820 (1981).

D.K. Smith and R.J. Marks II, "Closed form bandlimited image extrapolation." *Appl Opt*, 20, pp. 2476–2483 (1981).

R.J. Marks II, "Posedness of a bandlimited image extension problem in tomography." *Opt Lett*, 7, pp. 376–377 (1982).

D. Kaplan and R.J. Marks II, "Noise sensitivity of interpolation and extrapolation matrices." *Appl Opt*, 21, pp. 4489–4492 (1982).

R.J. Marks II, "Restoration of continuously sampled bandlimited signals from aliased data." *IEEE Transactions on Acoustics, Speech and Signal Processing, ASSP-30*, pp. 937–942 (1982).

R.J. Marks II and D.K. Smith, "Gerchberg-type linear deconvolution and extrapolation algorithms." in *Transformations in Optical Signal Processing*, W.T. Rhodes, J.R. Fienup and B.E.A. Saleh (eds.), SPIE 373, pp. 161–178 (1984).

K.F. Cheung, R.J. Marks II and L.E. Atlas, "Convergence of Howard's minimum negativity constraint extrapolation algorithm." *J Opt Soc Am A*, 5, pp. 2008–2009 (1988).

4. N.A. Barricelli, "Numerical testing of evolution theories, Part I: theoretical introduction and basic tests." *Acta Biotheor*, 16(1–2), pp. 69–98 (1962). Reprinted in David B. Fogel (ed.), *Evolutionary Computation: The Fossil Record* (IEEE Press, Piscataway N.J., 1998).

5. J.L. Crosby, "Computers in the study of evolution." *Sci Prog Oxf*, 55, pp. 279–292 (1967).

6. David J. Hand, *The Improbability Principle: Why Coincidences, Miracles, and Rare Events Happen Every Day* (Macmillan, 2014).

2

INFORMATION: WHAT IS IT?

"Every new body of discovery is mathematical in form, because there is no other guidance we can have."

Charles Darwin[1]

2.1 Defining Information[2]

The term *information* is commonly used in science but its precise definition varies widely. A number of questions arise in attempting to precisely define information:

- A Blu-ray disc is capable of storing about 50 GB. Is the amount of information on the disk different if the disc contains the movie *Braveheart* or a collection of random noise?
- When a ·book is shredded beyond recovery, is information being destroyed? Does it matter whether there is another copy of the book or not?
- Likewise, when a digital picture is taken, is digital information being created or merely captured?
- If you are shown a document written in Mandarin, does the document contain information even if you do not read Mandarin? What if the document is written in an alien language unknown to any human? If not, does the document suddenly contain information if we discover a Rosetta stone allowing for its translation?

The answers to these questions vary in accordance with the definition of information used.

Information can be written on energy. Examples include acoustic audio waves which are used by humans and other animals to audibly communicate, or electromagnetic waves which are used by radio stations to transmit their signal. As is the case with books and Blu-ray discs, information can also be etched onto matter. But energy and matter serve only as transcription media for information. Norbert Weiner,[3] the father of cybernetics, noted[4]

> "Information is information, neither matter nor energy."

Information is resident in design, and engineers and inventors copy nature's designs all the time. The idea for Velcro, for example, came from close examination of burrs stuck to the clothes of a Swiss engineer after a hunting trip. The function of the human eyelid was the inspiration for the invention of the intermittent windshield wiper.[5] The IEEE Computational Intelligence Society,[6] a professional electrical and computer engineering organization,[a] has as its motto, "Nature-inspired problem solving." Structure in nature, when examined, can be a rich source of useful information.

Matter and energy are modeled and well-studied by physicists. There is, though, no universal model of information. Claude Shannon recognized that his theory of Shannon information was not the last word in the mathematical modeling of information.[7]

> "It seems to me that we all define 'information' as we choose; and, depending upon what field we are working in, we will choose different definitions. My own model of information theory . . . was framed precisely to work with the problem of communication."

Shannon's definition of information suffers from an inability to measure meaning. A Blu-ray of random noise can have the same number of bits as a Blu-ray containing the movie *Braveheart*.

A frequently used example of design information is shown in Fig. 2.1. On the left is an image of an obviously designed Mount Rushmore. On the right, shadows resemble a man's face. The photo is from the surface of Mars taken during NASA's 1976 Viking 1 mission. Given the thousands of shadows on the surface of Mars which change according to the sun's angle of illumination, it is not surprising that some patterns should resemble a man's

---

[a] IEEE, the Institute of Electrical and Electronic Engineers, is the world's largest professional society. In 2016, there were 421,000 members in 160 countries.

Fig. 2.1. Mount Rushmore, on the left, displays design information. The shadow on the right resembling a man's face looks to be a chance shape.[8]

face. The image on the right is due to chance. The information property that allows us to differentiate the meaningful design of Mount Rushmore from the Mars face on the right is *specified complexity*. The Rushmore images are more than just the faces of men. They are specific men: Washington, Jefferson, Roosevelt and Lincoln. To most, the face on Mars resembles no one in particular. The images on Rushmore are complex. Details in the depiction of the eyes, the hair, the nostrils, the mouths and the facial hair are intricate and specified. As with Blu-ray discs of *Braveheart* and noise, pure Shannon information is unable to examine the two pictures in Fig. 2.1 and announce the presence or the absence of specified complexity from simple pixel statistics.

The presence of design in observation is obvious.[9] Behe's *irreducible complexity*,[10] Gitt's *universal information*,[11] Durston *et al.*'s *functional information*,[12] and Dembski's *specified complexity*[13] offer descriptions of the properties of meaningful information. A number of mathematical models address the measuring of meaning, including *sophistication*,[14] *pragmatic information theory*,[15] *functional information*,[16] *LMC information*[17] and *Kolmogorov sufficient statistics*.[18, 19] In Chapter 7.3, we present a model dubbed *algorithmic specified complexity* which can be used mathematically to successfully assess the meaning contained in a sequence of bits depicting an image, a sound, etc.

We can also apply the mathematics of information measures to (a) monitor the design process from which design arises and (b) measure the contextual complexity of the final design. A purpose of this monograph is to explain mathematical methods of measuring the information content of designed objects.

2.2   Measuring Information

There are many ways to quantify information. The most common are Shannon information[20] and Kolmogorov–Chaitin–Solomonov (KCS) information (or complexity). Shannon information is based on probability whereas KCS complexity deals with existing structures described by computer programs. The two measures are related and share the same unit of measure (bits), but are formalized differently.[21]

2.2.1   *KCS complexity*

Those familiar with computers know about compression software that produces zip files and JPG[b] images. Large files are made smaller by taking into account redundancy. Compressed files transmit more quickly and are reconstructed by the receiver. The rationale for compressing files is similar for dehydrated food. Water is removed at the factory. The waterless food is light and can be shipped inexpensively. The customer rehydrates and, ideally, reconstructs the original food at the receiving end. Likewise, compressed files can be transmitted using limited bandwidth and be rehydrated at the receiver.

Rehydrated food rarely tastes as good as the original. The dehydration process often loses or undesirably modifies the original food's taste, aroma or texture. Some image compression techniques, such as JPG image compression, are likewise lossy. As illustrated in Fig. 2.2, the recovered image is a slightly corrupted version of the original. If an original computer file can be recovered from a compressed file exactly, the compression is said to be *lossless*. Lossless dehydration would result in reconstituted food indistinguishable from the original. Portable network graphic (PNG) images are examples of lossless compression. KCS information is concerned only with lossless compression.

For a given file, we might expect that there is a way to compress maximally. The smallest lossless compression of a file, in bits, is the KCS

---

[b]Pronounced "JAY-peg".

  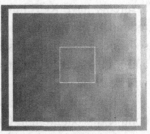

Fig. 2.2. JPG compression of images is lossy. Compression is performed in blocks of 8 × 8 pixels. A zoom of the JPG image on the left is shown in the middle where the 8 × 8 blocks can be seen. One of the blocks is outlined on the right. The boundaries on the boxes betray the lossy compression offered by the JPG algorithm. KCS compressed information, on the other hand, must be lossless. PNG files are lossless. Their compressed size can be taken as a bound for the KCS information. (The contrast of the right two images has been increased to allow for easier viewing.)

complexity of the file. The compression is typically cast in terms of a descriptive computer program able to reproduce the object. What is the shortest computer program able to accurately characterize the file?

How large can we expect the KCS information to be? A large file of B bits can obviously not be compressed into a single bit. And a file of B bits can obviously be represented with an uncompressed file about B bits long. We simply state the bits in the computer program and say PRINT and HALT. If Y denotes the shortest program for X, then we know that the length of Y lies somewhere between one and a few greater than B bits.[c] The size of the smallest file has a length, in bits, of $K(X)$. $K(X)$ is the KCS information (or complexity) content of the larger file. Chaitin calls these programs *elegant* programs.[22]

Structured sequences, like the repeating 01

$$X = 0101010101010101010101010101010101010101\ldots01$$

have a small KCS information. The program able to completely characterize the string is "repeat 01 a thousand times and halt." A sequence of 0's and 1's formed by flipping a fair coin B times will almost

---

[c]† A few additional bits are required for program commands such as PRINT. If B is a large number in the millions or billions, these bits are negligible in the final count.

assuredly have KCS information close to B bits. There is no structure or redundancy of which to take advantage. In other words, the coin flipping sequence is not compressible. We have to write the entire sequence of 0's and 1's in order to capture the sequence with no loss. The KCS complexity will be close to B bits.

There are deceptive strings that look to be random with large KCS complexity but are not. One is the Champernowne constant[23]

010001101100000101001110010111011100000010010...

This number, published when Champernowne was still an undergraduate student, passes many tests for randomness, but has a low KCS complexity. This is more clearly seen if the number is written as

0 1 00 01 10 11 000 001 010 011 100 101 110 111 0000 0001 0010...

This is simply a list of sequential numbers written in binary and, even for an infinite sequence, is described by a short program. For some value of N defining the length of the number,

```
For n=1 to N, write all binary numbers with n
              bits in order. Stop.
```

In base 10, the Champernowne Constant is

0123456789101112131415161718192021222324252627282930 31...

Another example of a complex-looking sequence is the binary string describing the number

$$\pi = 3.14159265358979323846264338327950288419716939 93751...$$

In binary,

$$\pi = 11.00100100001111110110101010001000100001011010 00110000$$
$$100011010011000100110001100110001010001011100000 0011011$$
$$1000001110011010001...$$

The string appears random. But since π can be computed from the simple formula $\frac{\pi}{4} = 1 - \frac{1}{3} + \frac{1}{5} - \frac{1}{7} + \frac{1}{9} + \cdots$, π can be generated to any accuracy desired by a short looping computer program.[d]

Formally, the KCS information of a string X of B bits is the length of the smallest computer program that will generate the string X and stop. This will depend on the computer language used. The shortest program to generate X using C++ will have a different length than if the computer language Python is used. However, there always exists in principle a translating program to convert C++ code into Python code. Assume the program to translate C++ into Python requires c bits. If $K_{C++}(X)$ is the KCS complexity of X using C++, then the KCS complexity in Python, $K_{Python}(X)$, can be no greater than $K_{C++}(X) + c$ bits.

For long strings, adding a translating computer program can be a negligible contribution to the KCS information.[e] In all cases, the KCS complexity between two computer languages can always be bounded by the number c that is independent of the object being described.[f] The KCS complexity is therefore a universal concept that translates seamlessly from one computer language to another. We adopt the notation[24]

$$K_{Python}(X) \underset{c}{=} K_{C++}(X)$$

to mean equality to within a constant c.

†2.2.1.1   *KCS information using prefix free programs*

Another illustration of KCS complexity is provided in Fig. 2.3. Shown is a binary tree where, going from left to right, new branches grow based on branching using 0's and 1's. In some instances, the branching ends. Terminated branches are called *leaves*. The sequences of 0's and 1's leading

---

[d]† For N sufficiently large to give the desired accuracy, we can use the following short program. S=1; for n=1:N; S=S+$(-1)^n$/$(2\times n+1)$; end; pi=4$\times$S; PRINT pi; halt.

[e]† KCS information is often expressed in big O notation. Let $|Y|$ be the number of bits in the binary string Y. The expression $|Y| = O(e^{|X|})$ means that, as $|X|$ increases, $|Y|$ asymptotically approaches a curve proportional to $e^{|X|}$. $O(c + e^{|X|}) = O(e^{|X|})$ since $e^{|X|}$ will soon dwarf c.

[f]† Specifically,

$$|K_{C++}(X) - K_{Python}(X)| \leq c.$$

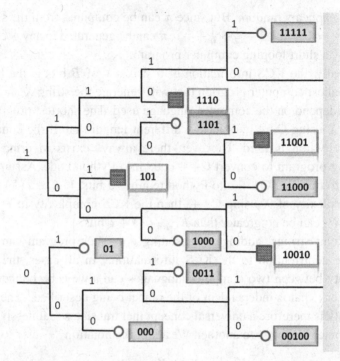

†Fig. 2.3. The leaves in this tree denote prefix free computer programs. The leaves marked with a square, █, result in printing $X = 0101010101$ and stopping. The shortest program in the tree that prints X contains three bits: 101. The KCS information of X is therefore $K(X) = 3$ bits.

to this termination are written as binary strings and correspond to bits comprising a computer program. For any meaningful computer language, this tree will branch billions of times and the tree will be enormous in size. The toy example tree in Fig. 2.3 does however serve as an illustration.

The computer language illustrated by the tree is dubbed *prefix free* to signify that no binary string corresponding to a leaf can form the beginning of another program. Since any computer language can be translated into any other computer language, a program in C++ or Python can always be translated into a prefix free computer language. To illustrate the nature of a prefix free code, consider the leaf labeled 101 in Fig. 2.3. The program 101 is a leaf in the tree. For a prefix free language, no other computer program can start with 101. In other words, 101 cannot be the *prefix* of any other computer program in the tree.

Consider, then, the string

$$X = 0101010101.$$

There are numerous programs that will generate X. We have depicted them in Fig. 2.3 as leaves with squares: ▓. Four such programs are shown. Since all of the leaves of the tree are not shown, there could be others deeper in the tree. The four bit program 1110 prints out X and might correspond to something like[g]

1110 → Print 0101 two times and stop.

The longer 5 bit program, 11001, might correspond to

11001 → Print 01, then Print 01 three times and stop.

The shortest program that prints X is the 3 bit program 101 which might correspond to

101 → Print 01 four times and stop.

Although a number of programs print $X = 0101010101$, this is the shortest. The KCS complexity for X is therefore

$$K(X) = 3 \text{ bits}.$$

†2.2.1.2 *Random programming and the Kraft inequality*

A prefix free coding tree is shown in Fig. 2.4. Interestingly, the tree suggests that we can randomly choose programs by repeatedly flipping a fair coin. If a head is assigned a logic one and a tail a zero, then repeated coin flipping can guide us from the left of Fig. 2.4 to the right. The coin is flipped until a terminal leaf is encountered. If the coin flip is HTTHT, for example, we arrive at the leaf 10010. Since each coin flip has a probability

---

[g]† The program 1110 is almost certainly too short to correspond to Print 0101 two times and stop. We could make the 1110 program longer or even offer the binary equivalent of Matlab code to generate $X = 0101010101$, but the tree in Fig. 2.3 would become too large to represent on a single page. So bear with us in our pedagogically expedient example using 1110 as a program.

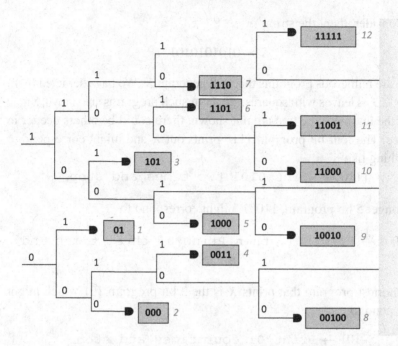

†Fig. 2.4. Illustration of the Kraft inequality for prefix free binary programs.

of $\frac{1}{2}$, the probability of flipping the five bit sequence HTTHT = 10010 is $\frac{1}{2} \times \frac{1}{2} \times \frac{1}{2} \times \frac{1}{2} \times \frac{1}{2} = \left(\frac{1}{2}\right)^5 = \frac{1}{32}$. It's easy to generalize this to any terminal leaf with l bits. The probability of flipping a coin and ending on a specific leaf with l bits is $\left(\frac{1}{2}\right)^l$. We can take advantage of this observation to derive an interesting property dubbed the *Kraft inequality*.[25]

The programs at the leaves in Fig. 2.4 can be numbered, i.e. lexicographically ordered, by placing all of the two bit programs in numerical order followed by the three bit programs, etc. The ordering would be as shown in Table 2.1. The first ($p = 1$) program on the list is the only two bit program. The length of this program is $l_1 = 2$ and the probability of getting this program by flipping a coin is $(\frac{1}{2})^{l_1} = \frac{1}{4}$. There are two 3 bit programs. Numerically, the smallest is 000. This is therefore program $p = 2$ with length $l_2 = 3$ bits. The chance of getting this program by a coin flip is $\left(\frac{1}{2}\right)^{l_2} = \frac{1}{8}$. We can repeat this by continuing down the list for all of the programs. The Kraft inequality results from recognizing that all of these programs are mutually exclusive, i.e. when you flip a coin, you can end

†Table 2.1. Lexiographic ordering of the programs in Fig. 2.4.
The ordering is shown in the Figure where leaves are numbered.

p	Program	l_p
1	01	2
2	000	3
3	101	3
4	0011	4
5	1000	4
6	1101	4
7	1110	4
8	00110	5
9	10010	5
10	11000	5
11	11001	5
12	11111	5
13	etc.	6

up at only one leaf (or program). Assuming all of the leaves are viable
programs and the tree is finite in depth, the probabilities must therefore add
to one. If not, the sum must add to a number not greater than one. The Kraft
inequality for binary codes is[h]

$$\sum_p \left(\frac{1}{2}\right)^{l_p} \leq 1. \tag{2.1}$$

2.2.1.3 *Knowability*

Finding the KCS complexity of arbitrary sequence of bits can be shown
to be algorithmically unknowable.[26,i] In other words, there is no computer

---

[h]† Probability mass functions with all masses only of the form $\left(\frac{1}{2}\right)^{l_p}$ where l_p is a positive
integer are called *dyadic*.

[i]† Unknowability can be proved using proof by contradiction. Assume a program C exist so
that when presented an arbitrary binary string X the program computes the KCS complexity
of the string. In other C(X) outputs the KCS complexity K(X). Given C, we can write the
following program that, including the function C, is M bits long. We'll call the program P.

Set B=M

program that when presented an arbitrary object outputs the object's KCS complexity. We can, though, bound the object's KCS complexity. If we are able to losslessly compress a billion bits into a thousand bits, we know that the KCS complexity of the original bit stream is, at most, a thousand bits. If the actual unknown KCS of a string X is K and we have successfully compressed the string losslessly to a length $\tilde{K}$, then we are assured that $K \leq \tilde{K}$.

2.2.1.4 *Application*

The Kraft inequality and the KCS measure of complexity will find use later in a model to measure algorithmic specified complexity (ASC).[j] Gregory Chaitin, the "C" in KCS, has proposed a model of evolution based on algorithmic information theory. We revisit KCS complexity and the Kraft inequality there also.[k]

2.2.2 *Shannon information*

Shannon information is based on probability rather than existing bit strings. There are links between KCS complexity and Shannon information,[27] but their foundations differ.

In his original and classic 1948 paper where the term "bits" was first used as a contraction for "binary digits," Shannon reasoned that quantified information should have two properties. First, the lower the probability, the greater the information. If I tell you the sun will rise tomorrow, I have

---

```
For all programs of length B bits, evaluate K=C(X)
If K>M,
   Print X and K
   Halt
Otherwise, increment B=B+1 and repeat
```

Since we are assured there are an infinite number of elegant programs of unbounded length, this program is guaranteed to halt.

Here is the problem. When the program P stops, it outputs a bit string X its KCS complexity of K(X) which is larger than the length M of the program P. But P computes the KCS complexity of X using less than K(X) bits! P only uses M<K(X) bits. This violates the definition of KCS as being the shortest program that can output the binary string X. The contradiction therefore shows there can be no computer program C of finite length that computes the KCS complexity of an arbitrary object X.

[j] In Chapter 7.3.

[k] As discussed in Chapter 6.3.

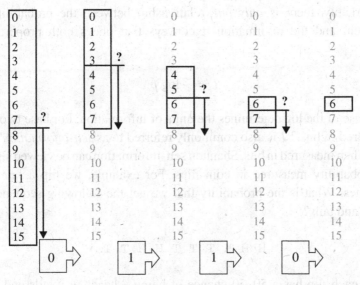

Fig. 2.5. There are 16 boxes. The quizmaster chooses one and the questioner must find it. The probability of choosing the target in one query is 1/16 corresponding to 4 bits of information. Using interval halving, the target can be isolated using interval halving and asking four "yes" (1) or "no" (0) questions. The sequence of answers, {0110}, is the binary representation for the final answer which is 6.

conveyed little information. It is a near certain event. If I tell you the sun will explode tomorrow, I'm giving you lots of information. The probability the sun will explode tomorrow is very very small. The second property information should have is additivity when two events are not related.[1] If "stuttering" conveys information I_1 and "professor" conveys information I_2, then "stuttering professor" should convey information $I_1 + I_2$. Thus, information should obey the following two properties.

1. The smaller the probability, p, of an event, the greater the information.
2. The information from two independent events should equal the sum of the information from each event separately.

---

[1]† In order to add, the information from two sources must be unrelated. The information from *jumping kangaroo*, for example, is the same as from *kangaroo* alone. All kangaroos jump. Statistically, in order to add, the events' occurrence must be *independent*. Events A and B are independent if $\Pr(A \text{ and } B) = \Pr(A) \times \Pr(B)$.

Remarkably, there is *only one* relationship between the probability of an event and the information it conveys that obeys both properties.[m] It is

$$I = -\log p. \tag{2.2}$$

The base of the log determines the units of information. For base two, I is measured in bits.[n] I is also commonly referred to as *self-information*.

When measured in bits, Shannon self-information can be viewed simply as probability measured in coin flips. For example, we flip a fair coin 10 times. What is the probability that we get the following sequence of heads and tails?

H H H T T T H H T T.

Since each flip has a 50–50 chance of being a heads or a tails and each flip's outcome is independent, the chance of getting this exact sequence of heads and tails is $p = \left(\frac{1}{2}\right)^{10} = \frac{1}{1024}$. And the corresponding information is $I = -\log_2 p = \log_2 2^{10} = 10$ bits. If the flip sequence is rewritten using a one for a heads and a 0 for a tails, we get

1 1 1 0 0 0 1 1 0 0.

This is, indeed, 10 bits of information.[o]

---

[m]† This satisfies Shannon's two requirements for information. (1) As p decreases, I increases. (2) For statistically independent events 1 and 2, the composite probability is $p = p_1 p_2$ and, from (2.2), $I = -\log p_1 p_2 = -\log p_1 - \log p_2 = I_1 + I_2$.

[n]† When the log is base 10, information is measured in *Hartleys*. For the natural log, information is in *nats* for natural logarithms. A base 3 log results in *trits* (**tri**nary di**git**). Base $2^{1/8}$ gives a *byte*. Like miles converted to inches, the various information measures have multiplicative conversion factors. Eight bits, for example, is a byte and one nat is $\log_2 e \approx 1.443$ bits.

[o]† Generally, the probability of forecasting any specified binary sequence of B bits is $\left(\frac{1}{2}\right)^B$ and

$$B = -\log_2 \left(\frac{1}{2}\right)^B.$$

This equation provides a translation from probability to bits. 10 bits equates to about one chance in a thousand, 20 bits to one in a million, and 40 to one in a trillion.

2.2.2.1 *Twenty questions: Interval halving and bits*

We can illustrate Shannon information with the familiar game of "twenty questions". A player chooses an arbitrary object and the opponent has up to 20 "yes–no" questions to identify it.

An example of a variation of the game of twenty questions (only six questions were asked) is the Genesis account of the destruction of Sodom.[28] God would spare Sodom if some righteous people lived there. Abraham wanted to find out the minimum number of righteous people and tried to find the answer by querying God with "yes or no" questions. Abraham's search can be paraphrased as follows.

1. Abraham: If there are at least 50 righteous people in the city of Sodom, will you spare the city?
   • God: Yes.
2. Abraham: What if the number of the righteous is at least 45?
   • God: Yes.
3. Abraham: What about 40?
   • God: Yes.
4. Abraham: Will you spare the city if there are at least 30 righteous people?
   • God: Yes.
5. Abraham: 20?
   • God: Yes.
6. Abraham: How about 10?
   • God: Yes.

We will never know the threshold God had in mind because the questioning stops here. We do know that 10 righteous people did not reside in Sodom because God destroyed the city.

In the game of twenty questions there are stupid and smart questions to ask. Suppose a game has just started and you are asking the first question. A specific initial question like "Is it the big toe on your left foot?" is generally not useful. An initial general question like "Is it in the North América?" is better. It splits the possible answers into two large groups. An answer of "yes" rules out all objects on other continents. Using such questions to zero in on one answer by sequentially cutting the possibilities into two groups is akin to *interval halving* and will generally guide the questioner to the correct answer with fewer queries.[p]

2.2.2.2 *Shannon information applied to interval halving*

Interval halving[q] divides all possibilities into two groups. By answering yes or no to a query, the questioner can eliminate half of the possibilities with each question.

Interval halving search is nicely described by Shannon information. Assume we are tasked to choose a box numbered between 1 and 16. If Bob and Monika choose a box unknown to each other, the chance Monika chooses Bob's box in one guess is

$$p = \frac{1}{16} \text{ corresponding to an information of } I = \log_2(16) = 4 \text{ bits.}^{\text{r}}$$

The value of 4 bits also dictates for this problem the minimum number of "yes–no" questions the questioner needs to ask the quizmaster to find the target box. There are 16 squares numbered from 0 to 15. Bob starts the game by saying "I am thinking of a box numbered between 0 and 15." Monika the questioner must guess this number by asking "yes" or "no" questions. Bob the quizmaster promises to be an *oracle* and correctly respond to each of her questions.

There are stupid sets of questions Monika can ask and smart sets. Here is a set of stupid questions.

"Is it square six?"
"No."
"Is it 15?"
"No."
"Is it square two?"
"No." etc.

---

[p]A foundation of *conservation of information* is that external sources of knowledge can get the questioner to an answer faster. If the quizmaster has stubbed the big toe on his left foot earlier in the day and has spent the day complaining that it was throbbing, "Is it the big toe on your left foot?" is no longer a stupid initial question.
[q]Interval halving is foundational in Chaitin's metabiology model as discussed in Chapter 6.3.
[r]In Chapter 5.4.1, we will formally dub this the *endogenous information*. It measures the difficulty of the questioner finding the box when there is no information about where the box might be.

The questioner might be lucky and get the right number on the second or third guess, but if she asks about one square per query, it will in general take her eight questions on average (half of the 16 possibilities) to guess the number. A smart set of "yes-no" questions uses the process of interval halving. The following process is illustrated in Fig. 2.5.

1. The questioner first asks "Is it eight or more?" No matter what the answer, the number of solutions is cut in half. Assume the quizmaster has picked six, so the quizmaster responds "No!".
2. Monika now knows the answer is between zero and seven. This new interval is likewise cut in two when Monika asks "Is the number between four and seven (inclusive)?" The answer is yes.
3. The number is between four and seven, so Monika asks "Is it six or seven?" Bob answers "yes".
4. Lastly Monika asks if the answer is seven. Bob says "no".

So Monika identifies box six as the correct one using four questions. Bob's answers were

No   Yes   Yes   No

Substituting a one for a *yes* and a zero for a *no* translates to $(0, 1, 1, 0)$ which specifies box six since in base 2

$$(0110)_2 = 6.$$

Four questions are required because there are 16 boxes each with a probability of $\frac{1}{16}$. The information corresponding to each box is therefore $\log_2\left(\frac{1}{16}\right) = 4$ bits. For box six, these bits are $(0, 1, 1, 0)$.

Abraham could have applied interval halving to his querying of God. Abraham asked six "yes or no" questions of God. Let's be presumptuous and assume the number of righteous people is somewhere between 0 and 63 inclusive. Using interval halving, Abraham could have found the exact number in $\log_2 64 = 6$ queries by using interval halving. Here is a hypothetical scenario.

1. Abraham: If there are 31 or more righteous people in the city of Sodom, will you spare the city?

- God: Yes.

  o We now know the answer lies between 0 and 31.

2. Abraham: What if the number of the righteous is at least 15?

   - God: Yes, I'll spare the city.

   o We now know the answer lies between 0 and 15.

3. Abraham: At least 7?

   - God: No.

   o We now know the answer lies between 8 and 15 inclusive.

4. Abraham: Will you spare the city if there are at least 11 righteous people?

   - God: Yes.

   o We now know the answer lies between 8 and 11 inclusive.

5. Abraham: At least 10 righteous people?

   - God: Yes.

   o We now know the answer is either 8 or 9.

6. Abraham: Will you spare the city if there are at least 8 righteous people?

   - God: No.

   o We now know the answer is nine or more righteous people.

The city will be spared if there are nine or more righteous people.

Each answer to a query by Abraham corresponds to a single bit of information. If we assign a zero to a "yes" and a one to a "no", the yes–yes–no–yes–yes–no sequence of God's hypothetical answers is the binary encoding of the answer of "nine righteous people." Specifically, the six bits of information are decoded as[s]

$$(001001)_2 = 9.$$

---

[s]† Generalizing, a number between 1 and 2^K can be identified in K guesses. Twenty questions can identify any number between 1 and $2^{20} = 1,048,576$. Thirty questions at most are required to specify a number between 1 and a billion $< 2^{30}$.

There are more interesting ways to play the number guessing game without directly revealing the interval is being used. A subtle set of a smart questions for guessing numbers is shown in Table 2.2.

Table 2.2. (*For caption see next page*)

32	16	8	4	2	1
33	17	9	5	3	3
34	18	10	6	6	5
35	19	11	7	7	7
36	20	12	12	10	9
37	21	13	13	11	11
38	22	14	14	14	13
39	23	15	15	15	15
40	24	24	20	18	17
41	25	25	21	19	19
42	26	26	22	22	21
43	27	27	23	23	23
44	28	28	28	26	25
45	29	29	29	27	27
46	30	30	30	30	29
47	31	31	31	31	31
48	48	40	36	34	33
49	49	41	37	35	35
50	50	42	38	38	37
51	51	43	39	39	39
52	52	44	44	42	41
53	53	45	45	43	43
54	54	46	46	46	45
55	55	47	47	47	47
56	56	56	52	50	49
57	57	57	53	51	51
58	58	58	54	54	53
59	59	59	55	55	55
60	60	60	60	58	57
61	61	61	61	59	59
62	62	62	62	62	61
63	63	63	63	63	63

Table 2.2. Here is an interval game to astonish those not technically inclined. Have a player choose a number between 0 and 63. Ask them if their number is the leftmost column of the numbers. The second column? The third, When a yes or no answer for the last column is offered, the chosen number can be stated *immediately*. For example, an answer of "Yes, no, yes, no, no, yes" is 41. A quick inspection confirms that 41 is the only number that is in the first, third, and last column. Most players will be astonished.

Here is how it works. The player is giving a binary number. "Yes, no, yes, no, no, yes" is $(101001)_2 = 41$.

But it's even simpler than that. There is no need of any knowledge of binary numbers. The top number in each "yes" column simply needs to be added. For example, $41 = 32 + 8 + 1$. Prior to the last column, the sum of the numbers to that point can be added mentally. The last answer for the last column tells whether to add one or not.

This is interval halving disguised. The numbers between 0 and 63 can all be expressed with six bits. There are 32 numbers per column. In asking whether a number is in a column, one is asking whether the chosen number has a one in the location corresponding to the column position.

The table can be easily extended to 127, or 255 or to any value of $2^n - 1$. Increasing n by one adds a column and doubles the number of rows.

2.3 Remarks

Neither the KCS nor Shannon models answer all of the questions about information posed at the start of this chapter. On a Blu-ray disc, $50\,GB = 400,000,000,000$ bits can correspond to the movie *Braveheart* or noise.

Likewise, neither KCS nor Shannon information measures whether the contents of the Blu-ray have meaning or were designed. However, these measures, as we will see, can be used as tools in making such assessments.

Notes

1. Quoted in Eric Temple Bell. *Men of Mathematics* (Simon and Schuster, 2014).
2. Portions of this section are taken from: Robert J. Marks II, "Information Theory & Biology: Introductory Comments," in *Biological Information — New Perspectives*, Cornell University, edited by R.J. Marks II, M.J. Behe, W.A. Dembski, B.L. Gordon, and J.C. Sanford (World Scientific, Singapore, 2013), pp. 1–10.
3. W. Gitt, R. Compton and J. Fernandez, "Biological Information — What is It?" in *Biological Information — New Perspectives*, Cornell University, edited by R.J. Marks II, M.J. Behe, W.A. Dembski, B.L. Gordon, J.C. Sanford (World Scientific, Singapore, 2013).

See also N. Wiener, *Cybernetics: Or Control and Communication in the Animal and the Machine* (Technology Press, MIT, 1968).

See also W. Gitt, *In the Beginning Was Information: A Scientist Explains the Incredible Design in Nature* (Green Forest, Master Books, 2005).

4. Stuart J.D. Schwartzstein. *The Information Revolution and National Security* (Center for Strategic and International Studies, Washington DC, 1992), p. 196.

5. J. Seabrook, "The Flash of Genius." The New Yorker, 11 January, 1993.

6. IEEE Computational Intelligence Society, http://cis.ieee.org/ (URL date May 2, 2016).

7. P. Mirowski, *Machine Dreams: Economics Becomes a Cyborg Science* (Cambridge University Press, 2002).

8. Photo credits: Mount Rushmore by Dean Franklin [CC-BY-2.0 (http://creativecommons.org/licenses/by/2.0)], via Wikimedia Commons. The image on the right is from the *National Aeronautics and Space Administration* (NASA): http://science.nasa.gov/science-news/science-at-nasa/2001/ast24may_1/ (URL date May 2, 2016).

9. J. Hübner, "A Christian Theory of Information," a *RPM Magazine*, 13(28), July 10 to July 16 (2011), http://www.reformedperspectives.org/ (URL date May 2, 2016).

10. Michael J. Behe, *Darwin's Black Box: The Biochemical Challenge to Evolution* (Free Press, 1998).

11. Werner Gitt, *op. cit.*

12. Kirk K. Durston, David K.Y. Chiu, David L. Abel and Jack T. Trevors, "Measuring the functional sequence complexity of proteins." *Theor Biol Med Modell*, 47(4) (2007).

13. William A. Dembski, *No Free Lunch: Why Specified Complexity Cannot Be Purchased without Intelligence* (Rowman & Littlefield Publishers, 2007).

14. H. Atlan and M. Koppel, "The Cellular Computer DNA: Program or Data," *Bull Math Biol*, 52(3), pp. 335–348 (1990).

15. Edward D. Weinberger, "A theory of pragmatic information and its application to the quasispecies model of biological evolution." *BioSystems*, 66(3), pp. 105–119 (2002).

16. Kirk C. Durston, *op. cit.*

17. R. López-Ruiz, "Shannon information, LMC complexity and Rényi entropies: a straightforward approach," *Biophys Chem*, 115(2–3), pp. 215–218 (2005). The initials LMC appear to refer to the authors of the original idea: López-Ruiz, Mancini and Calbet.

18. Thomas M. Cover and Joy A. Thomas, *Elements of Information Theory*, 2nd edition (Wiley-Interscience, Hoboken, NJ, 2006).

19. M. Li and P.M. Vitányi, *An Introduction to Kolmogorov Complexity and its Applications* (Springer, 2008).
20. C. Shannon and W. Weaver, *The Mathematical Theory of Communication* (University of Illinois Press, Urbana, Ill., 1949), p. 32.
21. Cover and Thomas, *op.cit.*
22. G. J. Chaitin, *Meta Math!: The Quest for Omega* (Vintage, 2006).
23. D. G. Champernowne, "The construction of decimals normal in the scale of ten." *J London Math Soc*, 8, pp. 254–260 (1933).
24. P.D. Grünwald and P. Vitányi, "Kolmogorov complexity and information theory," *J Logic Lang Inf*, 12(4), pp. 497–529 (2003).
    C.H. Bennett, P. Gács, M. Li, P.M. Vitányi, and W.H. Zurek, "Information distance," *IEEE Trans. Inf. Theory*, pp. 1–29 (1998).
25. Cover and Thomas, *op.cit.*
26. *Ibid.*
27. *Ibid.*
28. Genesis 18:20–33.

3

DESIGN SEARCH IN EVOLUTION AND THE REQUIREMENT OF INTELLIGENCE

"The formation in geological time of the human body by the laws of physics (or any other laws of similar nature), starting from a random distribution of elementary particles and the field is as unlikely as the separation of the atmosphere into its components. The complexity of the living things has to be present within the material [from which they are derived] or in the laws [governing their formation]."

Kurt Gödel[1]

3.1 Design as Search

Evolution is often modeled by as a search process.[2] Mutation, survival of the fittest and repopulation are the components of evolutionary search. Evolutionary search computer programs used by computer scientists for design are typically teleological—they have a goal in mind. This is a significant departure from the off-heard claim that Darwinian evolution has no goal in mind.

Information in computer search can be illustrated using engineering design. Engineering design invariably involves

- domain expertise,
- design criteria, and
- an iterative search.

A first prototype is constructed and tested. If the design criteria are not met, the prototype is refined and the test repeated. The design criteria constitute the teleological goal. The process is quicker when the problem is easier or the designer has greater domain expertise.

For those with domain expertise, success can occur on the first try or in only a few iterations. The domain knowledge of the designer reduces the possibilities that require exploring. When expertise is lacking, the design process is lengthier. Expertise saves time.

3.1.1 *WD-40^{TM} and Formula 409^{TM}*

Outcomes of iterative design are probably resident in your home. Formula 409^{TM}, the spray cleaner sold by the Clorox company, was perfected after 409 attempts at meeting a design criterion—hence the name.[3] A similar example is the petroleum-based lubricant and protectant, WD-40^{TM}, invented in 1953 by Norman B. Larsen. We know the design was iterative because WD-40^{TM} stands for[4] "water displacement, formulation successful in 40th attempt." The success of these designs is a function of the expertise of the designer. A high school student just completing an introductory course in chemistry, for example, will require far more that the 40 iterations required by industrial chemist Norman B. Larsen. We would instead be using something named WD-5120.

3.1.2 *Tesla, Edison and domain expertise*

Domain expertise requires general knowledge from experience and education. This knowledge needs to be folded intelligently into the process by the expert to simplify the design process. If the design is difficult and there is little expertise, then many iterations are typically required for success.

Inventor Thomas Edison had little experience in the properties of materials when searching for a light bulb filament that met his performance criteria.[5,6] Unable to bring expertise into his design, Edison resorted to a somewhat random search for possible solutions. An 1887 newspaper article lists some of the materials tried by Edison.

> "[E]ight thousand kinds of chemicals, every kind of screw made, every size of needle, every kind of cord or wire, hair of humans, horses, hogs, cows, rabbits, goats, minx, camels . . . silk in every texture, cocoons, various kinds of hoofs, shark's teeth, deer horns, tortoise shell . . . cork, resin, varnish and oil, ostrich feathers, a peacock's tail, jet, amber, rubber, all ores . . ." etc.[7]

Edison is famous for his quote:

> "Genius is one percent inspiration, ninety-nine percent perspiration."

Brilliant electrical engineer Nikola Tesla disagreed. Tesla felt that 99% perspiration is not necessary for those who know what they are doing. He admonished Edison for his lack of domain expertise and the consequent busywork required for Edison's invention process. In his own career, Tesla brilliantly manipulated visions and foundational theory in his creative mind and conceived of astonishing inventions such as brushless alternating current induction motors and wireless energy transfer. Tesla wrote that Edison required a large number of trials because of his lack of domain expertise. Tesla writes[8]

> "[Edison's] method [of design] was inefficient in the extreme, for an immense ground had to be covered to get anything at all unless blind chance intervened and, at first, I was almost a sorry witness of his doings, knowing that just a little theory and calculation would have saved him 90 percent of the labor. But he had a veritable contempt for book learning and mathematical knowledge, trusting himself entirely to his inventor's instinct and practical American sense."[a]

From the numbers he used, Tesla apparently believed that genius is $0.1 \times 90\% = 9\%$ perspiration and the remaining 91% inspiration.

In the quotation above, Tesla makes mention of *blind chance*. A blind search results when there is no domain expertise. We will hear much more about this later.

Tesla engaged in a famous battle against Edison concerning the use of alternating versus direct current. As witnessed by the output of the electrical outlets in your home today, Tesla's technology prevailed.

3.2   Design by Computer

With the advent of computer models, lab experimentation has been replaced in some instances by computer software simulations in the design process. The performance of antennas, for example, can be simulated

---

[a]† Tesla argues that Edison's lack of domain expertise resulted in a more lengthy design process. Edison would have invented WD-5120, not WD-40. In Chapter 5.4.2, we show that domain expertise in a design process is an information source that can be mined by the designer to contribute *active information* to the search. We will show the separation of expertise in the design of between WD-5120 and WD-40 can be estimated as active information

$$I_+ = -\log_2\left(\frac{40}{5120}\right) = 7 \text{ bits of active information.}$$

using long-established mathematical models describing propagation of electromagnetic waves. When a process can be modeled by software, the design process requires less laboratory simulation. Values of *design parameters* can be provided to the software which in turn provides, as an output, the design performance. As in laboratory testing, the human designer can look at the performance, refine the parameters, and try running the program with new parameters. The process, still iterative, now uses computer software simulations in place of laboratory experimentation.

A clever programmer can better the process by taking the human out of the design iteration loop. The programmer anticipates how a subpar design can be subsequently improved in future iterations and includes this in the software. The entire design process is then turned over to the computer. When the program is run, we expect the final result to meet the specified design criteria. The iterative process that looks for a successful design is dubbed *computer search*. Evolutionary programming is an example. Success, of course, depends on the successful transfer of the programmer's domain expertise into the software. As is the case in the writing of any software, garbage-in-garbage-out.

3.3   Designing a Good Pancake

To introduce search problems, we consider the problem of designing delicious pancakes and high-performance antennas. Pancakes are first.

3.3.1   *A search for a good pancake #1*

Here is the first search problem. Culinarily challenged Chef Ray is given pancake batter and must decide how long to cook a pancake on each of its two sides. To determine how good a pancake is, we employ the services of Bob, the Master Taster.[b] Bob will taste a pancake and tell us on a scale on one (terrible) to 10 (delicious) how good the pancake tastes. Chef Ray's job is to figure out how long to cook the pancake on each side to give a rating of nine or higher. The measure "nine or higher" is the *design criterion* for the pancake. It tells us beforehand what is considered an acceptable solution

---

[b]Coffee manufacturers engage *master tasters* to assess the quality of coffee beans. We are assuming an equivalent talent exists for pancakes.

of the search. Since the design goal is known, the search is teleological. When the design criterion is achieved the search is done and is announced a success.

In order to search for the best cooking times, let's assume Chef Ray can cook each side of the pancake in intervals of 15 seconds. We assign the numbers 1–10 to represent cooking times. A one is 15 seconds, two is 30 seconds, three is 45, all the way up to 10 which is two and a half minutes (150 seconds.) Each cooking time can be expressed as an ordered pair. The pair (5,3), for our example, means side one of the pancake is cooked 75 seconds on the first side, flipped and cooked 45 seconds on the second side. As shown in Fig. 3.1, there are a total of $10 \times 10 = 100$ ways to cook the pancake.

To search[c] for the best cooking times, Chef Ray chooses a random ordered pair, say (5,3) = (75 seconds, 45 seconds). He cooks the pancake for 75 seconds on one side, flips the pancake, and cooks for 45 seconds on the

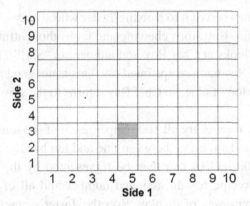

Fig. 3.1. A 10×10 grid showing the cooking times for the pancake on side one and side two. The shaded square corresponds to $(5, 3) = (75$ seconds on side one, 45 seconds on side two).

---

[c]Note that we can't use interval halving to search for the best looking pancake. Doing so would require numbering the recipes from one to one hundred and asking the first question "Is the best tasting recipe numbered between one and fifty?" To answer this and subsequent questions, the oracle, Bob the Taster, would need to know the identity of the best recipe prior to the start of the questioning. We are assuming we know nothing about the recipes and Bob the Taster can only respond with a ranking of pancakes he has tasted. Search using interval halving for problems of this type are simply not possible without intimate knowledge of the search domain.

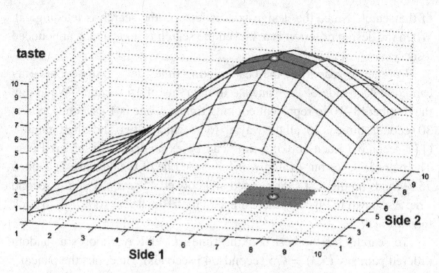

Fig. 3.2. The fitness landscape for cooking pancakes.

other side. He then serves it to Bob the Taster who slowly and thoughtfully chews a mouthful. Bob stops chewing and looks thoughtfully upward. He then swallows, looks at Chef Ray and announces "Six!" Thus, on a scale of 1 to 10, Chef Ray has a recipe rated six. This is not good enough to meet the design criterion of nine, so Chef Ray returns to the stove to try another ordered pair.

If Chef Ray were to try all 100 recipes, each of the squares in Fig. 3.1 would be assigned a number between one and ten by Bob the Taster. The fitness of all 100 recipes can then be represented by the plot shown in Fig. 3.2. Each recipe has an assigned number and all of the points are connected for purposes of display. Bob the Taster's ranking of a recipe can be viewed as fitness—bad-tasting pancakes have a low fitness and great-tasting pancakes have high fitness. For this reason, Fig. 3.2 is referred to as the *fitness landscape* of the search. Before the search begins, Chef Ray is totally ignorant of the fitness landscape. If he knew it, the search would not be necessary. To Chef Ray, knowledge of the fitness landscape comes only after repeated experiments.

Chef Ray does not have to test all 100 recipes to find an acceptable recipe. He only needs to find a recipe that Bob the Taster rates 9 or higher. He might be lucky and get a good recipe the first time. If, on the other hand, Chef Ray's goal is to find the absolutely best-tasting recipe, not just an acceptable recipe, he would need to try all 100 recipes.

Note that, prior to the search, Chef Ray does not even know if an acceptable solution exists. If Bob the Taster chooses to be finicky, none of the points in the fitness landscape would lie at 9 or above and there would be no pancake that meets the design criteria. In order to know this, Bob the Taster would need to taste all 100 recipes. On the other extreme, maybe all the recipes rate a 9 or a 10 and a single try gets an acceptable recipe.

Looking at the fitness landscape in Fig. 3.2, there are nine acceptable recipes ranking 9 or more. A value of 6, 7 or 8 translates to 90–120 seconds for side one, and 5, 6, 7, from 105 to 135 seconds, for side two. Since there are nine acceptable recipes, the chances of Chef Ray randomly choosing winning cooking times on his first query is 9 chances out of 100 which is a probability of success of

$$p = \frac{9}{100} = 0.09.$$

This number is unknown prior to the design process. It can be known exactly only if all 100 recipes are tried.

3.3.2 *A search for a good pancake #2: Cooking times plus range setting*

In our previous example, the stove was assumed to be set on a fixed heat level. We can make the search problem harder for Chef Ray by assuming we not only have to determine cooking times for the first and second sides of a pancake, but must also determine the heat setting of the stove. Suppose the stove is calibrated with heat settings from 1 (low heat) to 10 (high). With these 10 extra parameters, we now have $10 \times 10 \times 10 = 1,000$ recipes. This is illustrated in Fig. 3.3 where the large cube consists of 1,000 smaller cubes, each corresponding to a recipe. To assign a number to each little cube, Bob the Taster needs to taste 1,000 recipes. The idea of a fitness landscape is here not as evident as in Fig. 3.2. This is because we are in three rather than two dimensions. The fitness landscape in three dimensions (3-D) can be visualized as a cloud, dense when the fitness is high and clear when low. When we go to searches in even higher dimensions, the fitness landscape becomes difficult, if not impossible, to visualize.

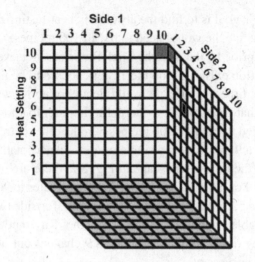

Fig. 3.3. The search space for cooking pancakes with three parameters.

Descriptions such as "smooth," however, are still often used as fitness landscape descriptors.

3.3.3 *A search for a good pancake #3: More recipe variables*

The search for the best solution when there are three parameters (time on side one, time on side two, and range setting) is more difficult than when there are two parameters. Fewer parameters can mean some of the design has already been done. In the pancake example, we have assumed the pancake batter has already been mixed. Searching for a pancake batter recipe in addition to cooking parameters makes the problem even more difficult. Assume there are nine search parameters. Three of the parameters are as before (cooking time on side one of the pancake, time on side two and the range's heat setting) and the remaining six parameters are recipe ingredients. Each of the parameters of the pancake recipe has 10 possibilities. Here's a list of parameters including the batter recipe.

1. *Pancake mix*: How much pancake mix do we use? One cup? Two cups? All the way to 10 cups is possible.
2. *Eggs*: How many eggs do we use? No eggs? One egg? Two eggs? All the way up to nine eggs, which makes 10 total possibilities.

3. *Milk*: How many cups of milk do we add? One cup? Two cups? All the way to nine cups.
4. *Water*: How many cups of water do we use? Maybe none. Let's start with zero cups of water and work our way to nine. There are a total of 10 possibilities.
5. *Salt*: How much salt do we add? 1 pinch to 10 pinches.
6. *Butter*: How much fresh butter do we melt in the skillet before putting in the pancake batter? Assume zero pats to nine.
7. *Side one*: How long do we cook the pancake on the first side? Let's assume, as before, that there are 10 possibilities starting at 15 seconds and increasing in intervals of 15 seconds.
8. *Side two*: Using the same timing that was used for the first side, how long do we cook the second side after the pancake is flipped?
9. *Temperature*: How hot do we heat the iron skillet? Assume, as before, the burner has 10 settings for heat.

With 9 parameters each divided into 10 possibilities, there are now $10^9 =$ one billion recipes! That's a lot of pancake possibilities.

Chef Ray's job to find a recipe for a delicious pancake is now much more difficult. (To put some meaning to the number, a billion seconds is almost 32 years.) We assume, as before, Chef Ray knows nothing about what makes a good recipe. As far as Chef Ray knows, a recipe that tastes like moldy pumpernickel could be made perfect by using one more pinch of salt, or that mixing one cup of pancake mix with five cups of milk and seven cups of water might make a good pancake. Knowing nothing about the recipe means we could try the same values next except add 10 cups of milk and 10 cups of water. The batter will be even more watery, but we try it anyway. That is the price of knowing "nothing." For this example, it is necessary to suspend all your culinarily knowledge and assume we are ignorant in the kitchen and don't know things like this.

How do we go about finding a good recipe for pancakes from the 1 billion possibilities? The only search option culinarily challenged Chef Ray has is as before. Choose one of the billion possible recipes, prepare the pancake, and present it to Bob the Taster. The design criterion, as before, is to find a recipe with a fitness of 9 or more.

Our simple pancake recipe example nicely illustrates the so called *combinatoric explosion* of solutions (recipes) as the number of parameters increases. In the language of search algorithms, the 9 ingredients of the recipe are dubbed *design parameters* and the set of all possible recipes is called the *search space*. For our example, there are 9 design parameters and the search space has 1 billion elements. If there are N parameters each with 10 possibilities, there are 10^N recipes. The number of elements in the search space thus increases exponentially with respect to the number of design parameters.

3.3.4 *A search for a good pancake #4: Simulating pancakes on a computer with an artificial tongue using a single agent*

Computers have replaced many workers. We now replace Bob the Taster with a computer program. Let's suppose that, using mathematical laws of physics and chemistry, the cooking of a pancake can be simulated by a software program called COOK. The input to COOK is an array of nine specific parameters needed to define the recipe. The output of COOK is data that defines the taste of the pancake. We will also assume that Bob the Taster is replaced by a taste simulation computer program dubbed TONGUE. TONGUE simulates what Bob the Taster does. The input to TONGUE is the output of COOK, namely the same taste parameters of the pancake used by Bob the Taster to rate the pancake's taste. The output of TONGUE is the rating of the pancake's taste on a scale of one to ten. Because Chef Ray has written these computer programs, he no longer needs to physically cook nor does he need to employ Bob the Taster's expensive finely tuned palate. Bob the Taster files for unemployment.

The cascaded COOK and TONGUE programs, as shown on the top of Fig. 3.4, is an example[d] of an *oracle*. For a price, an oracle will tell you how good something is. Bob the Taster was an oracle. For the pancake recipe search, the oracle input is the recipe. The output, the taste ranking, tells us how good the recipe is. The price we pay is computation time. Before computerizing the problem we paid Bob the Taster for his rankings.

---

[d]In the example of finding the secret square, the quizmaster is the questioner's oracle.

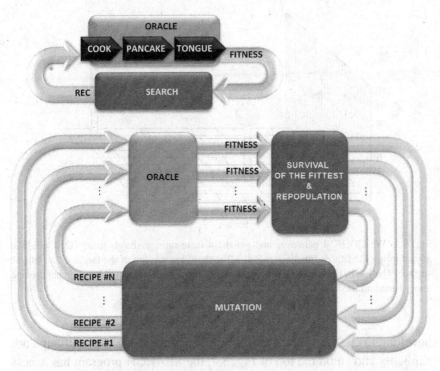

Fig. 3.4. (TOP) A single agent search for a good tasting pancake. The SEARCH algorithm is designed by the programmer to take advantage of any knowledge about the search. (BOTTOM) A generic evolutionary search.

In searches like the pancake search, the oracle typically consumes the vast majority of the computational resources. Time is the price we often pay.

Chef Ray is still faced with the problem of choosing recipes to input into the oracle. He could feed the computer the recipe, look at the result and decide which recipe to try next. Or he could write more computer code to examine each output and decide the next recipe to try. We will call a program that specifies the next recipe SEARCH. With the ability to use the results of previous queries, SEARCH has to determine which recipe to next feed to COOK. The design process can then be viewed as a loop shown at the top of Fig. 3.4. The loop exits when TONGUE announces a score that meets the design criterion.

We can't draw in nine dimensions, so let's return to the two-dimensional (2-D) search example shown in Fig. 3.1. Recall our job here is to determine

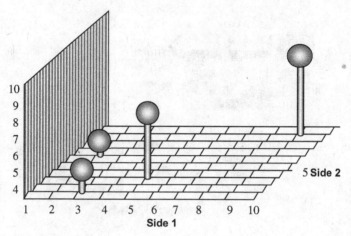

Fig. 3.5. We COOK 4 pancakes and get the 4 taste ratings shown from TONGUE. We are sampling the fitness function in Fig. 3.2 without knowledge of the target or the fitness surface. The job of the SEARCH program at the top of Fig. 3.4 is to choose the next recipe query based on the information we know.

how long to cook the pancake on side one and then side two. Although not explicitly shown on the top of Fig. 3.4, the SEARCH program has access to all or part of the previous query results. It can use this information to help choose the next query. In Fig. 3.5, the results of 4 recipes are shown. The job of SEARCH is to determine the next recipe to present to the COOK computer program. With no understanding of the shape of the fitness function or where the target is, there is not much guidance to choose the next recipe. The best we can do is not revisit a recipe that has already been tried. This is a type of blind search.

3.3.5 *A search for a good pancake #5: Simulating pancakes on a computer with an artificial tongue using an evolutionary search*

A blind search corresponds to a single sightless agent with a good memory walking around the search space and asking an oracle what the fitness is at its current location. For fast parallel computers, the situation can be improved. Instead of one agent, a team of agents can be searching the landscape, communicating with each other on walkie-talkies. A diamond necklace lost in a field is better found by a moving line of searchers holding hands than a single searcher walking the field in a Zamboni pattern.

Evolutionary search is a special case of multiple agent search.[9] For the pancake problem, a simple evolutionary search is shown on the bottom of Fig. 3.4. N recipes are first presented to the oracle (consisting of the COOK and TONGUE algorithms). Only recipes with high taste rankings are kept (survival of the fittest). Low taste rankings are discarded. To keep the population at a count of N, the discarded recipes are replaced with copies of recipes with higher rankings. We have repopulated. Each of the N recipes is now changed slightly. The changes are minor in hopes that the new recipe maintains the features that made it good in the first place. This corresponds to the *mutation* step in evolution.[e] One generation of evolution has occurred. The N new recipes are then subjected to a new cycle of selection (survival of the fittest), repopulation and mutation. The hope of evolutionary programs is that the population will become stronger and stronger as witnessed by ever increasing fitness scores and, in the case of the pancake design, ultimately result in a recipe for a delicious pancake.[f]

3.4 Sources of Knowledge

For many search approaches, there is generally no way to know how long a search program will run before finding an acceptable search result. Chef Ray could be lucky and find an acceptable pancake recipe with a taste of 9 on the first try. Or Chef Ray might end up testing every possibility and identify the good recipe on the last try.

---

[e]Another step in evolutionary search often used is *crossover*. It is loosely akin to the shuffling of father's, and mother's genes that ends up in the child. An example of crossover consists of (a) choosing two recipes, (b) choosing a set of ingredients, e.g. the number of eggs and the number of pinches of salt, and (c) swapping these values between recipes.

[f]Computer design must ultimately be implemented and tested. This is done in the laboratory. Before computers, more lab time was needed to tune a design to proper performance criteria. Computers allow initial stages of design on a computer. Even if the computer says the result is magnificent, the design needs to be tested. Chef Ray would not take a computer design of a pancake and invest millions to start a chain of *Ray's Pancake Houses* without testing the computer design by actually cooking and tasting a pancake himself. He might even tweak the computer's recipe a bit. Computer simulations can be accurate, but can miss subtleties that affect the outcome.

Introduction to Evolutionary Informatics

Knowledge concerning the search allows a reduction of search time. Here are some examples of knowledge Chef Ray can apply to simplifying the search for a good pancake:

- If the batter is too watery to cook with five cups of water and two of milk, there is no reason to try any recipes with additional cups of water or milk. That's a lot of recipes we need not try.
- Likewise, if 90 seconds on side two of the pancake burns it, there is no reason to try longer cooking times.
- If all of the cooking ingredients of the batter are doubled, we'll get the same batter—only twice as much. The rating of the pancake in both cases will be the same and the second recipe need not be tried.
- We can query the TONGUE software more in depth assuming it is willing to answer. If we are told "The pancake is too salty," there is no reason to test the same recipe using more salt.

Importantly, this prior knowledge must be accurate or it may steer us away from a good pancake. With incorrect information, the search could take longer than choosing random recipes, and the active information could be negative. Examples of misleading knowledge for the pancake recipe include (a) poorly written TONGUE software that gives us inaccurate fitness readings and (2) an unexpected fitness assessment contrary to our expectations, such as a high fitness assigned to severely burnt pancakes. (There is no accounting for taste.)

Knowledge about the fitness landscape can also help the search. Suppose, for example, we have a pancake with a low fitness of 2. With the prior knowledge of the smoothness of the fitness landscape, changing any one parameter either way will probably *not* result in a pancake with a fitness of 9. Indeed, changing parameters one unit each, either way won't provide success. What about two parameters away? Two parameters might work. The programmer writing the search software must decide what to do: exclude looking at all recipes with parameters one step either way, or two steps either way? Different programmers with different experience will choose differently. Such is the case for all prior knowledge about a search. The choice made by the programmer determines the active information infused into the search. Programmers with different skills and differing prior knowledge from domain expertise will infuse varying degrees of active information into the program.

Even after a search program is chosen, a clever pancake recipe programmer can have the freedom to transfer some of his prior knowledge about pancake recipes into the program. Most search algorithms have associated parameters that must be chosen. We can think of a search algorithm as a box with a number of knobs, each of which must be set by the programmer prior to implementation. An evolutionary search, for example, requires specifying the size of the population from generation to generation and the type and the severity of the mutations at each generation.

Proper choice of a search algorithm and its parameters can reduce the search time significantly. Different programmers will find different ways to fold prior knowledge into the search algorithm. When the search program produces a good pancake in a few hours, is it appropriate to say that the program is the source of intelligence that has reduced the time? Of course not. It is the computer programmer, i.e. the designer of the software that accelerates the search.

Every iterative search procedure has other components not illustrated in Fig. 3.4.

- **Memory.** A memory can store the results of previous queries.
- **Initialization.** The evolutionary loop in the bottom Fig. 3.4 must be initialized. If there is some knowledge of the region where the target is, for example, it makes sense to start the search in the region.
- **Stop Criterion.** No search can go on forever. Searches can go on for trillions of years before all possibilities are exhausted. The best *stop criterion*, of course, is finding an acceptable solution. No more iterations are required if we have found the recipe for a good-tasting pancake. Commonly used stop criteria include run time and iteration count. The iteration count is the number of times going through the evolutionary loop shown at the bottom of Fig. 3.4.

3.4.1 *Designing antennas using evolutionary computing*

The search for a good pancake, although presented solely for instructional purposes, describes what happens in computer search. A celebrated use of evolutionary computer search is the antenna design popularized by engineers at NASA. An antenna, designed by evolutionary computer search, is currently being used in space.

Here is a description. Assume we are given a paperclip-like length of stiff wire able to be bent in any and all ways. Once the wire is bent, it is tested to see how well, say, a cell phone signal is received. A success is declared when the cell phone signal strength is sufficiently strong. This is the design criterion. If a sufficiently strong signal is received, the design is a success and the search is complete. If not, the paperclip is bent differently and the experiment tried again. If the designer has no experience in antenna design, radio waves or cell phone electronics, the search is blind not unlike Edison's seeking of a light bulb filament. There is no assurance that a successful paperclip antenna even exists. Or it may turn out that almost any bent paperclip will do the job.

To perform this experiment, physical measurements using a cell phone are not required. The mathematical model of radio waves is well developed and the electromagnetic performance of a bent paperclip can be analyzed by a computer. All of the antenna design can thus be done on a computer. The computer is programmed to try millions of different bending geometries. The program is started. The programmer returns in a few days to see if any of the bending geometries works. The computer does nothing creative. The search is not substantively different than the performing painstaking bend-and-test experiments in the laboratory. The computer simply does things more quickly.

Designing an antenna using computer search is not simply a peda-gogical academic illustration of computer search. NASA scientists have designed antennas using evolutionary search where the results of previous failed designs are used to hone in to a successful design. One of the final designs is shown in Fig. 3.6.[10, 11]

What goes into such a design? In one evolutionary antenna synthesis by Venkatarayalu and Ray,[12] seven design parameters are used. Each parameter can be viewed as an ingredient for a recipe, akin to the ingredients for cooking a good pancake. We need to find out how much of each ingredient to use in order to make a sufficiently delicious pancake, or a good antenna. The final result must be good enough to meet prior design specifications.

Simulation software is often used as an oracle in search, including evolutionary search. NASA's evolutionary design of an X-band antenna,[13]

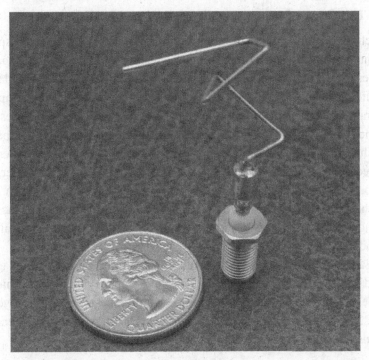

Fig. 3.6. An antenna designed by evolutionary search on a computer. The caption to the original web picture reads "Among the new technologies to be tested aboard the ST5 spacecraft is an antenna that was designed by a computer running a simulation of Darwinian evolution. This evolved antenna was discovered by an evolutionary algorithm running for days on a supercomputer. Its unusual shape is expected because most human antenna designers would never think of such a design."

for example, requires a mathematically involved fitness evaluation of every design proposed during the search. Akin to the COOK and TASTE oracles in the pancake search, NASA engineers used the *The Numerical Electromagnetics Code* (NEC-4)[14] as an oracle. NEC-4 is a widely used and powerful modeling software package for wire and surface antennas. Use of such software is essential in the computer design of the antennas. Note that evolutionary search is not the only search algorithm that can be used for the antenna design. Given the NEC oracle, for example, other search algorithms can be used to obtain a good antenna design. The evolutionary process itself creates no information.

3.5   The Curse of Dimensionality & the Need for Knowledge

Search algorithms guide us through our exploration of the search space. For human cooks and human tongues, testing up to a billion pancake recipes from 9 ingredients is not possible. For a computer model, simulating a billion pancakes is less of a problem. Suppose Chef Ray's computer program cooks and tests a virtual pancake at a rate of 100 recipes per second. Chef Ray can then examine all one billion 9 ingredient recipes in less than four months. If, though, we added only one more ingredient to our recipe, say adding 1 to 10 teaspoons of cooking oil to the batter, the number of possible recipes increases tenfold and becomes 10 billion. The search will take 10 times as long. Examining all of the possible pancakes will now take Chef Ray's program over 3 years. That's too long to wait for a good pancake.

Each ingredient we add to the recipe, assuming the step needs to be tested in 10 different ways, multiplies the computer simulation time by 10. Searching 16 parameters to a recipe would take over 3 million years. And 22 design parameters correspond to over 3 trillion years! The *curse of dimensionality* is evident from the numbers in Table 3.1.

Table 3.1. The number of years needed to try all recipes for various numbers of pancake ingredients.

Number of pancake ingredients	Years to try all possible recipes
9	0.32
10	3.2
11	32
12	317
13	3,169
14	31,688
15	316,881
16	3,168,809
17	31,688,088
18	316,880,878
19	3,168,808,781
20	31,688,087,814
21	316,880,878,140
22	3,168,808,781,403

A search for a pancake with 22 parameters without domain expertise is prohibitively time consuming. Chef Ray needs to be clever when he writes his computer program. Up to now, we have assumed Chef Ray knows nothing about cooking. His knowledge about cooking can be used to guide the search. Doing so infuses the search with *active information* to reduce its difficulty. Understanding and measuring active information is a fundamental precept of evolutionary informatics.

3.5.1 *Will Moore ever help? How about Grover?*

How about computers of the future? Will they allow large undirected blind searches within a reasonable amount of time? Even for problems of intermediate size, the answer is no.

Moore's law says that the number of transistors in a dense integrated circuit doubles approximately every two years. For discussion purposes, assume the speed of the computer doubles every year. Suppose there is a recipe with a 1500 design parameters, each of which takes on a value of one (use the ingredient) or zero (doesn't use it). Assume it takes a year to compute all of the recipes.[g] Let the speed of the computer double. How much larger a search can we now do in a year? If the speed of the computer has doubled, the disappointing answer is that a search can be done for only 1,501 ingredients.[h] *Only 1 more ingredient can be considered.* For the new search, we'd have to do the original search where the new ingredient is not used, and repeat the experiment for when the new ingredient is used. The effect of the addition of a single ingredient in the search is independent of the original search without the extra ingredient. Faster computers will not solve our problem.

What about the field of quantum computing? A quantum computer makes use of the strange and wonderful laws[i] of quantum mechanics such as superposition and entanglement[15] to perform operations on data. If implemented, Shor's algorithm[16] for quantum computers could rapidly decrypt many of the cryptographic systems in use today. In the area of

---

[g]For 500 ingredients that is $2^{500} = 3 \times 10^{150}$ recipes.
[h]For 501 ingredients, the number of recipes is $2^{501} = 2 \times 10^{500}$.
[i]Neils Bohr, a pioneer in quantum mechanics, famously stated "If quantum mechanics hasn't profoundly shocked you, you haven't understood it yet."

search, however, results are not yet that dramatic. Grover's algorithm[17] for search using a quantum computer reduces the search difficulty by only a square root. A trillion years on a traditional computer still translates to over a million years on a quantum computer. So Grover's algorithm helps a lot but does not solve the problem.

3.6 Implicit Targets

The search for a successful antenna design is explicitly *teleological*, meaning that specific design criteria are specified prior to the search. There is also *implicit teleology* wherein the structure of the search space or knowledge of the structure guides the search process to an implicit target.

Here is a simple example. Kirk is an armadillo foraging for grubs when he is bitten by a spider that makes him blind. Kirk wants to return to his armadillo hole, but is disoriented. He knows, though, that his hole is at the lowest elevation in the immediate area, so he balls up and rolls downhill to his hole. When Kirk does this, he is not explicitly seeking his hole. His surroundings are fortuitously designed to take him there. Kirk's target is thus implicit in the sense it is not specifically sought, but is a result of the environment's action on him. He can bounce off of trees and be kicked around by playful kids. And repeated trials of rolling down the hill might take drastically different paths. But ultimately, Kirk will end up in his hole at the bottom of the hill.[18] Kirk reaches his home because of information he acquires from his environment. The environment must be designed correctly for this to happen.

We can have *implicit target information* in the pancake example. Recall the first simple pancake example where the only two variables were the cooking times for sides one and two. The fitness landscape for this problem is in Fig. 3.2. Suppose Chef Ray's stove is electric and blows a fuse if either side of the pancake is cooked for more than a minute and half. That's equal to 6 intervals of 15 seconds. This constraint, imposed by the environment, changes the search to that pictured in Fig. 3.7. This constraint limits and thereby simplifies the search. Fortuitously, there is still a recipe that ranks sufficiently high to pass the design criterion. It is in the corner of the curve in Fig. 3.7 and marked with a small cube. The implicit

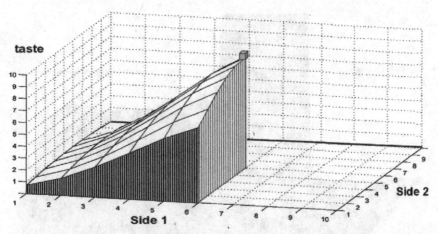

Fig. 3.7. This is how the search is changed from Fig. 3.2 on when the electric stove blows a fuse after 6 units of 15 seconds on either side. The search is now restricted. There is now a single recipe that ranks 9 or higher. It is marked by the small cube.

limitations imposed by the environment simplify the search by restricting the search space. Suppose, for some reason, the stove required that each side of a pancake had to be cooked for 6 minutes. If this is in addition to the constraint imposed by blowing fuses, then we find an acceptable recipe in one try! If, however, the environment is constrained in a negative way, the target may never be found even if it was available prior to the alteration.

So, like application of prior knowledge in cooking the pancake, fortuitous structure in the search space can likewise improve the search. As when applying prior knowledge to the search, the limitations on the search space must be such that an acceptable target can be found and will accelerate the search for the target. A change in the search without knowledge of the consequences will as likely have a positive as a negative impact.

Geographical maps can also illustrate the availability of active information from search space structure. In early 2014, Max was on a mission to raise funds for a politically liberal cause in the state of Texas. Texas is Max's search space. With no information about the politics of the state, Max is as likely to successfully raise his money in one part of the state as another. Suppose, however, Max has a copy of the results of the 2012 presidential election, as shown in Fig. 3.8. The lighter shaded areas went

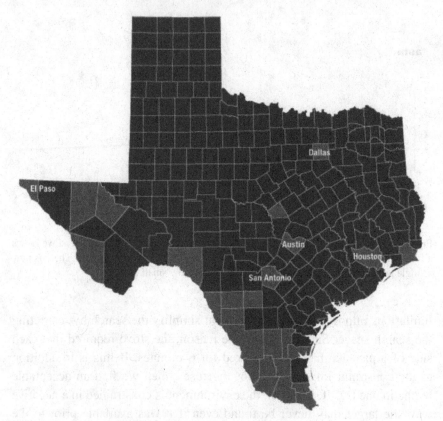

Fig. 3.8. A map of Texas counties. The darker shaded areas denote counties that voted for Mitt Romney in the 2012 presidential election and lighter shaded counties voted for Barack Obama. This map is helpful if you are raising funds for a liberal cause in Texas.

for Barack Obama and the darker shaded areas for Mitt Romney. Under the (very reasonable) assumption that Obama is more liberal than Romney, Max's best bet is to spend his fundraising time in the lighter shaded counties. The map can provide active information to Max's search for funding for his liberal cause.

3.7 Skeptic Fallibility

Critics of intelligent design more often than not have never designed anything. Their assessment of intelligent design from the viewpoint of design are often typically ill-formed or ill-informed.

Here is an oft-used critique from an anti-ID book:[19]

> "...ideal design is a lousy argument for evolution, for it mimics the postulated action of an omnipotent creator. Odd arrangements and funny solutions are the proof of evolution—paths that a sensible God would never tread but that a natural process, constrained by history, follows perforce."

This argument against an intelligent designer is founded on the premises "If I were the intelligent designer (e.g. God), I would design things in such and such a way. Things were not done this way, so there must be no intelligent designer."

Intelligent design critic Michael Shermer writes.[20]

> "...vestigial structures stand as evidence of the mistakes, the misstarts, and, especially, the leftover traces of evolutionary history."

Shermer claims weird design and leftovers in current organisms is evidence of evolution. Statements concerning suboptimal design presuppose that the intelligence behind evolution will choose to optimize to the best possible solution. Here are some problems with such statements.

1. Design can force tradeoffs so that an increase in effectiveness in one area necessitates a reduction of effectiveness of another. Effective design is, in part, an art of compromise. We'll discuss this more in depth in the *Pareto Optimization* section later in the chapter.
2. Optimization means finding the single absolutely best solution. Design engineers certainly don't do this. We've seen examples of single objective cases where engineers design in accordance with design criteria. The design is considered finished when fitness meets or exceeds these criteria. We did not search for the best pancake possible. We searched for any pancake with a taste rating of 9 or higher.
3. As witnessed by history, scientists make mistakes. Bloodletting does not make you healthier—it kills you. Ask George Washington. There is no aether in space that supports propagation of light. Debunking of that widely held belief contributed to the discovery of relativity.

Yesterday's vestigial structures often turn out to be today's prized necessity.

3.7.1 *Loss of function*

When environment changes, design can sometimes be improved by loss of function. A snake has no use for legs and a salamander in a dark cave has no use for eyes. Note, however, that loss of function does not correspond to infusion of information into the design, but is rather the removal of previous resident information. Selective loss of function can be beneficial for performance in temporarily changing environments and is a characteristic of good design. Rockets shed their emptied fuel stages to lighten the load and certain lizards shed their tails in order to avoid predators.

Loss of function is often erroneously diagnosed as proof of Darwinian evolution. But ignorance of function today is often replaced by newly discovered functional properties tomorrow. As the old saying goes, "absence of evidence is not evidence of absence." Just because we don't know whether or not an object has function doesn't mean it has no function.

A classic example is the human appendix, once thought to be a useless artifact of evolution. In 1912, Joseph McCabe wrote that the human appendix is "a large and normal intestine of a remote ancestor."[21] Modern medicine, however, has found the appendix assists the immune system,[22, 23] manufactures hormones during fetal development,[24] and provides a safe haven for flora bacteria.[25]

Another historical mistake concerning vestigial function concerns the role of DNA. Since most of our DNA does not encode proteins, the non-protein-coding portion was identified as useless vestigial "junk DNA." Junk DNA was thought to be the leavings of Darwinian evolution. It was later found to provide invaluable functions, including the transcriptional and translational regulation of protein-coding sequences.[26]

3.7.2 *Pareto optimization and optimal sub-optimality*

Often a search attempts to achieve two or more objectives. Besides a good-tasting pancake, we might also want an inexpensive pancake. These are conflicting criteria because delicious pancakes aren't cheap and cheap pancakes aren't delicious.

Conflicting criteria require application of the theory of multi-objective, or Pareto, optimization.[27, 28] Although there must be compromise, the final design can still be optimal in the sense it's the best we can get under conflicting design criteria.

An example is elementary detection theory. We are tasked to design a box where a red light flashes when we are being attacked by terrorists. A green light indicates we are safe. The performance of the detector can be discussed without knowing the details of its design. Here are two design criteria for our detector box:

1. *Maximize Detection Probability.* We want a detector whose probability of detection of a terrorist attack is high, i.e. when we are attacked the probability that the red light will flash should be high.
2. *Minimize False Alarm Probability.* When no terrorists are attacking we want the green light on with high probability. A red light flashing would be a false alarm when there is no attack.

Maximizing the detection probability alone is easy: always have the red light flashing. Then anytime we are being attacked by terrorists we will be 100% sure the red light is flashing. This, of course, is silly. The detector would be useless. It will also be useless if the false alarm probability is minimized in which case the green light is always left on. Since the red light never goes on, there are no false alarms. In detection theory, there is always a trade-off between detection and false alarm probabilities. When one goes up, so does the other. The Neyman–Pearson optimal detector maximizes detection probability for a fixed false alarm rate.[j,29–31] But there is no single best solution. The solution must be chosen in accordance with what the final user deems appropriate. One user's choice of an optimal design will often be different from another's.

Another example is the design of a personal motorized vehicle. If the design criterion is "inexpensive", a scooter is a good design. If the design criterion is "safety", however, then an armored SUV is the best design. But you can't have both extremes because cheap vehicles are not safe and safe vehicles are not cheap. The design tradeoff for this example is illustrated in Fig. 3.9.

---

[j]Equivalently, in the parlance of statistics, detection and false alarm probabilities relate to Type I and Type II errors, or false positives and false negatives.

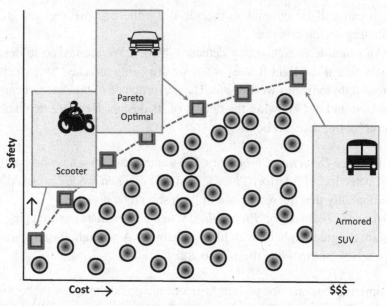

Fig. 3.9. An illustration of the design trade-off between safety and cost of a personal vehicle. In the example shown here, a number of vehicles are tested and assigned a number in accordance to safety. This number is plotted against the vehicle's cost. The squares are on the Pareto front and are connected with a dashed line. A vehicle makes the Pareto front if no other vehicle at the same cost is safer or no vehicle as safe cost less. Both the scooter and the armored SUV are on the Pareto front. Significantly, there is no single optimal design. The choice of the Pareto optimum on the Pareto front is a matter of informed choice. A frequently used solution is to fix one parameter and optimize the second. One might, for example, fix the maximum affordable cost and, under this constraint, purchase the safest possible vehicle. The circles below the Pareto front correspond to other vehicles that were tested. In the Pareto sense, these vehicles are suboptimal.

The final design must make a compromise. Design engineers are taught this art of compromise.

The field of multi-objective optimization is well-developed[31] in evolutionary search as elsewhere. A design is said to be optimal in the Pareto sense if the design is such that no individual design criterion can be bettered when the other criteria are fixed.

The lesson to be learned is this: in multi-objective or Pareto design, the critique of a design attribute cannot be made in a vacuum but must be made knowing the entire function of the final product and with consideration of other competing design criteria. Those criticizing design in nature by pointing to a less than optimal isolated performance of, say, the human eye without consideration of the entire physiology are unfamiliar with design and have probably never designed anything complex themselves.

3.7.3 *A man-in-the-loop sneaks in active information*

Computer programs, including evolutionary search, are invariably iteratively designed through debugging and tweaking.

3.7.3.1 *Evolving Tic-Tac-Toe to checkers to chess*

An interesting take on iterative design with a man-in-the-loop starts in 1993 when an evolutionary program "taught itself" to play tic-tac-toe.[32] The same researchers who developed the tic-tac-toe program published a paper eight years later in 2001 where a different evolutionary program they wrote learned to play checkers.[33] The skill of evolutionary programs they wrote had, in a sense, evolved to a higher level. Then in 2004 the team announced they had taught a computer using evolution to play chess.[34] Tic-tac-toe to checkers to chess is the type of information increase proponents of Darwinian evolution would celebrate. But the programming ability got better and better not because of evolution but primarily because of the increasing skill of the programmers.

This evolution in the capability of evolutionary programs would clearly not have happened without a man-in-the-loop.

3.7.3.2 *Replacing the man-in-the-loop with a*
computer-in-the-loop

Would it not be nice if we could program a computer to perform a search for a good search using a computer in the loop rather than a man in the loop? We show, however, that such a *search-for-a-search* (S4S) is a much more difficult problem than the search alone.[k]

The *man-in-the-loop's* contribution to the success of a search is rarely reported. More commonly, one hears only a report of the success of the final search algorithm followed by celebration and self-congratulations.

---

[k]Analysis of the search for the search is provided in Chapter 5.8.

3.8   A Smörgåsbord of Search Algorithms

We now return to the topic of the use of knowledge to generate active information in a single criterion search. If we do have knowledge about the search for a delicious pancake, there may be some clever ways to choose the next recipe. If, for example, the surface is known to be in some sense smooth, we can try *hill climbing*.[35,36] The fitness landscape for pancake cooking in Fig. 3.2 is smooth. Suppose two queries are taken close to each other in the' search space. If the fitness of the second query is smaller, we are going downhill and in the wrong direction. If the fitness is getting bigger, we are going up the hill and, hopefully, towards the maximum. In some search problems, measuring the slope (or gradient) of the fitness is possible. Knowing the slope means we know the steepest way up hill. This could be an efficient path to the maximum so the next step is taken in this direction. The occurrence of numerous hills on the search landscape, though, can be a problem. The search can be trapped on top of a hill at a *local maximum* which doesn't meet the design criterion and can be much lower than the *global maximum*. Such is the case in the two-dimensional fitness surface on the left in Fig. 3.10. There is a single global maximum. But on the right side of the landscape is a small hill. If the agent were to start on the right side of the search space and climb the hill, it very well could end up on the top of the smaller hill. The top of the smaller hill is an example of a local maximum.

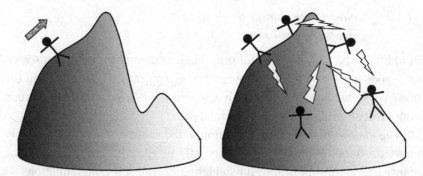

Fig. 3.10. Illustration of (left) stochastic hill climbing and (right) a multiagent search where agents can communicate their locations to one other. Evolutionary search is a special case of multiagent search.

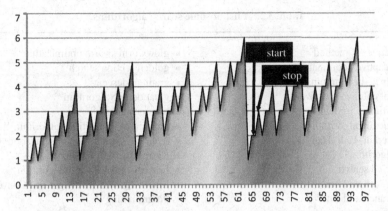

Fig. 3.11. A jagged landscape formed by the number of ones needed to express an integer in binary form. For example, $67 = (100011)_2$ has three ones.

Stochastic hill climbing and multiagent searches are a bit harder to visualize in higher dimensions, but the idea is the same. To find a yummy pancake recipe, we take a fairly successful recipe and change the recipe only slightly. If the new taste is better, we keep the new recipe and start changing the new recipe a bit. If the new taste is worse, we return to the original recipe and make some other slight changes.

All search landscapes are not smooth. Consider, for example, the one dimensional fitness landscape in Fig. 3.11. Our design criterion is to find an integer between 1 and 100 with fitness of 5 or above. There are 13 integers satisfying this constraint and they are well separated from each other in the search space. For this problem, there are initializations where strict application of stochastic hill climbing does not work. If, as shown in the figure, we start at 62 which has fitness of 2, we will climb a short hill and get stuck at the local maximum located at 63 which has a fitness of 3. This is a false maximum. The search procedure can be modified to get us out of this local maximum, but the performance of the fix will, in turn, depend on knowledge about the search space structure which itself must be accurate.

Hill climbing does not seem to be the appropriate search algorithm to explore the search space illustrated in Fig. 3.11. Stochastic hill climbing is only one of a large number of search algorithms. Different search algorithms work well on certain classes of optimization problems. Choosing

Table 3.2. A list of some search algorithms.

- active set method[38]
- adaptive coordinate descent[39]
- alpha–beta pruning[40]
- ant colony optimization[41]
- artificial immune system optimization[42]
- auction algorithm[43]
- Berndt–Hall–Hall–Hausman algorithm[44]
- blind search
- branch and bound[45]
- branch and cut[46]
- branch and price[47]
- Broyden–Fletcher–Goldfarb–Shanno (BFGS) method[48]
- Constrained optimization by linear approximation (COBYLA)[49]
- conjugate gradient method[50]
- CMA-ES (covariance matrix adaptation evolution strategy)[51]
- criss-cross algorithm[52]
- cross-entropy optimization[53]
- cuckoo search[54]
- Davidon's variable metric method[55]
- differential evolution[56]
- eagle strategy[57]
- evolutionary programs[58]
- evolutionary strategies
- exhaustive search
- Fibonacci search[59,60]
- firefly algorithm[61]
- Fletcher–Powell method[62]
- genetic algorithms[63]

- glowworm swarm optimization[64]
- golden section search[65,66]
- gradient descent[67]
- great deluge algorithm[68]
- harmony search[69]
- imperialist competitive algorithm[70]
- intelligent water drop optimization[71]
- Karmarkar's algorithm[72]
- Levenberg–Marquardt algorithm[73]
- Linear, Quadratic, Integer and Convex Programming[74]
- Nelder–Mead method[75]
- Newton–Raphson method[76]
- one-at-a-time search[77]
- particle swarm optimization[78]
- pattern search[79]
- POCS (alternating projections onto convex sets)[80]
- razor search[81]
- Rosenbrock methods[82]
- sequential unconstrained minimization technique (SUMT)[83]
- shuffled frog-leaping algorithm[84]
- simplex methods[85]
- simulated annealing[86]
- social cognitive optimization[87]
- stochastic gradient search[88]
- stochastic hill climbing[89]
- Tabu search[90]
- Tree search[91]
- Zionts–Wallenius method[92]

---

a good search algorithm and its parameters requires knowledgeable domain expertise of the computer programmer.

When computers became faster and were connected in parallel, effective multiagent search became possible. As we see on the right of Fig. 3.10, numerous agents are searching the fitness landscape. These agents are able to communicate with each other in order to coordinate their next move. Rules by which agents move, die and repopulate vary from search algorithm to search algorithm. Evolutionary search is an example of a multiagent search.

An incomplete list of search algorithms[37] is provided in Table 3.2. Search algorithms can have numerous variations. Each search procedure has various strengths and weaknesses depending on the character of the problem being solved. The good programmer will be able to use prior knowledge about the search to choose among the algorithms. The programmer seeks, as the saying goes, the right tool for the job.

3.9 Conclusions

Design is an inherently iterative search process requiring domain intelligence and expertise. Domain knowledge and experience can be applied to the search procedure to decrease the time needed for a successful search. Because of the exponential explosion of possibilities (i.e. the curse of dimensionality), the time and resources required by blind search quickly become too large to apply.

Undirected Darwinian evolution has neither the time nor computational resources to design anything of even moderate complexity. External knowledge is needed. Neither quantum computing nor Moore's law makes a significant dent in these requirements.

Notes

1. H. Wang, "On 'computabilism' and physicalism: some problems." In *Nature's Imagination*, J. Cornwall (ed.) (Oxford University Press, 1995), pp. 161–189.
2. For example:

    Thomas P. Schneider, "Evolution of biological information." *Nucleic Acids Res*, 28(14), pp. 2794–2799 (2000).

    R.E. Lenski, C. Ofria, R.T. Pennock, and C. Adami, "The evolutionary origin of complex features." *Nature*, 423(6936), pp. 139–144 (2003).

    G.J. Chaitin, *Proving Darwin: Making Biology Mathematical* (Pantheon, 2012).

    D. Thomas, "War of the Weasels: An Evolutionary Algorithm Beats Intelligent Design." *Skeptical Inquirer*, 43, pp. 42–46 (2010).

    D. Thomas, "Target? TARGET? We don't need no stinkin' Target!" http://pandasthumb.org/archives/2006/07/target-target-w-1.html (URL date May 2, 2016).

D. Thomas, "FORTRAN for Genetic Algorithm" (2006). http://www.nmsr. org/genetic.htm (URL date August 25, 2015).

D. Thomas (2006). "Steiner Genetic Algorithm-C++ Code." http:// pandasthumb.org/archives/2006/07/steiner-genetic.html (URL date May 2, 2016).

H.S. Wilf and W.J. Ewens, "There's plenty of time for evolution." *P Natl Acad Sci* 107, pp. 22454–22456 (2010).

R. Dawkins, *The Blind Watchmaker: Why the Evidence of Evolution Reveals a Universe Without Design* (Norton, New York, 1996).

3. Formula 409, http://www.formula409.com/ (URL date May 2, 2016).

4. D. Martin, "John S. Barry, Main Force Behind WD-40, Dies at 84." *New York Times*, July 22, 2009, http://www.nytimes.com/2009/07/22/ business/22barry1.html (URL date May 2, 2016).

5. M. Josephson, *Edison* (McGraw Hill, New York, 1959).

6. N. Baldwin, *Edison: Inventing the Century* (University of Chicago Press, 2001) ISBN 0-226-03571-9.

7. S. Shulman, *Owning the Future* (Houghton Mifflin Company, 1999), pp. 158–160.

8. *Thomas Edison: Life of an Electrifying Man*, Biographiq (Filiquarian Publishing, 2008).

9. David B. Fogel, *Evolutionary Computation: Toward a New Philosophy of Machine Intelligence*, 3rd edition (Wiley-IEEE Press, 2005).

Russell D. Reed and Robert J. Marks II, "An Evolutionary Algorithm for Function Inversion and Boundary Marking." *Proceedings of the IEEE International Conference on Evolutionary Computation*, pp. 794–797, November 26–30 (1995).

10. http://www.nasa.gov/centers/ames/news/releases/2004/antenna/antenna.html (URL date May 2, 2016).

11. Public domain, This work is in the public domain in the United States because it is a work of the United States Federal Government under the terms of Title 17, Chapter 1, Section 105 of the US Code.

12. N.V. Venkatarayalu and T. Ray, "Single and multi-objective design of Yagi-Uda antennas using computational intelligence." The 2003 Congress on Evolutionary Computation, CEC '03, 8–12 Dec., pp. 1237–1242 (2003).

13. J.D. Lohn, D.S. Linden, G.S. Hornby, A. Rodriguez-Arroyo, S.E. Seufert, B. Blevins, and T. Greenling, "Evolutionary design of an X-band antenna for NASA's Space Technology 5 mission." *IEEE Antennas and Propagation Society International Symposium*, 3, pp. 2313–2316 (2004).

J.D. Lohn, D.S. Linden, G.S. Hornby, and W.F. Kraus, "Evolutionary design of a single-wire circularly-polarized X-band antenna for NASA's Space

Technology 5 mission," *2005 IEEE International Symposium Antennas and Propagation Society*, 2B, pp. 267–270 (2005).

14. Gerald J. Burke, *Numerical Electromagnetics Code NEC-4, Method of Moments, Part I: User's Manual*, Lawrence Livermore National Laboratory (1992).
    Gerald J. Burke, *Numerical Electromagnetics Code NEC-4, Method of Moments, Part II: Program Description Theory*, Lawrence Livermore National Laboratory (1992).
15. I. Hiroshi and H. Masahito, *Quantum Computation and Information* (Springer, Berlin, 2006).
16. Peter W. Shor, "Polynomial-Time Algorithms for Prime Factorization and Discrete Logarithms on a Quantum Computer." *SIAM J Comput* 26(5), pp. 1484–1509 (1997).
17. L.K. Grover, "A fast quantum mechanical algorithm for database search." *Proceedings, 28th Annual ACM Symposium on the Theory of Computing*, p. 212 (1996).
18. This example was suggested to us by Walter Bradley.
19. J.B. Foster, B. Clark, and R. York, *Critique of Intelligent Design: Materialism versus Creationism from Antiquity to the Present* (Monthly Review Press, 2008).
20. M. Shermer, *Why Darwin Matters: The Case Against Intelligent Design* (Times Books, 2006).
21. J. McCabe, *The Story of Evolution* (Hutchinson & Co., London, 1912).
22. Loren G. Martin, "What is the function of the human appendix? Did it once have a purpose that has since been lost?" *Sci Am* (1999). http://www.scientificamerican.com/article/what-is-the-function-of-the-human-appendix-did-it-once-have-a-purpose-that-has-since-been-lost/ (URL date May 2, 2016).
23. M.L. Everett *et al.*, "Immune exclusion and immune inclusion: a new model of host-bacterial interactions in the gut." *Clin Appl Immunol Rev*, 5, pp. 321–32 (2004).
24. A. Zahid, "The vermiform appendix: not a useless organ." *J Coll Physicians Surg Pak*, 14(4), pp. 256–258 (2004).
25. R.R. Bollinger *et al.*, "Biofilms in the large bowel suggest an apparent function of the human vermiform appendix." *J Theor Biol*, 249(4), pp. 826–831 (2007).
26. J. Wells, *The Myth of Junk DNA* (WA Discovery Institute Press, Seattle, 2011). Also, "Not junk after all: non-protein-coding DNA carries extensive biological information." *Biological Information — New Perspectives* (World Scientific, Singapore, 2013), pp. 210–231.

27. Kay Chen Tan *et al.*, *Multiobjective Evolutionary Algorithms and Applications* (Springer, 2005).
28. Altannar Chinchuluun *et al.*, eds, *Pareto Optimality, Game Theory and Equilibria* (Springer, 2008).
29. R.J. Marks II, G.L. Wise, D.G. Haldeman and J.L. Whited, "Detection in Laplace noise." *IEEE Transactions on Aerospace and Electronic Systems*, (14), 1978, pp. 866–872.
30. C.F. Bas and R.J. Marks II, "The layered perceptron versus the Neyman-Pearson optimal detection." *Proceedings of the International Joint Conference on Neural Networks* (IEEE Press, Singapore, 18–20 Nov 1991), pp. 1486–1489.
31. For example, Paolo Di Barba, *Multiobjective Shape Design in Electricity and Magnetism* (Springer, 2009).
32. David B. Fogel, "Using evolutionary programing to create neural networks that are capable of playing tic-tac-toe." 1993 IEEE International Conference on Neural Networks, pp. 875–880.
33. Kumar Chellapilla and David B. Fogel, "Evolving an expert checkers playing program without using human expertise." *IEEE Transactions on Evolutionary Computation*, 5(4), pp. 422–428.
    See also David B. Fogel, *Blondie 24: Playing at the Edge of AI* (Morgan Kaufmann, 2001).
34. David B. Fogel, Timothy J. Hays, S. H. Hahn, and James Quon, "Self-learning evolutionary chess program." *Proceedings of the IEEE*, 92(12), pp. 1947–1954 (2004).
35. Richard O. Duda, Peter E. Hart, and David G. Stork, *Pattern Classification*, 2nd edition (Wiley-Interscience, 2000).
36. Olle Häggström, "Intelligent design and the NFL Theorem." *Biology & Philosophy* (2007).
37. Donald E. Knuth, *Sorting and Searching (The Art of Computer Programming volume 3)* (Addison Wesley, 1973).
38. J. Nocedal and S. Wright, *Numerical Optimization* (Springer Science & Business Media, 2006).
39. I. Loshchilov, M. Schoenauer, and M. Sebag, "Adaptive Coordinate Descent." In *Proceedings of the 13th Annual Conference on Genetic and Evolutionary Computation* (ACM, 2011), pp. 885–892.
40. Donald E. Knuth and Ronald W. Moore, "An analysis of alpha-beta pruning." *Artif Intel*, 6(4), pp. 293–326 (1976).
41. M. Dorigo, V. Maniezzo, and A. Colorni, "Ant system: optimization by a colony of cooperating agents." *IEEE Transactions on Systems, Man, and Cybernetics — Part B*, 26(1), pp. 29–41 (1996).

42. Leandro N. de Castro and J. Timmis, *Artificial Immune Systems: A New Computational Intelligence Approach* (Springer, 2002), pp. 57–58.

43. Dimitri P. Bertsekas, "A distributed asynchronous relaxation algorithm for the assignment problem." *Proceedings of the IEEE International Conference on Decision and Control*, pp. 1703–1704 (1985).

44. Ernst R. Berndt, Bronwyn H. Hall, Robert E. Hall, and Jerry A. Hausman, "Estimation and inference in nonlinear structural models." *Annals of Economic and Social Measurement*, 3(4), pp. 653–665 (1974).

45. Patrenahalli M. Narendra and K. Fukunaga, "A branch and bound algorithm for feature subset selection." *IEEE Transactions on Computers*, 100(9), pp. 917–922 (1977).

46. M. Padberg and G. Rinaldi, "A branch-and-cut algorithm for the resolution of large-scale symmetric traveling salesman problems." *SIAM Rev*, 33(1), pp. 60–100 (1991).

47. Cynthia Barnhart, Ellis L. Johnson, George L, Nemhauser, Martin W.P. Savelsbergh, and Pamela H. Vance, "Branch-and-price: Column generation for solving huge integer programs." *Operations Research*, 46(3), pp. 316–329 (1998).

48. J. Nocedal and Stephen J. Wright, *Numerical Optimization*, 2nd edition (Springer-Verlag, Berlin, New York, 2006).

49. Thomas A. Feo and Mauricio G.C. Resende, "A probabilistic heuristic for a computationally difficult set covering problem." *Op Res Lett*, 8(2), pp. 67–71 (1989).

50. A.V. Knyazev and I. Lashuk, "Steepest descent and conjugate gradient methods with variable preconditioning." *SIAM J Matrix Anal Appl*, 29(4), pp. 1267–1280 (2007).

51. Y. Akimoto, Y. Nagata, I. Ono, and S. Kobayashi. "Bidirectional relation between CMA evolution strategies and natural evolution strategies." *Parallel Problem Solving from Nature*, PPSN XI, pp. 154–163 (Springer, Berlin Heidelberg, 2010).

52. Dick den Hertog, C. Roos, and T. Terlaky, "The linear complimentarity problem, sufficient matrices, and the criss-cross method." *Linear Algebra Appl*, 187, pp. 1–14 (1993).

53. R.Y. Rubinstein, "Optimization of computer simulation models with rare events." *Eur J Ops Res*, 99, pp. 89–112 (1997).
R.Y. Rubinstein and D.P. Kroese, *The Cross-Entropy Method: A Unified Approach to Combinatorial Optimization, Monte-Carlo Simulation, and Machine Learning* (Springer-Verlag, New York, 2004).

54. X.S. Yang and S. Deb, "Cuckoo search via Lévy flights." *World Congress on Nature & Biologically Inspired Computing* (NaBIC 2009). IEEE Publications, pp. 210–214. arXiv:1003.1594v1.

55. W. C. Davidon, "Variable metric method for minimization." *AEC Research Development Rept.* ANL-5990 (Rev.) (1959).

56. P. Rocca, G. Oliveri, and A. Massa, "Differential evolution as applied to electromagnetics." *Antennas and Propagation Magazine, IEEE*, 53(1), pp. 38–49 (2011).

57. Xin-She Yang and Suash Deb, "Eagle strategy using Lévy walk and firefly algorithms for stochastic optimization." *Nature Inspired Cooperative Strategies for Optimization (NICSO 2010)* (Springer Berlin Heidelberg, 2010), pp. 101–111.

58. Jacek M. Zurada, R.J. Marks II and C.J. Robinson; Editors, *Computational Intelligence: Imitating Life* (IEEE Press, 1994).
    M. Palaniswami, Y. Attikiouzel, Robert J. Marks II, D. Fogel, and T. Fukuda; Editors, *Computational Intelligence: A Dynamic System Perspective* (IEEE Press, 1995).

59. David E. Ferguson, "Fibonaccian searching." *Communications of the ACM*, 3(12), p. 648 (1960).

60. J. Kiefer, "Sequential minimax search for a maximum." *Proceedings of the American Mathematical Society*, 4(3), pp. 502–506 (1953).

61. Xin-She Yang, "Firefly algorithms for multimodal optimization." In *Stochastic Algorithms: Foundations and Applications* (Springer Berlin Heidelberg, 2009), pp. 169–178.

62. R. Fletcher and M.J.D. Powell, "A rapidly convergent descent method for minimization." *Computer J.* (6), pp. 163–168 (1963).

63. David E. Goldberg, *Genetic Algorithms in Search Optimization and Machine Learning* (Addison Wesley, 1989).
    R. Reed and R.J. Marks II, "Genetic Algorithms and Neural Networks: An Introduction." *Northcon/92 Conference Record* (Western Periodicals Co., Ventura, CA, Seattle WA, October 19–21, 1992), pp. 293–301.

64. K.N. Krishnanand and D. Ghose. "Detection of multiple source locations using a glowworm metaphor with applications to collective robotics." *Proceedings of the 2005 IEEE Swarm Intelligence Symposium (SIS 2005)*, pp. 84–91 (2005).

65. A. Mordecai and Douglass J. Wilde. "Optimality proof for the symmetric Fibonacci search technique." *Fibonacci Quarterly*, 4, pp. 265–269 (1966).

66. Jack Kiefer, *op. cit.*

67. Jan A. Snyman, *Practical Mathematical Optimization: An Introduction to Basic Optimization Theory and Classical and New Gradient-Based Algorithms* (Springer Publishing, 2005).

68. Gunter Dueck, "New optimization heuristics: the great deluge algorithm and the record-to-record travel." *J Comp Phys*, 104(1), pp. 86–92 (1993).

69. Zong Woo Geem, "Novel derivative of harmony search algorithm for discrete design variables." *Applied Mathematics and Computation*, 199, (1), pp. 223–230 (2008).

70. Esmaeil Atashpaz-Gargari and Caro Lucas, "Imperialist competitive algorithm: an algorithm for optimization inspired by imperialistic competition." *2007 IEEE Congress on Evolutionary Computation (CEC 2007)*, pp. 4661–4667 (2007).

71. Shah-Hosseini Hamed, "The intelligent water drops algorithm: a nature-inspired swarm-based optimization algorithm." *Int J Bio-Inspired Comp*, 1(1/2), pp. 71–79 (2009).

72. Karmarkar Narendra, "A new polynomial-time algorithm for linear programming." *Proceedings of the Sixteenth Annual ACM Symposium on Theory of Computing*, pp. 302–311 (1984).

73. Kenneth Levenberg, "A Method for the Solution of Certain Non-Linear Problems in Least Squares." *Quart App Math*, 2, pp. 164–168 (1944).

74. Alexander Schrijver, *Theory of Linear and Integer Programming* (John Wiley & Sons, 1998).
    Yurii Nesterov, Arkadii Nemirovskii, and Yinyu Ye, "Interior-point polynomial algorithms in convex programming." Vol. 13. *Philadelphia Society for Industrial and Applied Mathematics* (1994).

75. K.I.M. McKinnon, "Convergence of the Nelder–Mead simplex method to a non-stationary point." *SIAM J Optimization*, 9, pp. 148–158 (1999).

76. E. Süli and D. Mayers, *An Introduction to Numerical Analysis* (Cambridge University Press, 2003).

77. A.H. Boas, "Modern mathematical tools for optimization," *Chem Engrg* (1962).

78. J. Kennedy and R. Eberhart, "Particle Swarm Optimization." *Proceedings of IEEE International Conference on Neural Networks* IV, pp. 1942–1948 (1995).
    J. Kennedy and R. Eberhart, *Swarm Intelligence* (Morgan Kaufmann, 2001).

79. A. W. Dickinson, "Nonlinear optimization: Some procedures and examples." *Proceedings of the 19th ACM National Conference* (ACM, 1964), pp. 51–201.

80. Robert J. Marks II, *Handbook of Fourier Analysis & its Applications* (Oxford University Press, 2009).

81. J.W. Bandler and P.A. Macdonsdd, "Optimization of microwave networks by razor search." *IEEE Trans. Microwave Theory Tech.*, 17(8), pp. 552–562 (1969).

82. H.H. Rosenbrock, "An automatic method for finding the greatest or least value of a function." *Comp. J.*, 3, pp. 175–184 (1960).

83. John W. Bandler, "Optimization methods for computer-aided design." *IEEE Transactions on Microwave Theory and Techniques*, 17(8), pp. 533–552 (1969).

84. Muzaffar Eusuff, Kevin Lansey, and Fayzul Pasha, "Shuffled frog-leaping algorithm: a memetic meta-heuristic for discrete optimization." *Engineering Optimization*, 38(2), pp. 129–154 (2006).

85. M.J. Box, "A new method of constrained optimization and a comparison with other methods." *Computer J.*, (8), pp. 42–52 (1965).
     J.A. Nelder and R. Mead, "A simplex method for function minimization." *Computer J.*, 7, pp. 308–313 (1965).

86. S. Kirkpatrick, C.D. Gelatt, and M.P. Vecchi, "Optimization by simulated annealing." *Science*, 220(4598), pp. 671–680 (1983).

87. X.-F. Xie, W. Zhang, and Z. Yang, "Social cognitive optimization for nonlinear programming problems." *Proceedings of the First International Conference on Machine Learning and Cybernetics*, 2, pp. 779–783 (Beijing, 2002).

88. James C. Spall, *Introduction to Stochastic Search and Optimization* (2003).

89. Brian P. Gerkey, Sebastian Thrun, and Geoff Gordon, "Parallel stochastic hill-climbing with small teams." *Multi-Robot Systems. From Swarms to Intelligent Automata*, Volume III, pp. 65–77. (Springer Netherlands, 2005).

90. F. Glover, "Tabu Search — Part I." *ORSA J Comput*, 1(3), pp. 190–206 (1989).
     "Tabu Search — Part II", *ORSA J Comput*, 2(1), pp. 4–32 (1990).

91. Athanasios K. Sakalidis, "AVL-Trees for Localized Search." *Inform Control*, 67, pp. 173–194 (1985).
     R. Seidel and C.R. Aragon, "Randomized search trees." *Algorithmica*, 16(4–5), pp. 464–497 (1996).

92. S. Zionts and J. Wallenius, "An interactive programming method for solving the multiple criteria problem." *Manage Sci*, 22(6), pp. 652–663 (1976).

4

DETERMINISM IN RANDOMNESS

"We could have come from anything — fish, maybe, but not monkeys. I don't believe in the evolution of fish to monkeys to men. It's absolutely irrational garbage. They set up these idols and they knocked them down. It keeps all the old professors happy at the University. He gets something to do . . . Everything they told me as a kid's already been disproved by the same type of Experts who made them up in the first place."

John Lennon[1]

All evolutionary processes are stochastic. They use randomness and make some decisions, as it were, by flipping a weighted coin. Depth of mutation is an example.

Although it sounds paradoxical, randomness as modeled by standard probability theory has many fixed almost deterministic properties. Randomness need not imply unguidedness. When this is the case, one is led to ask who is steering this randomness to its ultimate end?

We will show how random evolutionary processes are constrained to both limited and bounded results. For this reason, no matter how long you let an evolutionary process run in a fixed environment, a solution will never get smarter than is allowed by the process. An evolutionary program written to design an antenna will never develop the ability to play chess. And a fixed environment to guide a stochastic process into evolving complexity on the scale of man is unimaginably improbable.

But couldn't we write a computer program to dynamically change the environment and therefore the fitness in such a way as to guide an evolutionary process to evolve a single cell, then a guppy, a frog, a monkey and then man? If so, the scheduling of the environmental changes must themselves be carefully designed. It is more likely that an environmental change will destroy previous gains than that it will advance them to a new level of sophistication.

The steel ball bouncing about in a pinball machine is an example of a random process with a single fixed point: The ball always ends up in the little hole behind the flippers. A variation of this illustration is a hand-held maze with a rolling BB whose goal is to get the BB to the end of the maze. For simple mazes, random tilting corresponding to environment changes may occasionally find the end of the maze target. For a standard 4.75 mm BB in a complex maze with walls separated by 5 mm, randomly solving a maze the size of a football field would be more difficult. As the complexity of the maze grows, the more difficult success becomes. Intelligence monitoring the maze from above can tilt the maze purposefully, i.e. change the environment, to roll the BB to a desired target. Doing so, however, requires precise planning of the environmental changes. The process must be carefully designed (see Fig. 4.1).

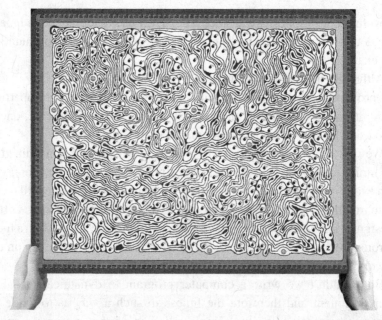

Fig. 4.1. Get the BB through the maze from A to Z passing through various stages of functional viability (☺) and avoiding extinction (☻※). Extinction is allowed once. "It is possible to fail in many ways . . . while to succeed is possible only in one way." Aristotle.

4.1 Bernoulli's Principle of Insufficient Reason[2]

To search for a pancake with nine ingredients, domain expertise is needed to perform the search through 1 billion recipes in reasonable time. For any but the simplest search problems, domain expertise is mandatory. But what if we have no expertise? It may sound trite, but if there is no domain expertise, we know *nothing*. Probabilistically, this means the solution is equally likely to exist anywhere in the search domain. In terms of Shannon information, the initialization is at maximum entropy, e.g. maximum uncertainty.

4.1.1 *"Nothing is that which rocks dream about"*[a]

What does knowing "nothing" mean? It might sound like a paradox, but "nothing" means something[b] — it means "absolutely nothing" or, more literally, "nothing," The idea of "nothing" can be difficult to grasp.

As an example, consider the theory of the Big Bang creation of the universe. It is common to picture the universe before the Big Bang as a large black void empty space. No sound, no matter, no energy. Just a never-ending expanse of empty space. No. This is a flawed image. Before the Big Bang there was *nothing*[c] and a never ending expanse of empty space is *something*.[d] Claims about matter spontaneously appearing in an empty space due to quantum effects, therefore, do not explain the Big Bang. Before the Big Bang, there was *nothing*. So space must be purged from our visualization of reality prior to the creation of the universe.

Okay. Visualize no space. It's hard, but we can do it. Maybe. We think "There was nothing. No sound, no matter, no energy. No space. Nothing. Then, all of a sudden . . ."

---

[a]Variously sourced to Plato, Aristotle and Socrates.

[b]Word play around "nothing" can be fun here. The meaningful statement "nothing means something" appears at first to be an oxymoron. The phrase "nothing means nothing," interestingly, means the same thing, or alternatively can be interpreted as a tautology.

[c]Nothingness prior to creation is also consistent with the biblical account of creation in Genesis.

[d]Arguments based on the premise that matter spontaneously appearing in empty space due to quantum effects therefore do not apply to the Big Bang. The argument has a faulty presupposition. Prior to the creation of the universe, there was no space. Physics says space did not exist prior to the Big Bang. So do most Christian theologians.

No. This doesn't work either. *All of a sudden* presupposes a surprising event that occurs within the flow of time. Modern cosmology says that time in our universe was also created[e] at the Big Bang.[3] So besides space, the idea of time must be purged from our imagination before comprehending the nothing that existed before the Big Bang. Comprehension of no space and no time is not a trivial intellectual exercise.[f] We have always existed in time and space and have difficulty visualizing their absence. The meaning of the nothing prior to the Big Bang is seen to be difficult to intuitively grasp.

4.1.2 *Bernoulli's Principle (PrOIR)*

In computer search, Bernoulli's *Principle of Insufficient Reason* (PrOIR) assumes *nothing* is known about a search problem except for the search space domain, including its cardinality. When a point in the search space is queried, the fitness can be ascertained. Otherwise we should have no method to keep score on the queries. Foundationally, the idea of nothing in the search space is not as difficult to comprehend as the *nothing* that existed before the Big Bang, but the rigor of interpretation of *nothing* remains strict. We know nothing about where the target is located. We know nothing about the structure of the search space. We don't know if it's smooth, ragged, or flat everywhere. It could be that every point in the search space is a viable solution to the problem. Maybe there is no solution whatsoever. We don't know. We know *nothing*.

Bernoulli's PrOIR, published in 1713, reads[4,5,g]

> "... in the absence of any prior knowledge, we must assume that the events [in a search space] have equal probability."

---

[e]Phrases such as "before the beginning of time" are in the Bible. See, for example Titus 1:2 in the NIV translation.

[f]Proponents of M-theory would argue the possibility of parallel universes existing "before" the Big Bang. The absence of time as we know it, though, begs the question of the meaning of "before." The meaning of "before" conceptually lies even beyond the concept of *nothing* in our universe.

[g]*Bernoulli's PrOIR*, credited to Jakob Bernoulli (1654–1705) and published after his death, is not to be confused with the *Bernoulli's principle* of fluid dynamics. The fluids principle is credited to Jakob's nephew, Daniel Bernoulli (1700–1782).

Pierre-Simon Laplace, noted 18th century mathematician/astronomer and atheist, agreed.[6]

> "[When] we have no reason to believe any particular case should happen in preference to any other"

If we know *nothing* about the search, each of the elements in the search space should be considered equally probable.

4.1.2.1 *Examples*

We use Bernoulli's PrOIR in everyday calculations of chance:

1. *The Lottery:* If a 1000 lottery tickets are sold, we assume the chance of any ticket being drawn is the same as any other. If you buy one ticket, your chance of winning is one in a thousand. Bernoulli's PrOIR has been applied. Cheating lottery officials can skew the results, but if you don't know about it, i.e. you know *nothing* about the selection process, the equally probable outcomes are your best estimate of your chances.
2. *Roulette:* A similar example is the roulette wheel. Odds of winning are based on Bernoulli's PrOIR which says the chance of the roulette ball falling in any slot is the same as falling in any other. If the casino operator has an unknown control over the wheel, the assumption may not be true. If, though, you know *nothing* about the process of the spinning roulette wheel, the uniform probability assumption is the right one.
3. *Dice:* When we roll a fair die, all six sides are assumed to be equally probable. The chance of three dots showing are thus one in six.
4. *Casting lots*: The practice of casting lots in the Bible presupposed all outcomes had equal probability and was fair to all participants. We read:

> "Casting lots causes contentions to cease, and keeps the mighty apart." (Proverbs 18:18)

Better to roll the dice and impose Bernoulli's PrOIR than fight a war.

4.1.2.2 *Criticisms of Bernoulli's principle*

Although Bernoulli's PrOIR seems obvious, there are those who object. Let's address these criticisms.

4.1.2.2.1   Model variations

A valid criticism of Bernoulli's PrOIR is improper modeling. The distribution is either interpreted improperly or has been knowingly manipulated to be non-uniform.[h] Here are some examples.

Star Trek: Fans of Star Trek are familiar with the Kobayashi Maru,[i] a test given to Starfleet cadets in the command track at Starfleet Academy. The test was administered as a virtual reality battle simulation and was designed to be difficult or even impossible to pass. James T. Kirk, the future Captain of the Starship Enterprise, took the test and became the first to ever pass. He did so by changing the model underlying the test and thereby invalidating assumptions normally associated with the game. To do so, he sneaked away with and rewrote some of the software controlling the simulation.

Our takeaway is this: The outcome of an event is often modelled by our presupposition of the event's representation. If the model is invalid, then our prediction of an outcome will also be invalid. Probability is a mathematical model. When a coin is flipped, the detailed physics of the flip, the coin and the environment totally determine whether the outcome will be a heads or tails. The physical analysis can be too detailed for analysis or, more significantly, environmental parameters such as impact elasticity that controls the coin's bounce, are unknown.

But what if we constructed a machine in a vacuum that flipped a coin the exact same way each time? We should get the same result each time. But coin flipping is *ill-conditioned*.[7] Even small variations in the flip or the environment quickly revert the solution back to a 50–50 probability of a heads or tails. Thus, the probability model is applied and the outcome of heads or tails is, according to Bernoulli's PrOIR, 50–50. In the coin flip, as in other probability applications, the determination of probability must

---

[h]Bernoulli's PrOIR is applied in the examples of *active information* in Chapter 5.4.2. The definition of active information, however, need not use a uniform distribution as a baseline, but can measure added information from any distribution. The idea is the same as measuring dB (decibels) which, like active information, is proportional to the logarithm of a ratio. The denominator of the ratio, the reference, can be any value desired.

[i]The Kobayashi Maru test, well known to Trekkies, was first administered in the opening scene of the film *Star Trek II: The Wrath of Khan*. It also is mentioned in the 2009 film *Star Trek*.

be considered a model. Bernoulli's PrOIR indicates that, in the absence of any knowledge about the outcome of an experiment, equal probability is assigned to each possible result.

When considering the previous lottery, roulette and dice examples, one can point to the failure of the uniform probability assumption after model-discrediting experimentation. Experimentation, however, creates knowledge and we know something, i.e. we no longer know *nothing*.

Roulette: In one of the first attempts to use a computer to skew odds, Claude Shannon[8] and Edward O. Thorp[j] used a wearable computer in 1961 to experimentally measure the deviations from uniformity of a roulette wheel.[9] Shannon and Thorp challenged the model of uniformity. By learning something about the roulette wheel process, they were able to place bets on outcomes more favorable than uniform. Today, roulette wheels are balanced frequently and realigned to keep the result of the spins as random as possible. Also the table is now closed for betting before the spin begins.

Blackjack: When playing blackjack at a casino, the casino's chance of taking your money when dealing from a freshly shuffled deck is about 51%. Although these are not overly favorable odds, the law of large numbers dictates that if you play blackjack long enough, the casino will end up with all your money. But blackjack is typically not dealt from a freshly shuffled deck. A number of decks are shuffled together and the cards are flipped over sequentially over a number of games. Information gained from remembering what cards were played can decrease the casino's odds below 50%. The tables are turned. If you play long enough, you'll take all of the casino's money.[k]

Simple methods of accounting for cards played in blackjack are dubbed *card counting* as shown in the documentary *Holy Rollers*.[10]

†*Loaded Die and Proportional Betting:* The mathematics of optimal gambling is well defined using the language of Shannon information theory.

---

[j]Thorp was a developer of card counting and an early hedge-fund pioneer.

[k]This assumes that your initial stash of betting money is large. The volatility (variance) in winning at probabilities close to 50% is big and, although the law of large numbers is applicable, there might be a significant amount of loss before asymptotic winnings are achieved.

Shannon and Thorp knew that the roulette wheel did not conform to a uniform probability of outcome, yet payout is based on the assumption that it does. Consider the two extremes. If the probabilities of outcomes are all the same, prospects of winning extra money are bleak. Consider for example six possible outcomes, as there are on the roll of a fair die. Then each outcome would have odds of 1 in 6. Assumed when you place a successful bet, your winnings are six times the amount of the wager. If you had $12 and put $2 bets on each of the six outcomes, you always end each game with your $12 back, whether or not the die is fair. This is neither a very exciting nor a lucrative pastime. But things get more exciting if the die is not fair and you have knowledge of the probability of the outcome of each event. Money can be made.

The optimal long term strategy when you know the probability of each outcome is dubbed *proportional betting*. Here's an example. You roll a die and no matter what number shows after a roll, the payoff is 6:1 for winners. The house is assuming that the die is fair and the chance of any face is one out of six.[1] But you know the die is loaded and has the following outcome probabilities:

$$p_1 = \frac{1}{2}, \quad p_2 = \frac{1}{3}, \quad p_3 = p_4 = \frac{1}{12}, \quad p_5 = p_6 = 0.$$

The probability of rolling a 2 is, for example, $p_2 = \frac{1}{3}$ Proportional betting dictates you should spread your bets proportional to the probabilities of success. If you initially had $12, proportional betting would be

$$b_1 = \$6, \quad b_2 = \$4, \quad b_3 = b_4 = \$1, \quad b_5 = b_6 = \$0.$$

Here are the possible outcomes and your next spread of bets:

- If the die is rolled and shows one, you collect $36. The chance of this happening is $p_1 = \frac{1}{2}$ Your second wager using proportional betting is

---

[1]† At this payout, the house is also apparently not interested in making any money in the long run. It would, on the average break even. For the house to win, it would need to pay something less, say $5.50 for every one dollar bet, when the die outcome is successfully predicted.

then

$$b_1 = \$18, \quad b_2 = \$12, \quad b_3 = b_4 = \$3, \quad b_5 = b_6 = \$0.$$

- If the die is rolled and shows 2, you collect $24 which you again spread proportional to the odds. The second round of betting is then

$$b_1 = \$12, \quad b_2 = \$8, \quad b_3 = b_4 = \$2, \quad b_5 = b_6 = \$0.$$

- If either a three or a four shows on the roll of the die, you get paid $6 and have lost half of your money. That's okay. You still have money to bet and your second wager is

$$b_1 = \$3, \quad b_2 = \$2, \quad b_3 = b_4 = \$0.50, \quad b_5 = b_6 = \$0.$$

- Since you know the probability of the five or six showing is zero, five and six are never bet on.

In the long run, proportional betting maximizes your returns faster than any other method.[11,m] But the probabilities must be accurate. If not, you could lose everything quickly.

Since outcomes are stochastic, different games of proportional betting will result in different outcomes. Starting with only one dollar, simulations of repeated wagering using these probabilities and proportional betting

---

[m]† Here's the math. For N possible outcomes, the *doubling rate* for proportional betting is

$$W(\vec{p}) = \log_2 N - H(\vec{p}),$$

where $\vec{p} = [p_1, p_2, p_3, \ldots, p_N]^T$ denotes a vector of the probability of outcomes for each occurrence and

$$H(\vec{p}) = -\sum_{n=1}^{N} p_n \log_2 p_n$$

is the entropy of the probability spread. The quantity $W(\vec{p})$ is dubbed the doubling rate because, after $M \gg 1$ games using proportional betting, your expected winnings are

$$S_G = S_0 2^{M\,W(\vec{p})},$$

where S_0 is the money you started with. When all p_n's are the same, $W(\vec{p}) = 0$, and your money never doubles. When one p_n is one and the rest are zero, $W(\vec{p}) = \log_2 N$ and $S_G = S_0 N^M$. Each game multiplies your winning by a factor of N.

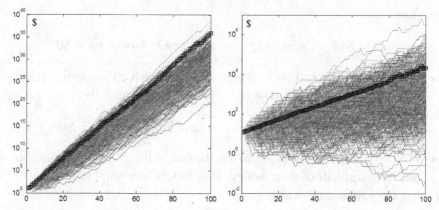

Fig. 4.2. Simulation of proportional betting for 100 games starting with \$12. The thick black line is the average. On the left, the outcomes of six possibilities are $p_1 = \frac{1}{2}$, $p_2 = \frac{1}{3}$, $p_3 = p_4 = \frac{1}{12}$, $p_5 = p_6 = 0$. In 100 games, you can on average pay off the national debt, pay 50% taxes and still be the richest person in the world. On the right is the more modest case of $p_1 = \frac{1}{12}$, $p_2 = \frac{3}{12}$, $p_3 = p_4 = p_5 = p_6 = \frac{1}{6}$. You can make a few thousand dollars on average, but note that in the worst case you end up with about $\$10^{-2}$ = a penny.

are shown on the left in Fig. 4.2. Winnings accumulate rapidly using proportional betting. Note that 10^{10} corresponds to 10 billion dollars and 10^{15} to one quadrillion (1000 trillion) dollars.

The further the probabilities are from uniform, the faster money is accumulated. This is measured by the doubling rate parameter, W, which tells how long on the average it takes to double your initial stash.[n] It is given by

$$W(\vec{p}) = \log_2 N - H(\vec{p}),$$

where N is the number of possible outcomes of the experiment and $H(\vec{p})$ is the Shannon entropy corresponding to the probability distribution. For an unloaded die (i.e. a uniform distribution), $H(\vec{p}) = \log_2 N$ and $W = 0$. In other words, neither you nor the house makes money on average in the long run. The game is breakeven, which is what the game was initially designed to do.

The same equation describes the active information in the case where we have N possible outcomes in a search space and compute the active

---

[n]† See the previous footnote for math details.

information corresponding to choosing outcomes proportional to the probability that the search space element is the target. Then the active information from knowledge of the probabilistic distribution is $I_+ = W$ as given in the equation above. In gambling, active information can be very profitable.

Simulations for repeated proportional betting with probabilities closer to uniform are shown on the right hand side of Fig. 4.2. The accumulation of winnings is still remarkable but occurs at a much more modest rate. When all the probabilities are equal to each other and the distribution is uniform, the winning curve is no longer random. For proportional betting, your winnings each game will exactly replenish your initial stash. The winning curve will therefore be a constant horizontal line.

The performance of proportional betting is akin to that of a search algorithm. For proportional betting, you want to extract the maximum amount of money from the game in a single bet. In search, you wish to extract the maximum amount of information in a single query. The mathematics is identical.

The Broken Die: Proportional betting is an example where probability knowledge about a search space can be used to make money. Here is an historical example where the fundamental model of a fair die was shown to be inaccurate.

The illustration is an account documented in Ivar Ekeland's *The Broken Dice*.[12] Ekeland describes how the kings of Norway and Sweden back in the Middle Ages decided to cast a pair of dice to determine ownership of a settlement on the Island of Hising, a settlement that had alternately belonged to both countries. The highest totaling sum was to determine the winner. The king of Sweden went first and rolled double sixes. It would therefore seem that the king of Norway could at best tie the king of Sweden, though the more likely outcome was that the Hising settlement would end up in the hands of Sweden. With six faces on a die and faces numbered one through six, the sum of any pair of faces from a pair of dice could total no less than two and no more than 12. The reference class of possible outcomes for the pair of dice could therefore be represented by the set {2, 3, 4, 5, 6, 7, 8, 9, 10, 11, 12}. What's more, the king of Sweden had just rolled the best possible result in this set, namely, 12.

What happened next was therefore remarkable:

> "Thereupon Olaf, king of Norway, cast the dice, and one six showed on one of them, but the other split in two, so that six and one turned up; and so he took possession of the settlement."[13]

Since in this game of dice higher sums trump lower sums, $13(= 6 + 6 + 1)$ trumps $12(= 6 + 6)$, so the king of Norway was declared the winner. Typically, any game with a pair of dice reckons with at most a pair of faces on any throw. Given this constraint, the reference class of possible sums for a pair of dice faces will be $\{2, 3, 4, 5, 6, 7, 8, 9, 10, 11, 12\}$. Yet given the possibility of a die splitting in two and showing two faces, the reference class of possible sums would have to be expanded to include at least $\{2, 3, 4, 5, 6, 7, 8, 9, 10, 11, 12, 13\}$.

Could it be that King Olaf orchestrated his win? Possibly he knew the die was made from some brittle material that would break if thrown forcefully to the ground. By doing so he altered the space of possible outcomes in variance with the assumptions of the king of Sweden and other spectators. Later in this chapter will see that chances of winning in a sweepstakes drawing are independent of their spatial distribution or method of selection. But as seen in Fig. 4.3, we can apply *Olaf's principle* to increase our chances of winning in a drawing of paper ballots.

4.1.2.2.2   Vague definitions & ambiguity: Bertrand's paradox

Critics of Bernoulli's PrOIR include John Maynard Keynes,[o] who renamed Bernoulli's PrOIR the *Principle of Indifference*.[14] Keynes appeals to *Bertrand's paradox* as a counterexample. Bertrand asks the following question.

> "If a cord in a circle is chosen randomly, what is the probability that its length exceeds $\sqrt{3}$ of the circle's radius?"

Bertrand shows there are at least 3 solutions depending on the application of Bernoulli's PrOIR: $p = \frac{1}{2}, \frac{1}{3}$ or $\frac{1}{4}$. As shown in Fig. 4.4, and discussed in its caption, however, this is not the problem. In one case

---

[o]John Maynard Keynes (1883–1946) was a British economist who advocated interventionist government policy. His ideas provide the foundation for *Keynesian economics*.

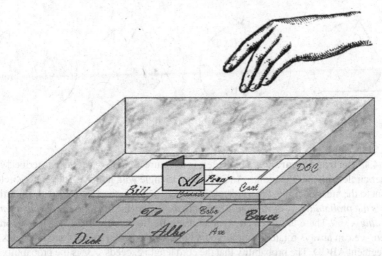

Fig. 4.3. How to win at drawings using Olaf's principle. The only way to increase your chance of winning a drawing is, like King Olaf, to concoct a clever plan to change the contest to be outside of the laws and assumptions of a uniform probability model, either by acquiring knowledge about the process or, like the king of Norway, manipulating the system so that the assumption of uniformity is no longer applicable. Here's a way to beat uniform odds in a drawing. When selecting slips of paper from a hat, Bernoulli's PrOIR is assumed. If there are N slips of paper in the hat and you have one entry, then there is one chance out of N you will win. That is, unless the selection process is manipulated. An effective way to do this is by folding or crumpling your entry so it takes up more space. Try it next time the opportunity presents itself. It does not guarantee a win, but certainly increases the probability of a win. The authors admit to seeing this procedure work successfully on numerous occasions (but choose not to confess whether or not they have used the method themselves) We leave the discussion of the ethics of this practice for another venue.

the circle is bisected with a diameter length line in the random cord was chosen from the set of all possible perpendicular bisectors. In the second case the cord was specified by randomly choosing two points on the circle circumference and connecting them to form the cord. In the third case the cord was defined by its midpoint in that the midpoint is chosen as a random point within the circle. The failure is not a failure of Bernoulli's PrOIR[15] but is due to an ambiguity in the meaning of the word "random" in the statement of Bertrand's paradox.

Keynes also noted Bernoulli's PrOIR does not work when a search space is ill-defined or heuristically uncertain, as is typical in the social sciences.[16,17] Consider a social scientist who categorizes the primary

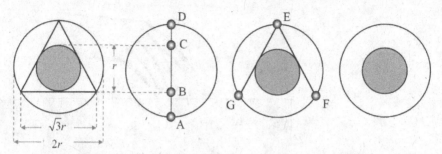

†Fig. 4.4. **Bertrand's paradox**. On the left is a picture a circle of radius r inscribed with another circle with half the radius. An equilateral triangle with points on the larger circle is tangent to the smaller circle. Each side of the triangle has length $\sqrt{3}r$. We ask the question: *What is the probability, p, of randomly choosing a cord intersecting the circle with a length exceeding $\sqrt{3}r$?* There are three answers all using Bernoulli's PrOIR. (1) When a cord is chosen, we can always rotate the circle so that the perpendicular bisector arc intersects the line segment ABCD. The probability that the cord length exceeds $\sqrt{3}r$ is the probability the cord intersects the line segment BC. By Bernoulli's PrOIR, the probability of intersecting any point on the line segment AD is uniform. Since the line segment BC is half the length of that of AD, we conclude the answer is $p = \frac{1}{2}$. (2) When a cord is chosen, it can always be rotated so that one end intersects with E. The probability the cord length exceeds $\sqrt{3}r$ is the probability the other end of the cord intersects the clockwise circle arc FG. Applying Bernoulli's PrOIR gives each point on the circumference of the circle equal probability of being the other end of the cord. Since the arc FG is one third that the circle's circumference, we conclude the answer is $p = \frac{1}{3}$. (3) Lastly, the probability the cord exceeds $\sqrt{3}r$ in length is the probability that, in the rightmost figure, the cord's midpoint lies in the smaller shaded circle. According to Bernoulli's PrOIR, the distribution of points within the circle is uniform. The smaller shaded circle is one fourth the area of the larger circle so we conclude that $p = \frac{1}{4}$.

There are three different answers using Bernoulli's PrOIR. Each answer is different. Keynes suggested that Bertrand's paradox is an example of Bernoulli's PrOIR. A more reasonable explanation is that the term *randomly* in the original question is not precisely defined. The three answers in Bertrand's paradox are due, instead, to different interpretations of the meaning of the word *randomly*. Once defined, Bernoulli's PrOIR applies with no ambiguity.

causes of juvenile delinquency to (a) poverty, (b) peer pressure, or (c) "other causes." Does this warrant a $\frac{1}{3}, \frac{1}{3}, \frac{1}{3}$ split? Suppose a second social scientist absorbs peer pressure into the "other causes" category. There are now only two categories: poverty and other causes. The Bernoulli's PrOIR for poverty is now one half instead of one third. Frequentists argue that with no prior knowledge of the search space, assignment of probabilities is inappropriate and falls outside of the scope of probability theory.[18]

4.1.2.2.3 Continuous versus discrete probability

Keynes offers yet another criticism of Bernoulli's PrOIR.[19],p

"Consider the specific volume of a given substance. Let us suppose that we know the specific volume to lie between 1 and 3, but that we have no information as to whereabouts in this interval its exact value is to be found. The Principle of Indifference [Bernoulli's PrOIR] would allow us to assume that it is as likely to lie between 1 and 2 as between 2 and 3; for there is no reason for supposing that it lies in one interval rather than in the other. The specific density is the reciprocal of the specific volume, so that if the latter is v the former is 1/v. Our data remaining as before we know that the specific density must lie between 1 and 1/3, and, by the use of the Principle ... as before, that it is as likely to lie between 1 and 2/3 as between 2/3 and 1/3."

Keynes argues that Bernoulli's PrOIR cannot apply to both the specific density and the specific volume because the 50–50 division results differ in each case.

Keynes's objection at first seems troublesome. If we have a random variable that has a uniform distribution, then any function on that random variable except for degenerate cases, will not produce another random variable with a uniform random variable.

Gädenfors and Sahlin[20] note that many criticisms of Bernoulli's PrOIR, such as Keynes's, focus on cases where the underlying random variable is continuous.q

---

p† Here is the math behind Keyne's objection. The original specific volume random variable, v, is uniform on the interval of one to three. Applying Bernoulli's PrOIR, there is a 50–50 chance that v lies between 1 and 2 or between 2 and 3. The specific density is $d = \frac{1}{v}$ and, using a standard transformation on a random variable, has a probability density function of $f_d(x) = \frac{1}{2}x^{-2}$ for $\frac{1}{3} \leq x \leq 1$. This is different, of course, than if we started with d and assumed it was uniformly distributed on the interval $\left[\frac{1}{3}, 1\right]$, in which case there is a 50–50 chance it landed in intervals $\left[\frac{1}{3}, \frac{2}{3}\right]$ and $\left[\frac{2}{3}, 1\right]$, i.e. $\Pr\left[\frac{1}{3} \leq d \leq \frac{2}{3}\right] = \Pr\left[\frac{2}{3} \leq d \leq 1\right] = \frac{1}{2}$. But using $f_d(x)$, we calculate $\Pr\left[\frac{1}{3} \leq d \leq \frac{2}{3}\right] = \frac{3}{4}$ and $\Pr\left[\frac{2}{3} \leq d \leq 1\right] = \frac{1}{4}$. Keynes objects to the answers being different.

q† Even the definition of Shannon information varies from the discrete to the continuous case. For a probability mass function p_n we have seen that entropy is defined as

$$H = -\sum_n p_n \log_2 p_n.$$

"[Bertrand[21] was] so much impressed by the contradictions of geometrical probability that he wishes to exclude all examples in which the number of alternatives is infinite."[22]

We can show, however, that this is not the case for discrete random variables in the sense that the expected value of the transformation is preserved. Indeed, Bernoulli's PrOIR is unbreakable in the discrete case when the search domain is properly defined and we know nothing.

For example, if we have a standard shuffled deck of 52 cards, then the chance of picking the A♠ is independent of the methodology used to sequentially draw cards. Bernoulli's PrOIR holds. It also holds in all variations of its execution. Consider, first, the "some to many" mapping illustrated in Fig. 4.5. Some of the cards from the deck are identified and duplicated in a new deck. We'll even assume some of the cards can be duplicated more than once. From the new deck, what is the probability of choosing the A♠ in a single query? The same as in the old deck: 1 out of 52.[r]

For a continuous random variable described by a probability density function $f(x)$ the continuous entropy, often called the *differential entropy*, is

$$H = - \int_x f(x) \log_2 f(x) dx.$$

Differential entropy is not a limiting case of the discrete case. Indeed, the unit of the two entropy measures are different. Since probability is unitless, the unit of entropy for discrete events is bits. Alternately, if x for example has units of meters, then $f(x)$ has units of reciprocal meters and differential entropy has units related to length. Another difference is that differential entropy can be negative. Discrete entropy cannot.

[r]† Here is a thumbnail version. If the probability of success in the original deck of cards is p, then drawing k cards gives a binomial probability mass distribution of $\binom{n}{k} p^k (1 - p)^{n-k}$.

The median and mean of the corresponding random variable is np. (More rigorously, the median is the rounding of np to the nearest integer. (See K. Hamza, "The smallest uniform upper bound on the distance between the mean and the median of the binomial and Poisson distributions," *Statist. Probab Lett*, 23, p. 2125 (1995)). Dividing by n reveals that the expected value of the probability of success in the new deck is p: the same as in the original deck. Likewise, the chance of success from the new deck is the same as the old, i.e. the chance of getting better equals the chance of doing worse equals $\frac{1}{2}$. The generalization to cases where a card from the original deck can be duplicated more than once in the new deck is straightforward. Since the location of the target is unknown, the replication of any element in the original deck to make the space larger will result in a new deck, where the expected probability of success, p, remains the same.

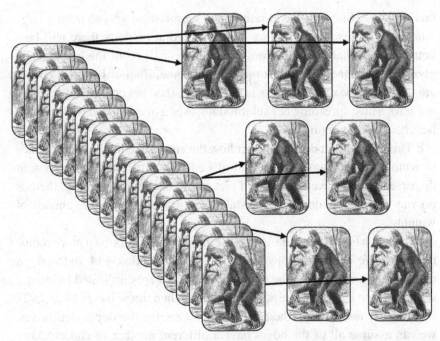

Fig. 4.5. A "some to many" mapping using a deck of playing cards. (Not all of the cards in the deck of 52 are shown.)

A similar example illustrating the robustness of Bernoulli's PrOIR for discrete events arises in the analysis of sweepstakes entries. Lenore is a sweepstakes hobbyist who identifies profitable contests and sends in multiple entries. Sweepstakes sponsored by commercial products cannot require the purchase of their product to play their game. Otherwise, the contest would be a lottery and would be illegal where gambling is prohibited. Thus, all sweepstakes will specify in small print how to submit entries without purchasing the product. Lenore is one of many sweepstakes enthusiasts who spend hours submitting entries. When the entry is mailed, the only cost to Lenore is her time, stationery, and postage.

To increase the odds of winning a sweepstakes, one self-help book for sweepstakes gamers notes that entries are typically placed in different boxes. The boxes, possibly of different sizes, are sequentially filled until the entry deadline. If, the book argues, Lenore spreads her submissions over the duration of the contest, then she will not have "all her eggs in one basket.''[s] She will have, rather, her submissions spread over a large number of boxes. Thus, when a box is picked at random, there will be a better chance that a submission from Lenore will be in the box thereby giving her a chance to win. At the other extreme, if all of Lenore's entries are in a single box and that box is not chosen, then her chances of winning are zero. Thus, spreading her submissions over a number of days increases her chances of winning.

This is wrong. It doesn't matter how the entries are mailed. The chance of winning is the same whether all of Lenore's entries are in one box or dispersed among several boxes. In fact, when one knows nothing, there is no way to manipulate the sweepstakes entries to increase the chance of winning.

Indeed, as illustrated in Fig. 4.6, Bernoulli's PrOIR is even more robust than this. We can photocopy all of the entries in Box #14 and make a duplicate box of entries. The contents of Box #5 are duplicated twice and we have three identical copies of Box #5. We then throw boxes #8 and #27 into the fire and destroy their contents. Except for the duplicated boxes, we can assume all of the boxes have a different number of entries. After

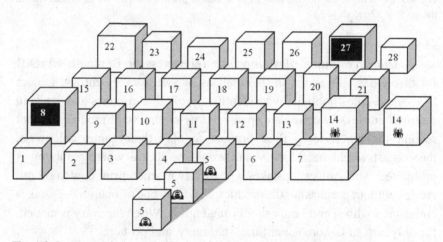

Fig. 4.6. In sweepstakes, unequally sized boxes are sequentially filled with entries. At the drawing, a box is chosen and an entry is randomly chosen from the box.

---

[s]Contrary to Mark Twain's advice to "Put all your eggs in one basket—and watch that basket!"

all of the duplicating and burning is finished, we choose a random box from those available and from the box choose an entry. The probability of Lenore winning is *exactly* the same as before the duplicating and the burning. Indeed, the probability Lenore is the winner is the same as if all the entries were placed in one big barrel and an entry chosen. There is no way to beat Bernoulli's PrOIR by duplicating and destroying boxes. The chance of winning is the same.[t]

Here is a thought process to illustrate this. Consider 1000 sweepstakes entries being placed in one large box and an entry drawn. Let the probability of winning be p. equal to the number of entries you make divided by $N = 1000$. Assume, now, that someone had come in the previous night and, without looking at the entries, marked 300 entries with a ❶, 20 with a ❷, 280 with a ❸, and 400 with a ❹. After we draw the winning entry, does the ❶, ❷, ❸, or ❹ marks on the winning entry tell us anything? Of course not. The chance of the mark being a ❹ is the greatest, but the mark of the entry and whether or not it is the winner are independent events.

Next, consider placing all the entries with the same marking in different boxes. The 300 entries marked ❶ go in one box, the 20 marked ❷ go in a second box, etc. We still have not looked at whether any entry is a winner. We only look at the markings. Now choose one of the boxes using any method you desire. We choose an entry from that box. No matter what box we choose, the chance of your entry being drawn is the same.

This holds true in the case when there are 1000 entries and 999 of them are placed in one box with a single entry placed in a second box. Choosing the second box and drawing the single entry from the box has the same chance of winning as choosing an entry from the box with 999 entries.

---

[t]† The case for duplication is treated in Fig. 4.6. For varying entries in each box, we consider the special case where Lenore has a single entry. Assume the mth box contains k_m entries and there are $n = \Sigma_m k_m$ total entries. If all entries are placed in a single large barrel, the chance of Lenore winning is $1/n$. This is the same as if a box is chosen at random and an entry drawn. This follows from Pr[Winning | Box m chosen] = Pr[{Winning | Box m chosen} | Lenore's entry is in Box m] = $(1/k_m)(k_m/N) = 1/n$. If we have two entries, #1 and #2, then Pr[Winning | Box m chosen] = Pr[Winning with #1 OR Winning with #2 | Box m chosen]. Since the events are mutually exclusive, Pr[Winning | Box m chosen] = $2/n$. More generally, with r entries, Pr[Winning | Box m chosen] = r/n.

Here's another way to look at it. Each of the entries prior to the drawing can be considered being marked with a p for the probability of that entry being the winner. It matters not whether you choose the entry from one big box or a 100 little boxes, the entry you draw has a p on it and the chance of it being a winner is the same no matter how you choose it. Using this reasoning, it is easy to see why destroying some of the entries and making copies of others still does not change your chance of winning. In the end, all of the entries have the same chance, p, of winning. Bernoulli's PrOIR cannot be broken.

Having inside (active) information on sweepstakes can help to win with a chance other than that afforded by a uniform distribution. Here are two examples.

- If we have inside information about the stuffing of the boxes with sweepstakes entries, we could alter the odds. If we knew *when* the smaller boxes will be filled and are able to time the entries to go into the smaller boxes, the chances of winning increase. To convince ourselves of this, consider the extreme case where there is one box so small it can contain only one entry. If we are able to manipulate our single submission so that it is placed in the very small box, then our chance of winning is one in M where M is the number of boxes. This is much better than one chance out of N where N is the number of entries.
- If entries are accepted for a week in bags and the Friday bag close to the door has a better chance of being chosen than the Monday bag across the room next to the wall, then the uniformity assumption is no longer valid and we can increase our odds of winning by submitting all our entries on Friday.

Without any knowledge of the lottery to create active information, Bernoulli's PrOIR can't be beat. A source of knowledge is always mandatory for the creation of active information.

4.2   The Need for Noise

Randomness is an important component of evolutionary search.

Consider steepest descent optimization for finding a minimum. A single agent, exploring the search landscape, computes which way is downhill and takes a step in that direction. The problem is that the search can get stuck in a local minimum far inferior to a deeper minimum elsewhere in the search space. If a random component is added to each step downhill, there is a possibility the search could skip the local minima and land in a better minima. In this sense, noise can help the accuracy of a search.

Simulated annealing[23] is an example of the use of randomness in optimization. Annealing in metallurgy cools a molten metal according to a cooling schedule so that the metal acquires desired properties. The general principle is the same as we find with water. Rapidly cooled water, for example, turns into ice with physical flaws. The ice cracks and is opaque. Slowly cooled water, on the other hand, turns into a clear block of ice. In metallurgy, heat corresponds to a random fluctuation of molecules. In simulated annealing, lowering temperature corresponds to reducing the amount of noise[u] added to the search process. Mutation in evolutionary search can be viewed as a kind of simulated annealing. In standard evolutionary algorithms, mutation is not annealed however. The mutation rate, i.e. heat, often remains fixed.

Although not a perfect analogy, here is another description. Imagine a bowl whose shape describes a smooth search landscape but has numerous indentations corresponding to false minima. If a BB is dropped into the bowl there is a good chance it will roll into and then stop in a local minima. Instead, imagine shaking the bowl after the BB is dropped. Initially, there is a lot of shaking (i.e. a lot of random heat) and then the shaking reduces in intensity corresponding to an annealing schedule. The shaking of the bowl should knock the BB out of local minima and, when the shaking is done, land the BB in a spot more favorable than if the bowl had not been shaken.

4.2.1 *Fixed points in random events*

Evolutionary processes are dynamic stochastic processes. Although we are dealing with outcomes of chance, probability often follows almost deterministic laws. Randomness introduced by quantum mechanics, for example, is modeled by probability models derived from the solution of Schrödinger's equation. The probability density functions are deterministic.

---

[u]As typically measured by the standard deviation of the random variable describing the noise.

A simpler example is the probability that the flip of a fair coin shows heads. The probability $p = \frac{1}{2}$, although describing a random variable, is itself deterministic.

The most commonly used deterministic[v] property of probability is the *law of large numbers*.[24] Political pollsters, insurance companies, casinos and quality control engineers rely on it. Although there are various forms of the law of large numbers, it can be stated at a high level as follows:

The Law of Large Numbers: In the limit, the *average* approaches the *mean*.

Until we define the terms, the definition might appear vague because of the similarity of the terms *mean* and *average*. So let's illustrate the law with some examples. We flip a fair coin. If a heads occurs, we score one. If a tails shows, zero. Since the coin is fair, the mean value of a flip is $\mu = \frac{1}{2}$. The law of large numbers says that the more times a coin is flipped, the closer the average approaches the mean. Outcomes of HHTHTHT correspond to 1101010 or an average of $a = \frac{4}{7} = 0.571$. A simulation of five coin flippers is shown in Fig. 4.7. After every flip, the coin flipper evaluates the ratio of the number of heads to the total number of coin flips. This is what is

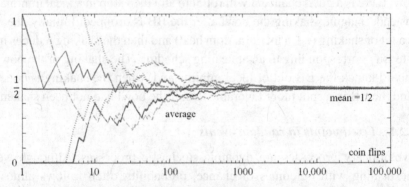

Fig. 4.7. Five coin flippers flip a fair coin 100,000 times. The paths are different, but as the number of flips increases, the average approaches the mean of one half.

---

[v]† We here use "deterministic" in a loose mathematical sense. Mean square convergence and convergence with probability one are both deemed deterministic in the context of our discussion.

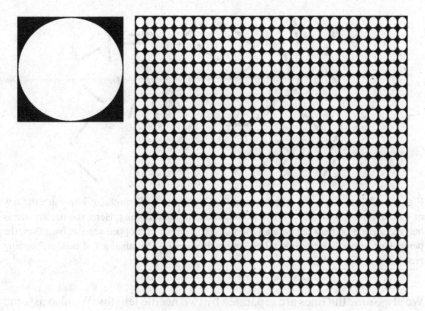

Fig. 4.8. Calculating π by throwing darts.

plotted in Fig. 4.7 for 100,000 coin flips. As the number of flips increases, the average approaches the mean of $\frac{1}{2}$. The paths are different but the end result is the same.

Using the law of large numbers, we can estimate $\pi = 3.14159\ldots$ to an arbitrary accuracy by throwing darts. Consider the circle in a square pictured on the left Fig. 4.8. If the circle has a radius of r, then the ratio of the area of the circle to the square is $\frac{\pi}{4} = 0.7853981\ldots$ If we have a dart board as shown on the right in Fig. 4.8, then, under the assumption we have no control over where the dart lands, the number of times a dart lands inside a circle divided by the total number of dart throws will approach $\frac{\pi}{4}$ according to the law of large numbers.

An even more interesting example of evaluating π by random experiments is *Buffon's Needle*,[25] an 18th century problem illustrated in Fig. 4.9. Needles are dropped onto a floor where parallel lines are drawn.[w]

---

[w]† If the needle is of length a and the separation between lines is $b > a$, then $\mu = \frac{2a}{\pi b}$. We have chosen $b = 2a$ so $\mu = \frac{1}{\pi}$.

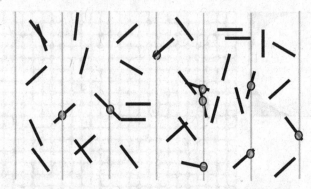

Fig. 4.9. Calculating π by dropping needles. Buffon's needle problem illustrates the law of large numbers with a less obvious outcome than coin flipping. Here, the needle size is half the separation between parallel lines. As the number of dropped needles increases, the percentage of needles crossing a line approaches $\mu = \frac{1}{\pi}$. Simulations of needle dropping are shown in Fig. 4.10.

We'll assume the lines are separated by two needle lengths. We also assume the needle dropper does not have the ability to control the needle and it lands randomly.[x] If a needle intersects a line, we score a one. Otherwise, a zero. When the distance between lines is twice the length of a needle, the curious result is that the mean of this experiment is $\mu = \frac{1}{\pi} = 0.3183$. In Fig. 4.9, a third of the needles intersect the parallel lines and the average is $a = \frac{1}{3} = 0.3333$. As the number of dropped needles increases, the average will approach $1/\pi$. This is illustrated in Fig. 4.10, where five simulations of averages of the outcomes of needle dropping are all shown to converge to the same point. Buffon's needle shows, fascinatingly, that one can estimate π by throwing needles at a target consisting of straight lines. There are no circles or arcs.

4.2.2 *Importance sampling*

Writing programs to converge to a desirable fixed point is the goal of evolutionary programming. The task can be much more complex than

---

[x]We learned from Bertrand's paradox that care must be taken in using the term "random." For Buffon's needle, Bernoulli's PrOIR is applied. The location of the middle of the needle is assumed to be uniform between lines and the angle of the needle is also assumed uniform.

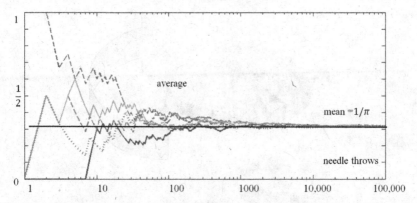

Fig. 4.10. Five needle throwers throw a needle 100,000 times. The paths are different, but as the number of throws increases, the average approaches the mean of $\mu = \frac{1}{\pi} = 0.3183\ldots$

those illustrated thus far and convergence may not be possible with available computing resources. Active information in the program can be used to accelerate the process. In determining percentages, this can be accomplished using *importance sampling*.[26]

Rather than random sampling of voters, political pollsters will sample independent and undecided voters with greater frequency. Knowledge that Democrats will probably vote for Democrats and Republicans will probably vote for Republicans is translated into active information by the pollsters, allowing more accurate estimates with fewer queries. And that's why there is such interest in the so-called swing voters. They are more important in determining the outcome and are therefore polled more heavily.

Another example of importance sampling is shown in Fig. 4.11. A wheel is divided into five sections: *A*, *B*, *C*, *D* and *E*. What is the probability that, when the top wheel is spun, the marker P points to the pie slice marked *D*? In order for *D* to be selected let alone have its probability estimated, it will take a large number of spins. Suppose, though, we know the probability of the large segment marked *A*. This is knowledge that can be used to decrease the number of queries required to find the probability of *D* to a given accuracy. We remove *A* and, as shown in the bottom of Fig. 4.11, form a new wheel of the remaining segments. Now the chance of getting *D* on a spin is higher so the estimation of its probability will require fewer spins.

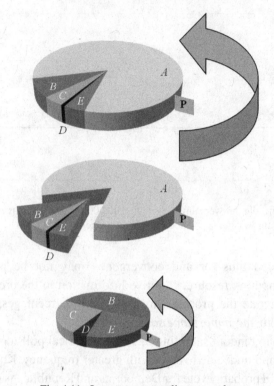

Fig. 4.11. Importance sampling example.

4.2.3 *Limit cycles, strange attractors & tetherball*

Coin flipping, dart throwing and Buffon's needle exemplify cases where randomness converges to a single fixed solution. Other stochastic phenomena can converge to two or more final values, called *fixed points*. An example we call *tetherball* is illustrated in Fig. 4.12 for 10 games. The goal is to get to the top for player 1 and to the bottom for player 2. A player is chosen to serve at random and hit the ball a quarter of the way to one of the walls.[y] On the next turn, the player has a 25% chance to hit the ball an eighth of the way to the walls. There is a 75% change the player will lose the same distance to their opponent. The closer a player is to a wall, the greater chance the player has to get the ball even closer. In each case, a success moves the ball a quarter of the distance between the ball and the wall. When the ball is

---

[y]We use one-fourth. In general any fraction of the distance can be used.

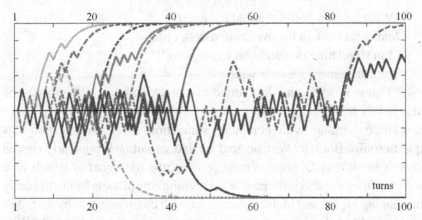

Fig. 4.12. Ten simulations of tetherball. The end result is at either one of two fixed points at the top or the bottom.

90% to the wall, the rule is that there is a 90% chance that, in the next step, a quarter of the 10% will be covered, leaving the ball at 92.5%. There is a $100\% - 90\% = 10\%$ chance the ball will move in the opposite direction and end up at 87.5%. When the ball is almost at the wall, say 99% of the distance, the chance it will move closer to the wall in the next iteration is 0.99. Eventually, every game will commit to one of the two walls.

Ten tetherball games are shown in Fig. 4.12 for 100 turns. In all cases but one, the ball ends up either at the top or the bottom. The top and bottom are the two fixed points of the process. For the single unresolved process left in Fig. 4.12, additional turns are required to determine which of the two walls will be the final destination.

Iterations can also approach solutions of repeated periodic patterns called *greedy limit cycles*.[27] A similar phenomena is found in deterministic chaos where iterations can approach *strange attractors*.[28] Markov processes can have numerous *absorbing states*[29] to which the process converges. The performance of these operations is akin to that seen in evolutionary computing. Different runs of the program can result in convergence to different fixed points.

4.3 Basener's ceiling

A colleague walked into the office of Robert Marks, one of your humble authors. Marks finished typing on his computer and turned to greet his guest.

"What are you doing?" asked the guest.

Marks sat back in his overstuffed desk chair.

"I'm simulating evolution on a computer."

The colleague's eyes got wide.

"That is so exciting!" he blurted in a mocking tone. "When will I be able to talk to it?"

Those familiar with computer simulations of evolution find this question silly. But is it? With no goal in mind, evolution is popularly viewed as a dynamic greedy improvement process, the only goal of which is to increase fitness. If this is the case, what prohibits the process from ultimately developing higher and higher information-rich complexity? Why wouldn't we expect Marks's program to become self-aware and ultimately talk? Why will an evolutionary program written to design an antenna never design a delicious pancake or play chess? From a computer programmer's point of view, the answer is obvious. The computer programmer who wrote the antenna design program designed the program to evolve antennas. It was not designed to evolve skill at playing chess.

Mathematician William F. Basener shows that models of Darwinian evolution have limited capability.[30] Applying basic topology and dynamical systems results, Basener proves "that every such evolutionary dynamical system with a finite spatial domain is asymptotic to a recurrent orbit; to an observer the system will appear to repeat a known state infinitely often. In an evolutionary system driven by increasing fitness, the system will reach a point after which there is not observable increase in fitness." In other words, a ceiling of improvement is hit and the evolutionary process or any other search can proceed no higher. The "point after which there is not observable increase in fitness" is the implicit target in such searches.

After exploring evolution as a dynamic process, Basener makes the following observation.

"Our first conclusion is that chaos and nonlinear dynamical systems contribute nothing to the ongoing increase in complexity or evolutionary fitness of biological systems. Statements . . . suggesting that complexity of life results from nonlinear chaotic systems, are contrary to mathematics."

"Second, the evolutionary process driven by mutation-selection, in both mathematical models and directly observed behavior, is that of a system going to an equilibrium and staying there. It seems the discussion of evolution in biology is that of an ongoing process but the study of mathematical models of evolution is that of equilibrium dynamics. There is nothing inherent in the fitness-driven mathematical system that leads to ongoing progress; to the contrary, mathematical systems, both those which are specific models such as the quasispecies equation and very general classes of models, have limits on the amount of increase in fitness that occurs."

In Chapter 6, we will talk about computer programs that purport to demonstrate Darwinian evolution. The Avida and EV programs have clearly defined Basener ceilings. So does Dawkins's Weasel Ware. Once the desired target is achieved, neo-Darwinists raise their voices in celebration and shout "Eureka! Evolution has succeeded!" None of these computer programs, however, are capable of evolving further. The very idea is ludicrous.

Basener's Ceiling is manifest in evolutionary simulations. Its applicability to Avida and EV in Chapter 6 is obvious. Let's spend some time here with some other illustrative examples.

4.3.1 *Tierra*[31]

Thomas Ray's celebrated evolutionary algorithm *Tierra*[32] was created in 1989 to test the claims of Darwinian evolution by computer simulation. Historically, it was the first celebrated computer program to make such an attempt. Ray was specifically interested in the information creation in the Cambrian explosion where a diversity of complex organisms appeared in a short period of time[z] although no such complexity had existed before. The Cambrian explosion is an event recorded in the fossil record during which there was a breathtaking shift in the appearance of life on earth. Prior to this point, biological life consisted almost entirely of single-celled organisms. However, in a brief period of geological time, there was an "explosion" of biological forms in which most of the phyla now in existence appeared suddenly in the fossil record. The causes behind this geological event are debated within biological circles. Darwin viewed the Cambrian explosion as a possibly viable objection to his theory of evolution.[33] Stephen Meyer has given a detailed analysis of why the Cambrian explosion is

---

[z]A short time in relation to evolution. The Cambrian explosion occurred over about 75 million years.

more troublesome than ever for the theory of Darwinian evolution in light of the recent understanding of the complexity of the rapidly developed life forms.[34] A quarter century before Meyer's book though, Ray was enthusiastic about his project. He wrote[35]

> "While the origin of life is generally recognized as an event of the first order, there is another event in the history of life that is less well known but of comparable significance: the origin of biological diversity and macroscopic multicellular life during the Cambrian explosion 600 million years ago."

Ray's goal was to simulate this historical evolutionary event on a computer.

If artificial evolution could reproduce the exciting complexity observed in the Cambrian explosion, researchers might also be able to produce a plethora of fascinating forms analogous to those found in biology. Essentially, once evolution (whether biological or artificial) has produced a Cambrian explosion, the rest of evolution should proceed easily.

Ray's hope was that the complexity of his system would reach a critical mass. Once past this point, evolution's creativity would be unleashed. Tierra was Ray's attempt to give evolution the critical mass it needed. Ray was not initially deterred by failure. He reformulated Tierra three times each starting with more complexity in an attempt to kick start the evolutionary process.

Tierra produced a variety of interesting phenomena, including parasites, hyper-parasites, social behavior, cheating, and loop unrolling. However, 25 years after the introduction of Tierra, there has been no Cambrian explosion or open-ended evolution. Tierra kept bumping into Basener's ceiling.

Though Ray described Tierra's evolution as generating "rapidly diversifying communities of self-replicating organisms exhibiting open-ended evolution by natural selection"[36] others disagreed.[37]

> "Artificial life systems such as Tierra and Avida produced a rich diversity of organisms initially, yet ultimately peter out. By contrast, the Earth's biosphere appears to have continuously generated new and varied forms throughout the 4×10^9 years of the history of life."

These strong increasing trends imply a directionality in biological evolution that is missing in the artificial evolutionary systems.[38]

The absence of a Cambrian explosion in artificial life at the hands of a skilled programmer demands an explanation. If biological evolution produced a Cambrian explosion, why does artificial evolution not do the same? Our inability to mimic evolution in this regard suggests a deficiency in our understanding of it. In the words of Feynman: "What I cannot create, I do not understand."[39]

Evolution in Tierra can be characterized as an initial period of high activity producing a number of novel adaptations followed by barren stasis. It would appear that Tierra easily produced the novel information required for a variety of adaptations. Why did it cease? If Tierra could produce novel information, it should continue to do so as long as it was run.

A closer look at Tierra's evolution reveals an important characteristic of the adaptations. Tierra started with a designed ancestor to seed the population. In other words, it presupposed something like an origin of life and was concerned with the development of complexity after that point. The ancestor provides initial information to Tierra. Adaptations primarily consist of rearranging or removing that information, i.e. a loss of function. Open-ended evolution requires adaptations which increase information. However, such adaptations are rare in Tierra. Tierra's informational trajectory is the opposite of what evolution requires. It is dominated by loss and re-arrangement with only minimal new information, instead of being dominated by the production of new information, with minimal cases of removal or rearrangement of information. Long-term evolutionary progress is dependent on the generation of new information.

If Tierra is capable of generating new information even in small amounts, does this not provide evidence that Darwinism can account for new information? Many small gains will eventually accumulate into a large amount of information. However, if that were true, we would see evidence of it within Tierra. There ought to be a steady stream of information gaining adaptations rather than the stasis actually observed.

Subsequent high-level analysis of Tierra confirms it hits the Basener's ceiling.[40] Ewert et al.[41] documents the history and performance of Tierra and indicates that Ray now recognizes that Tierra's performance is bounded. Ewert *et al.* cites a recent podcast with Ray[42] and writes

> "Ray has recently stated that he regards Tierra as having failed to reach its goal. He describes the evolution seen within Tierra as transitory. He no longer considers himself part of the artificial life community, and is now studying biological questions rather than those of artificial evolution."

Ray's Tierra hit Basener's ceiling.

4.3.2 *The edge of evolution*

Biochemist Michael Behe notes that observed biological adaptation limits the ability of evolution to generate diversity. A compelling case is made in his book "*The Edge of Evolution: The Search for the Limits of Darwinism.*"[43]

The ability of a system to adapt is a sign of good engineering. Like a banker shedding their suit coat when walking outside into 100° heat, creatures can lose function to better interface with their environment. Cave-dwelling salamanders lose operational eyes which are useless in their ponds with no light. Loss of function is certainly adaptation, but not the kind of adaptation that causes increased complexity.

Humans have had ample opportunity to adapt to the parasite that causes malaria. Through billions of trials and potential for mutation, humans have developed immunity to malaria. But, like some strong drugs, the immunity has side effects that can kill you. One immunity humans have evolved is sickle-cell anemia, a hereditary blood disorder where red blood cells are abnormally shaped like sickles. The bad news is that sickle cell anemia is a debilitating disease which, without careful management, will severely shorten a human lifespan. The good news is that sickle-cell anemia provides immunity to malaria. In quinine-free, malaria-infested areas, those with sickle-cell anemia will be fit and begin to dominate the population. But, like the salamander without eyes, the sickle-cell anemia occurred because of loss of function. Malaria's cure occurred at the cost of broken performance. Any estimate of the required number of mutations required for primates to evolve into man is dwarfed by several orders of magnitude by the chances for evolution to create a constructive immunity to malaria.

In 1988, Richard Lenski at Michigan State, started an attempt to evolve *E. coli* bacteria. Behe documents in detail the failure of the experiment from the viewpoint of the creation of new information structures within the organism.[44] The journal *Science* celebrated the 25th anniversary of Lenski's experiment.[45] Lenski's experiment has tracked 58,000 generations (corresponding to over a million years for humans) using trillions of cells and is the "most detailed source of information on evolutionary processes available anywhere, dwarfing rival lab projects and swamping field studies." Like a cave salamander losing the use of its unneeded eyes[46]

> "... the bottom line is that the great majority of even beneficial mutations have turned out to be due to the breaking, degrading, or minor tweaking of pre-existing genes or regulatory regions. There have been no mutations or series of mutations identified that appear to be on their way to constructing elegant new molecular machinery of the kind that fills every cell. For example, the genes making the bacterial flagellum are consistently turned off by a beneficial mutation (apparently it saves cells energy used in constructing flagella). The suite of genes used to make the sugar ribose is the uniform target of a destructive mutation, which somehow helps the bacterium grow more quickly in the laboratory. Degrading a host of other genes leads to beneficial effects, too."

This is evidence that Lenski's experiment has hit Basener's ceiling.

4.4 Final Comments

Computer-modeled evolution and computer search almost always uses randomness. An iterative random process is modeled by determinism in the form of laws such as the Law of Large Numbers and Basener's ceiling.

Can a computer program be constructed such that Basener's ceiling is not applicable? We can certainly evolve an organism to the ceiling and use the evolved entity as an initialization to a different more advanced evolutionary pressure. Doing so could, in principle, generate unbounded specified complexity. Note, though, that each stage of the evolution must itself be carefully designed. For example, if the earth is hit with a meteor that wipes out the dinosaurs and alters the evolutionary environmental pressure to guide a subsequent stage in evolution, the change in direction must be just right. If the meteor is too big, all life will be wiped out and the evolutionary process stopped. If too small, dinosaurs will survive and the next stage in evolution will not be sparked. G.K. Chesterton notes, "It is always simple to fall; there are an infinity of angles at which one falls, only one at which one stands." Although there are potentially many ways to steer an evolutionary process to higher complexity, there will be many more ways the process can be derailed.

Evolvability with shifting fitness landscapes requires viable design at each stage. In the next chapter, we dub this piecewise contribution that guides the evolutionary process to high levels of specified complexity as *stair step* active information. The Avida computer program uses stair step active information on a small scale. The concept of gradually applying new environmental pressure, dubbed *evolution of evolvability*,[47] makes the staircase into a ramp. Either way, the path to significant specified complexity must be carefully designed in order to succeed and does not easily punch a hole into Basener's ceiling.

Notes

1. D. Sheff, *All We are Saying: The Last Major Interview with John Lennon and Yoko Ono* (Macmillan, 2010).
2. Portions of this section previously appeared in William A. Dembski, and R.J. Marks II, "Bernoulli's Principle of Insufficient Reason and Conservation of Information in Computer Search." *Proceedings of the 2009 IEEE International Conference on Systems, Man, and Cybernetics*, October 11–14, San Antonio, Texas, USA (2009).
3. For a more thorough high-level explanation, see: S. Hawking, *A Brief History of Time* (Bantam Books, 1996).
4. J. Bernoulli, *Ars Conjectandi* (The Art of Conjecturing) (1713).
5. A. Papoulis, *Probability, Random Variables, and Stochastic Processes*, 3rd edition (McGraw-Hill, New York, 1991), pp. 537–542.
6. A. Fisher, C. Dickson, and W. Bonynge, *Mathematical Theory of Probabilities & Its Applications to Frequency Curves & Statistical Methods* (Macmillan, 1922).
7. R.J. Marks II, *Handbook of Fourier Analysis and Its Applications* (Oxford University Press, 2009).
   For some specific examples of ill-posedness, see K.F. Cheung and R.J. Marks II, Ill-posed sampling theorems. *IEEE Transactions on Circuits and Systems*, CAS-32, pp. 829–835 (1985).

R.J. Marks II, Posedness of a bandlimited image extension problem in tomography. *Opt Lett*, 7, pp. 376–377 (1982).

8. With his classic 1948 paper, Claude Shannon single-handedly founded the field of information theory. This is the topic of Chapter 2.2.2.

9. K.L. Jackson and L.E. Polisky, "Wearable computers: Information tool for the twenty first century." *Virtual Real*, 3(3), pp. 147–156 (1998).

10. *Holy Rollers: The True Story of Card Counting Christians* (2011 Documentary). Director: B. Storkel.

11. Cover and Thomas, *op. cit.*

12. I. Ekeland, *The Broken Dice* (University of Chicago Press, Chicago, 1993).

13. *Ibid.*

14. J.M. Keynes, *A Treatise On Probability* (Macmillan Co., 1921).

15. Papoulis, *op. cit.*

16. E. Kasner and J.R. Newman, *Mathematics and the Imagination* (Dover Publications, 2001).

17. D. Howie, *Interpreting Probability: Controversies and Developments in the Early Twentieth Century* (Cambridge University Press, 2002).

18. *Ibid.*

19. Keynes, *op. cit.*

20. P. Gädenfors and N.E. Sahlin, *Decision, Probability, and Utility* (Cambridge University Press, 1988).

21. J. Bertrand, *Calcul Des Probabilités* (1896).

22. W. Ewert, W.A. Dembski and R.J. Marks II, "Evolutionary synthesis of Nand logic: Dissecting a digital organism." *Proceedings of the 2009 IEEE International Conference on Systems, Man, and Cybernetics*. San Antonio, TX, USA, pp. 3047–3053 (2009).

23. Simulated annealing was first proposed in: N. Metropolis, A.W. Rosenbluth, M.N. Rosenbluth, A.H. Teller, and E. Teller, "Equation of state calculations by fast computing machines." *J Chem Phys*, 21(6), p. 1087 (1953).
    See also R.D. Reed and R.J. Marks II, *Neural Smithing: Supervised Learning in Feedforward Artificial Neural Networks* (MIT Press, 1999).

24. R.J. Marks II, *op. cit.*

25. Papoulis, *op. cit.*

26. See, for example, R. Srinivasan, *Importance Sampling* (Springer, 2002).

27. R.J. Marks II, *op. cit.*

28. D. Ruelle, *Chaotic Evolution and Strange Attractors* (Cambridge University Press, 1989).

29. J.G. Kemeny and J. Laurie Snell, *Finite Markov Chains* (Springer, 1976).

30. W.F. Basener, "Limits of chaos and progress in evolutionary dynamics." In *Biological Information: New Perspectives*, R.J. Marks II, M.J. Behe, W.A. Dembski, B.L. Gordon and J.C. Sanford (eds.) (World Scientific, Singapore, 2013).

31. Portions of this section were first presented in: W. Ewert, W.A. Dembski, and R.J. Marks II, "Tierra: The character of adaptation." In *Biological Information — New Perspectives*, R.J. Marks II, M.J. Behe, W.A. Dembski, B.L. Gordon and J.C. Sanford (eds.) (World Scientific, Singapore, 2013).

32. T. Ray, "Overview of Tierra at ATR Technical Information." *Technologies for Software Evolutionary Systems*, No. 15 (2001).
    T.S. Ray, "An approach to the synthesis of life." In *Artificial Life* II, C.G. Langton, C. Taylor, J.D. Farmer, and S. Rasmussen (eds.), pp. 371–408 (Addison Wesley Publishing Company, 1992).
    T. Ray, "Evolution of parallel processes in organic and digital media." In *Natural & Artificial Parallel Computation*: *Proceedings of the Fifth NEC Research Symposium*, p. 69. Soc for Industrial & Applied Math (1996).

33. C. Darwin, *On the Origin of Species by Natural Selection* (Murray, London, United Kingdom, 1859), pp. 315–316.

34. S.C. Meyer, *Darwin's Doubt: The Explosive Origin of Animal Life and the Case for Intelligent Design* (Harper Collins Publishers, 2013).

35. T.S Ray, "An approach to the synthesis of life." In *Artificial Life*, C.G. Langton, C. Taylor, J.D. Farmer, and S. Rasmussen (eds.), 2, pp. 371–408 (Addison Wesley Publishing Company, 1992).

36. *Ibid.*

37. R.K. Standish, "Open-ended artificial evolution." *Int J Comp Intel* Appl, 3(2), pp. 167–175 (2003).

38. M.A. Bedau, E. Snyder, C.T. Brown, and N.H. Packard, "A comparison of evolutionary activity in artificial evolving systems and in the biosphere." *Proceedings of The Fourth European Conference on Artificial Life*, pp. 125–134 (MIT Press, Cambridge, 1997).

39. *Ibid.*

40. *Ibid.*, R.K. Standish, *op. cit.*

41. Ewert *et al.*, *op. cit.*

42. T. Ray and T. Barbalet, Biota live #56, "Tom Ray on twenty years of Tierra." (2009) podcast http://poddirectory.com/episode/2485604/biota-live-lite-56-tom-ray-on-twenty-years-of-tierra-present-and-future-october-16-2009 (URL date May 2, 2016).

43. M. Behe, *The Edge of Evolution* (Free Press, New York, 2008).

M. Behe, "Experimental evolution, loss-of-function mutations, and the first rule of adaptive evolution." *Quart Rev Biol*, 85(4), pp. 419–445 (2010).

44. *Ibid.*
45. E. Pennisi, "The man who bottled evolution." *Science*, 342, pp. 790–793 (2013).
46. M. Behe, "Lenski's long-term evolution experiment: 25 years and counting." November 21, 2013 2:50 PM, *Evolution News & Views*. http://www. evolutionnews.org/2013/11/richard_lenskis079401.html (URL date May 2, 2016).
47. N. Colegrave and S. Collins, "Experimental evolution: Experimental evolution and evolvability." *Heredity*, 100(5), pp. 464–470 (2008).
    M. Kirschner and J. Gerhart, "Evolvability." *Proceedings of the National Academy of Sciences of the United States of America* 95(15), pp. 8420–8427 (1998).

5

CONSERVATION OF INFORMATION IN COMPUTER SEARCH

"I have deeply regretted that I did not proceed far enough to understand something of the great leading principles of mathematics, for men thus endowed seem to have an extra sense."

Charles Darwin[1]

5.1 The Genesis

When a new paradigm is introduced, there is often skepticism and criticism. At times critics sharpen a theory. At other times the paradigm is distracting and wrong and critics rightfully bury it. As time passes and a valid new idea is vetted, a once controversial idea often becomes surprisingly obvious. Such is the case with the law of *conservation of information* (COI) in computer learning and search as popularized by the *No Free Lunch Theorem* (NFLT).[2]

Great ideas often have a distributed genesis. Calculus was independently discovered by Newton and Leibniz. The Kolmogorov–Chaitin–Solomonov model of algorithmic information theory was independently proposed by three men.[a] Other examples are numerous. The Karhunen–Loève expansion,[3] the Papoulis–Gerchberg algorithm[4] and the Whittaker–Kotelnikov–Shannon sampling theorem[5] are examples of hyphenated tributes to 20th century mathematical landmarks discovered independently by more than one person.

Likewise, COI looks to have been independently identified by a number of researchers. Perhaps the earliest statement concerning COI in computers comes from Lady Lovelace (Augusta Ada King), recognized as the first

---

[a]As we noted in Chapter 2.2.1.

computer programmer and namesake of the computer language Ada. Bringsjord *et al.*[6] paraphrase Lovelaces's view from the 19th century.

> "Computers can't create anything. For creation requires, minimally, originating something. But computers originate nothing; they merely do that which we order them, via programs, to do."

Likewise, in 1956, without mathematical elaboration, information theory pioneer Leon Brillouin wrote[7]

> "The [computing] machine does not create any new information, but it performs a very valuable transformation of known information."

Mitchell seems to have originated a mathematical basis for COI in 1980.[8] He noted that, in order for computer programs to learn, the programmer must insert their own *bias*.

> "If consistency with the training instances is taken as the sole determiner of appropriate generalizations, then a program can never make the inductive leap necessary to classify instances beyond those it has observed. Only if the program has other sources of information, or biases for choosing one generalization over the other, can it non-arbitrarily classify instances beyond those in the training set."

> "[We] use the term *bias* to refer to *any basis for choosing one generalization over another, other than strict consistency with the observed training instances.*"[b]

Without bias in the design of the program, learning cannot occur beyond data already observed.

More recently, COI has been popularized by Schaffer[9] and Wolpert & Macready.[10] Schaffer showed that a computer program that learns well in some instances will work poorly in another:

> "[P]ositive performance in some learning situations must be offset by an equal degree of negative performance in others."

After proving his proposition, Schaffer compares the ability of a program that learns well in all instances to a perpetual motion machine. Specifically:

> "... a learner [without prior knowledge] ... that achieves at least mildly better-than-chance performance ... is like a perpetual motion machine."

---

[b]Italics are in the original quotation.

And Wolpert and Macready,[11] who coined the term *No Free Lunch* in regard to computer search originality, write that search can be improved only

> "... [by] incorporating problem-specific knowledge into the behavior of the [optimization or search] algorithm."

Indeed,

> "... unless you can make prior assumptions about the ... [problems] you are working on, then no search strategy, no matter how sophisticated, can be expected to perform better than any other."[12]

Conservation of information was initially controversial. After an oral presentation of his paper, *A Conservation Law for Generalization Performance*, Cullen Schaffer noted[13]

> "About half of the people in the audience to which my work was directed told me that my result was completely obvious and common knowledge—which is perfectly fair. Of course, the other half argued just as strongly that the result wasn't true."

We now show that, in agreement with the first half of Schaffer's audience, conservation of information is "completely obvious".

5.2 What is Conservation of Information?

To introduce the obviousness of COI, consider the following illustration.[14] If we enter a room where cards from a well shuffled standard 52-card poker deck are laid randomly face down on a table, our chances of turning over the ace of spades (A♠) in less than five card flips is not dependent on how the cards are chosen. Using the result of the first flipped card, say the K♣, is there any way to determine the location of the next move that improves the probability of success? Obviously not. After five card flips, no matter how clever the method used and no matter what set of rules used by a search algorithm, the probability, p, of choosing the A♠ is the same, namely

$$p = \frac{5}{52} = 0.0962.$$

COI states that, without knowledge of a target or search space structure, one search procedure will work, on average, as well as any other search. The

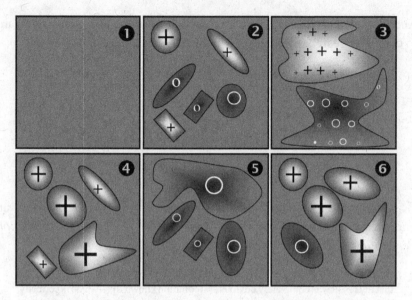

Fig. 5.1. Illustration of conservation of information on a waterbed.

choice of the search algorithm is immaterial. There is no reason to suspect that one algorithm will perform better than another.

Here is an illustration of COI using a waterbed metaphor. Because water is incompressible, if you push down on a framed waterbed at one point, it will bulge somewhere else. Consider Fig. 5.1 which is similar to a figure in Schaffer's seminal paper.[15, 16] Each of the six images in the figure corresponds to a specific search algorithm across a space of problems. The square marked 1 is flat, illustrating an algorithm that performs exactly the same on all problems. In 2, every place the waterbed is pushed in is labeled with a "o" and every place it bulges with a "+". A bulge means that the algorithm performs better than average on a set of problems. An indentation indicates the algorithm does worse. For every place there is a bulge in 2, COI dictates there must be a corresponding indentation so that, on average, the algorithm here illustrated performs, on average, like the algorithm illustrated in 1. The amount of water in the waterbed remains the same, so the average water depth is the same in both cases. As seen in square 3, the shapes of the indentations and bulges need not be the same. They need to, rather, average to the same level as in 1. Design expertise or other sources of knowledge are needed to choose a better than average search on a bulge and away from indentations.

Squares 4, 5 and 6 illustrate violations of the law of information conservation. In 4, the algorithm performs better than that in 1 for a number of problems without doing worse anywhere else. A waterbed cannot bulge at a number of points without being indented somewhere else. Likewise, square 5 illustrates many indentations without any bulges. Conservation of information requires a balance between better and worse performing algorithms. Square 6 violates this requirement because the waterbed bulges more than indents.

This property was intuitively obvious to artificial intelligence pioneer Marvin Minsky who, in a transcribed exchange with proponents of evolutionary programming published in 1970, comments on evolutionary learning algorithms[17]:

> "When one talks about a learning machine of this type [evolutionary search], one really ought to characterize the class of problems for which it is good, ... What class of problems is your technique [evolutionary search] good at solving? It is not enough to say it is good at [solving] all."

Minsky went on to emphasize

> "I am asking you what class of problems you think this technique [evolutionary search] is good at solving, and I am saying, in effect, that *I will not accept all as an answer.*"[c]

Subsequent development of the law of COI confirmed Minsky's concerns.

5.2.1 *Deceptive counterexamples*

There are search scenarios that look like they violate COI, but they don't. Indeed, COI, as demonstrated by its codiscovers, is a mathematical law that cannot be violated. One example that appears to defy COI but doesn't is coevolution,[18] a search algorithm we will deal with in detail later in this chapter. Here is another simpler deceptive example.

---

[c]Italics added.

Fig. 5.2. Can searching for the treasure get you a free lunch?

Illustrated in Fig. 5.2 is an example that, on first impression, seems to violate conservation of information.[19] One search seems to always give better results than any other. Consider a treasure buried in one of three possible locations on a desert island. Two rival pirates, X and Y, arrive at the island with the intent of digging up the treasure. Each pirate has to pick a strategy consisting of choosing the order of locations to be visited. If one of the pirates searches a location after his rival has already looked, he will not find the treasure. We will assume that the treasure is equally likely to be found in any of the locations. As illustrated in the figure, assume Pirate X searches for the location in a specific order such as (1,2,3). Assuming the location of the treasure at each point is equally probable. Pirate Y uses a related but different search order: (2,1,3). Again, the probability of finding the treasure at any of the locations is one out of three. Each strategy alone will thus have the same performance, as dictated by COI.

However, this changes if both pirates are hunting for treasure at the same time. Pirate Y has chosen locations such that in two of the three cases, he will have searched a location and taken the treasure because Pirate Y is always one step ahead of Pirate X. If the treasure is at location 1, Pirate X will get the treasure. However, if the treasure is located in either location 2 or 3, Pirate Y will have checked the locations first, and thus Pirate Y will win. Pirate X's strategy gets the treasure one in three times, whereas Pirate Y will claim the treasure two out of three times. In this sense, the strategy of Pirate Y is better than the strategy of Pirate X. This is true despite the two strategies performing the same when considered separately.

Due to the generality of the conservation of information results, any exception to the general COI principle, such as these unbalanced performance results, gives pause. Does such a basic and simple variation cause conservation of information to cease to be universally valid? And if conservation of information is violated here, should there not be ways to exploit the failure to construct superior search algorithms?

The answer to these questions is no. The apparent advantage of Pirate Y over Pirate X is not a failure of COI. One strategy may beat another head-to-head, but when compared to a group of related strategies, losses and wins will balance out. Victories against one strategy are paid for by losses against another. Consequently, there exists no generally superior search algorithm.

The transitive property necessary to establish an overall superior search algorithm is inapplicable to search.[20] Pirate Y has the advantage over Pirate X. A third treasure hunter, Pirate Z, chooses the sequence (3,1,2) which beats Pirate Y. Thus Pirate Z beats Pirate Y who beats Pirate X. If transitivity applies, Pirate Z beats Pirate X. But the opposite is true, Pirate X beats Pirate Z. Details are in Table 5.1.

Every strategy has an advantage against some other strategy, but also has another strategy with an advantage over it. Thus, no way exists to gain

Table 5.1. **Inapplicability of transitivity example. As shown in Fig. 5.1, Pirate X's search order is (1,2,3) and Pirate Y's order is (2,3,1). Not shown is Pirate Z with order (3,2,1). All possible orders are now represented. This table shows who wins (always with a probability of $\frac{2}{3}$) when the Pirates are paired. Z beats Y and Y beats X. Transitivity would dictate then that Z beats X. but the opposite is true. Transitivity does not hold in search.**

Teams → Treasure Location ↓	ZY	YX ↓Winner↓	XZ
1	Z	X	X
2	Y	Y	X
3	Z	Y	Z
Overall Winner →	Z beats Y	Y beats X	X beats Z

an absolute advantage over all other strategies. The lack of an absolute advantage limits the sense in which one strategy can be better than another. One can beat a specific algorithm, but not in a way that actually performs better against all other algorithms. Pirate Y is only able to outperform his rival X if he somehow knows the strategy his rival will employ. Thus, as would be expected from the idea of the COI, knowledge of the rival's strategy is necessary in order to beat it. This is externally applied knowledge about the search that can be used to Pirate Y's advantage.

Consider a randomly chosen search algorithm. This is equivalent to randomly choosing which strategy to employ. Playing against this strategy will produce the average performance of all other strategies. This average is the same regardless of the opposing strategy, so no way exists to consistently best a random search algorithm.

To make a point with an extreme example, consider an alternate game scenario where Pirate X and Y decide who keeps the treasure by the majority of wins in three quick games of rock-paper-scissors. If Pirate Y knows the strategy of Pirate X, e.g. X always shows "rock", Pirate Y can win all three games. One search's knowledge of the details of another can assist in winning the contest but does not violate COI. Knowledge of an opponent's strategy can be translated into a comparatively better search.

5.2.2 *What does learning have to do with design?*

Mitchell and Schaffer both refer to COI in regard to learning. But our topic deals with search algorithms with attention to evolutionary processes. What does learning have to do with search? The answer is that most machine learning is done by a search. In this section, we'll give a short example. The topic is a digression from our central theme, so impatient readers might want to skip this section.

5.2.2.1 *Sumo wrestlers can't play basketball*

Here's an example of learning. Sumo wrestlers are very different in appearance from professional basketball players. Sumo wrestlers are heavier than average and basketball players are taller than average. We want to design a black box classifier to differentiate between the two. When a person's physical data is input into the classifier box, the box will tell us whether that person is a sumo wrestler or basketball player. In the case of supervised learning,[21,22] the box has tunable knobs whose values are set in accordance to examples of sumo wrestlers and basketball players. We are given a group of example sumo wrestlers and basketball players specifying their identity as such. We use these examples to turn the knobs so the classifier operates accurately. Here is where the computer search comes in. The values to which the knobs are eventually set are determined by a search procedure, possibly evolutionary, to tune the box's performance in accordance to some design criterion.

The first step is to define features. What features separate sumo wrestlers from basketball players? Height and weight immediately come to mind. So we collect some data and form the plot shown in Fig. 5.3. Next we choose a method of classification. Suppose we decide we would like to separate the two classes with a line. The fitness is determined by the number of misclassifications. But which line? With attention again to Fig. 5.3, we can choose a point **A** on the left side and **B** on the right, connect them with a line and count the number of misclassifications. Since there are 30 each of

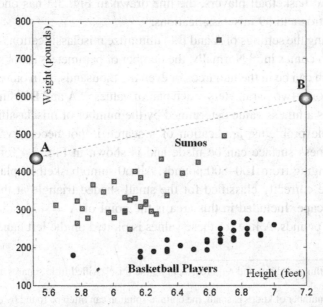

Fig. 5.3. Examples of the height and weight of 30 sumo wrestlers (squares) and 30 basketball players (circles).

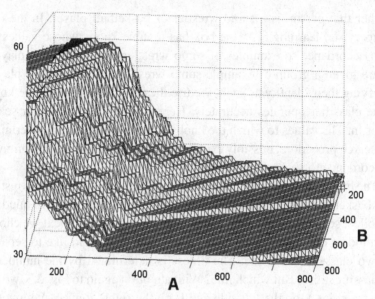

Fig. 5.4. The number of accurate classifications for different choices of **A** and **B** in Fig. 5.3.

sumos and basketball players, the line drawn in Fig. 5.3 has one correct classification and 39 misclassifications.[d]

Finding the settings of **A** and **B** to minimize misclassifications is where the search comes in.[23] Normally, the number of parameters (knobs to turn) in a search can be in the hundreds or even the thousands.[24] In our example, there are only two parameters. Each pair of values of **A** and **B** defines a line which has a fitness value determined by the number of misclassifications. For simple problems, application of a search is not necessary.[e] A plot of the fitness surface can be made and is shown in Fig. 5.4 for both **A** and **B** ranging from 100–800 pounds. All 60 sumo/basketball player data points are correctly classified for the small shaded triangle at the top of the landscape. Included in this area is the point of **A** = 175 pounds and **B** = 330 pounds. A line for these values is plotted on the left hand side of

---

[d]Verifying this is tedious and requires counting the misclassified little squares and circles in the figure.
[e]When the number of knobs is small, the optimal solution can often be found by examining all possible settings. This is what is done in computing the fitness function in Fig. 5.4. Doing so is called *exhaustive search*.

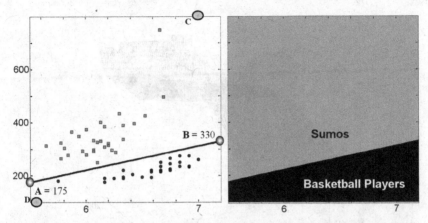

Fig. 5.5. (LEFT) A plot of sumo and basketball player data repeated from Fig. 5.3. The line of **A** = 175 pounds and **B** = 330 pounds, corresponding to a maximum of the fitness curve in Fig 5.4, cleanly separate the two classes. (RIGHT) The data is discarded and the line now becomes the foundation of our classifier. Give me an athlete's height and weight and I will announce Sumo or Basketball player depending on whether the point is above or below the line in the right hand figure.

Fig. 5.5. The line is seen to cleanly differentiate the sumo wrestlers from the basketball players.

The line dividing the sumo wrestlers from the basketball players has been *learned* from the data. In fact, the data can be discarded and the classifier shown on the right hand side of Fig. 5.5 results. When a new person enters, we take their height and weight. If the point lies above the line, they are a basketball player. If below the line, it's a sumo wrestler.

After we looked at the data plot, we restricted ourselves to a line separating the two data sets. From our examination of the problem it seemed like a good idea. This is a very restrictive classification approach[25] but happens to work in this case. Note that because we placed the sumos above the line and basketball players below the line, we have introduced a bias. What if we had done the opposite? Let's place the sumo wrestlers below the line and the basketball players above. Knowing what we know, this is not a wise thing to do, but certainly is a classifier option. Repeating the same process as before, the fitness function for the reversal is shown on the top of Fig. 5.6. The optimum now is only 35, a bit over half of the available data points. Here, **A** = 510 and **B** = 100. Previously, we were able to separate all 60 data points. The new "best" line is shown at the bottom of Fig. 5.6.

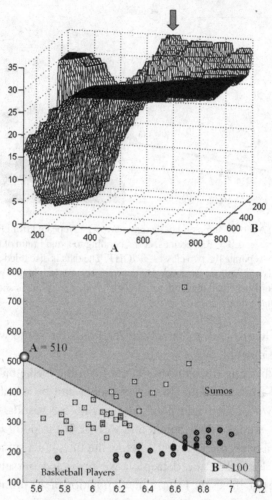

Fig. 5.6. A poor classifier optimized for discriminating sumo wrestlers from basketball players.

There are certainly performance biases imposed by the classifier choice. We see the need for knowledge about our simple choice of whether the sumo wrestlers or basketball players are above the discrimination line. If, on the left figure in Fig. 5.5, we always choose a line connecting the points **D** on the bottom horizontal line and **C** on the top, we will never end up with a very good classifier.

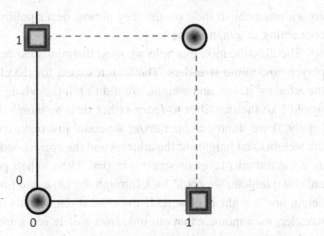

Fig. 5.7. An "exclusive or" (XOR). The circles correspond to a logic value of 0 and the squares to a logic value of 1.

An often cited and simple example where the choice of a line classifier will never give 100% accuracy was suggested by Minsky and Pappert.[26,f] Consider the four points shown in Fig. 5.7. Two squares and two circles are in diagonally opposite corners. This represents an *exclusive or* (XOR) logic operation.[g] The circles represent zeros and the squares represent ones. There exists no line which can successfully separate the squares from the circles. For this and many other cases, a linear classifier will not work. So the classifier chosen must be matched to the problem to be solved. The linear classifier doesn't work here. But for discrimination between sumo wrestlers and basketball players, a line works fine.

5.2.3 *A man-in-the-loop sneaks in active information*

Those who write software can spend hours debugging their programs. Authors of evolutionary programs can spend significant time tuning the parameters of their search algorithms. When proponents of search

---

[f] Both Minsky and Pappert are pioneers in the field of artificial intelligence.

[g]† The XOR operator is commonly denoted by the symbol $\oplus$. It is defined by four relationships: $0 \oplus 0 = 0$, $0 \oplus 1 = 1$, $1 \oplus 0 = 1$ and $1 \oplus 1 = 0$. These are the four points shown in Fig. 5.7.

algorithms publish their results they almost never publish documentation concerning this man-in-the-loop.

The classification example we used distinguished between basketball players and sumo wrestlers. The features used for the classification were the athletes' height and weight. We didn't tell the whole story though. We would like the classifier to *learn* rather than *memorize* the examples we supply. If we wanted to memorize, we could just make a database of all of the weights and heights of the athletes and the corresponding classification as a basketball player or sumo wrestler. Then, when presented with an unknown athlete, we could look through the table and find which athlete's height and weight is closest. If the closest data points belong to a sumo wrestler, we announce that our unknown athlete is a sumo wrestler.

Learning, on the other hand, attempts to recognize examples outside of the provided training set. The true measure of the performance of the sumo wrestler/basketball player classifier is how the classifier works on athletes the classifier has not seen before. For this reason, a common practice is to set aside some of the examples for the purpose of *testing*. The data is therefore separated into two parts: the testing set and the training set. After training the classifier as best we can, the test data is applied to see how well the classifier performs on athletes it has never seen before. Doing so is a test of how the classifier performs outside of the training data and therefore how well it learns rather than memorizes.

One of your humble authors (Marks) co-founded and co-chaired the first IEEE conference on application of computational intelligence, including classifiers, to financial data.[27] Initially, some novice participants were excited that they had trained an artificial neural network[28] to forecast the market. Neural networks are trained using a search algorithm. The trainers of the neural network followed the prescribed method of randomly separating the data into the training and testing sets.[h] In some instances, the results were remarkable. We were all going to be rich! As is often the case with things that are too good to be true, these results were too good to be true. The problem was this. Neural networks have a number of parameters, including the number of hidden layers and the number of

---

[h]A third corruptible data set, dubbed the *validation data*, is commonly used to test the classifier after training.

neurons in each hidden layer. Each parameter can be viewed as a knob to tune. Each neural network responds differently to the financial data. So the computer programmer who was training the neural networks would choose its architecture, train, and then test the result. The performance of the trained neural network on the testing data then informed the programmer how well the neural network did. But maybe the programmer could do better. In hopes of finding a better neural network, another neural network architecture was chosen and the process was repeated. The programmers were performing a search for a search with a man-in-the-loop. After repeating this process several times, the programmers happened upon a neural network architecture that worked quite well on their financial data. The problem, however, was that repeated use of test data from the same financial data set had corrupted the impartiality of the test data. The test data had become training data for the man-in-the-loop. When the programmers placed their neural networks online and tried to trade with real-time data, they were discouraged. Their program didn't work and they lost money. In terms of learning versus memorization, this is not surprising. The programmers use of a man-in-the-loop essentially resulted in a neural network that memorized *both* the training and test data.

Will a neural network or any other learning machine ever be able to make significant profit in stock trading? Retired St. John's University Professor John F. Marshall,[29] the first ever Professor of Financial Engineering and founder and first President of the *International Association of Financial Engineering*, was asked how to judge a programmer who claimed they trained a computer to beat the market. Marshall's wise response was not to look at the theory and methodology by which their machine was trained, but rather to simply assess the programmer's income by asking what kind of car they drove.[30] Ultimately, the proof of a design is in its performance.

5.2.3.1 *Back room tuning*

Search algorithms have numerous parameters that require tuning. After one search algorithm has been applied unsuccessfully, the programmer can tweak the parameters of the search algorithm or even try a different search algorithm.

Here's a specific example. David Thomas, an intelligent design critic, offered a software implementation of an evolutionary algorithm he claimed toppled intelligent design.[31] Thomas wrote[32]:

> 'If you contend that this algorithm works only by sneaking in the answer into the fitness test, please identify the precise code snippet where this frontloading is being performed."

So we did.[33] Many sources of active information were identified. One was code showing that Thomas was using a man-in-the-loop. We identified a smoking gun snippet of code. Here's an excerpt from our critique:

> "Thomas published a C++ version of his algorithm[34] after posting his original description. Our focus has been on the Fortran version of the algorithm because that is where the most detailed results were presented. For the most part, the C++ algorithm works the same as the Fortran algorithm but some differences should be noted. The minimum interchange count system has been modified. The initialization restricts the interchange used count to always be at the maximum.[35]

```
x = (double) rand() / (double)RAND_MAX; num =
(int)((double)(m_varbnodes*x); num = m_varbnodes; //
                    over-ride!!!
```

> "The claim that no design was involved in the production of this algorithm is very hard to maintain given this section of code. The code picks a random count for the number of interchanges; however, immediately afterwards it throws away the randomly calculated value and replaces it with the maximum possible, in this case, 4. The code is marked with the comment "over- ride!!!," indicating that this was the intent of Thomas. It is the equivalent of saying "go east" and a moment later changing your mind and saying "go west." The most likely occurrence is that Thomas was unhappy with the initial performance of his algorithm and thus had to tweak it."

We will revisit Thomas's work in Chapter 6.4.1

5.3   The Astonishing Cost of Blind Search in Bits

COI states that any search algorithm performs, on average, as well as any other search algorithm if there is no knowledge about the location of the target or the search space structure. Thus, random sampling of the search space (blind search) can be as good as any other in such a case. If one is performing a search with only a small number of outcomes, such as looking for A♠, this is not a problem. We are assured of success in no more than 52 trials.

For even intermediately sized problems, though, random sampling of the search space cannot be performed without knowledge about the search. The universe is neither big enough nor old enough to allow such searches. Neither is a googol of parallel universes. In regard to evolutionary search, artificial intelligence pioneer Seymour Papert said as much in the following comment from a dialog transcribed in 1970[36]:

> "If you are looking for a function about which you know nothing except that it is in some very, very large space of functions, I contend it will take a *very, very long time* to find it. The only way out of the exponential blowup is by avoiding the model of a blind hunt in an arbitrary space of functions, for example, by building very specific structured knowledge into the system, but what you have described [evolutionary search] is a blind hunt."[i]

Papert was wrong in equating evolutionary computing to a blind hunt in the sense each is a different search algorithm. COI dictates that evolutionary programming will work better than average on some problems and worse than average on others. But he is right in stating that blind search will take a "very, very long time."

We will now measure the difficulty of a blind search in bits rather than seconds. The result is astonishing.

†5.3.1 *Analysis*

Let's analyze the proverbial "monkeys at a typewriter" problem of producing prose by chance by using a blind search. Consider the phrase METHINKS*IT*IS*LIKE*A*WEASEL from Shakespeare's *Hamlet*. The phrase contains $L = 28$ letters chosen from an alphabet of $N = 27$ characters (26 letters and a space.) If we repeatedly choose 28 letters randomly, how many trials will we need to reach the target WEASEL phrase? There are

$$N^L = 27^{28} = 1.20 \times 10^{40}$$

possible outcomes from the characters available. If we take queries without duplication (i.e. once a random phrase is generated, it is never tested again) we expect to, on the average, find the phrase after half of the possible

---

[i]† Italics added.

solutions have been queried.

$$\bar{Q} = \frac{1}{2}N^L = 0.60 \times 10^{40}.$$

Recall that Shannon information can be thought of as measuring probability in terms of coin flip predictions. Six bits of information is equivalent to the probability of successfully forecasting six flips of a fair coin.[j] To differentiate $N = 27$ different characters, a total of $b = \log_2 N = \log_2 27 = 4.75$ bits per character is needed. For a string of $L = 28$ letters, then a total of $L \log_2 N = 28 \log_2 27 = 133$ bits is needed. If $Q = 0.60 \times 10^{40}$ queries are made, each requiring $\log_2 N^L = 133$ bits, the total number of bits assigned to the search is

$$B = Wb = 8.0 \times 10^{41} \text{ bits.} \tag{5.1}$$

That's a lot of bits! A Blu-ray disc stores 50GB and is 1.2 mm thick. Incredibly, in order to store 8.0×10^{41} bits, one would need about 24,000 stacks of discs each as tall as the Milky Way galaxy is wide.[k] All of this for a search for the simple phrase

METHINKS*IT*IS*LIKE*A*WEASEL.

In general, if we have an alphabet of N characters and a message of length L characters, the number of bits required for a successful search without replacement from Equation (5.1) is on average

$$B = \frac{1}{2}N^L \log_2 N^L \text{ bits.} \tag{5.2}$$

For a given number of bits, B, and an alphabet with N characters, this transcendental equation can be solved to find the length L of a specific phrase that can be found using a blind search.

---

[j]† From the equation for information, $p = 2^{-I}$. Six bits of information thus corresponds to odds of $2^6 = 64$ to one.

[k]† There are 8 bits per byte so the Blu-ray stores 400 giga bits. For 8.0×10^{41} bits, that's 2.0×10^{29} Blu-ray discs. At a thickness of 1.2 mm per disc, this translates to a stack of discs 2.4×10^{23} km. Using a Milky Way diameter of 10^{41} km gives a stack of Blu-rays equal to 24,000 Milky Way diameters.

5.3.2 *The cost*

We will now show that, with no prior knowledge, there are not enough computational resources in the universe to produce a meaningful target phrase.

Given B bits, the length of a specific message for which we can search is given in Table 5.2. For perspective, we can relate the number of bits to the number of cubic millimeters[1] in various volumes. The volume of an Olympic-sized swimming pool is about 10^{12} cubic millimeters. This is the number of bits, on average, required to search for a phrase only $L = 7$ letters long. The entries in Table 5.2 increase stepwise in volume starting from the swimming pool and ending with the observable universe. The volume of the observable universe, in cubic millimeters, is about 10^{89}. For $B = 10^{89}$ bits and $N = 27$, Equation (5.2) dictates a message of only length $L = 61$ letters can be found. Ronald Reagan's quote

> ## "FREEDOM IS NEVER MORE THAN ONE GENERATION AWAY FROM EXTINCTION"

is 62 characters long including spaces. We're one character short.

Table 5.2. The number of bits, B, to search for a message of length L, when the alphabet is of size $N = 27$. For perspective, corresponding sizes are given for various volumes in cubic millimeters.

Size (cubic mm)	B	L
Olympic Swimming Pool	10^{12}	7
Volume of Lake Superior	10^{21}	11
Volume of the earth	10^{30}	20
Volume of Jupiter	10^{33}	22
Volume of the Sun	10^{36}	24
Volume of the Milky Way	10^{69}	47
Observable universe	10^{89}	61

---

[1]A cubic millimeter is equal to a microliter.

Maybe we are thinking too small. Assume the age of the universe is 14 billion years. We divide that time up into picoseconds[m] and assume, for each picosecond, there are 10^{89} cubic millimeters. In space-time, that's over 10^{115} cubic millimeter — picoseconds. How far does $B = 10^{115}$ bits get us? Only to $L = 79$ characters — one short of the C.S. Lewis quote:

"A YOUNG MAN WHO WISHES TO REMAIN AN ATHEIST CANNOT BE TOO CAREFUL OF HIS READING"

We are not even close to the letters on a single page of a book. And we are not even using numbers or punctuation. Perhaps the millimeter is too large a measurement. Let's measure the volume of the universe, instead, in cubic Planck units. One Planck volume $= 17.692557 \times 10^{-104}$ m^3 and the age of the universe in Planck time ($=5.39 \times 10^{-44}$ seconds). We obtain the space-time volume measure of 10^{244} Planck volume $\times$ Planck time units. And $B = 10^{244}$ bits allows us to search for a phrase of only a length of about $L = 169$.

When stripped of punctuation, Lincoln's short *Gettysburg Address*[37] contains $L = 1422$ characters, including spaces. We are not even close using Planck time and volume. The computational resources for a blind search are astonishingly large. Our universe is too small and too young.

So let's assume an even bigger number. Suppose there are of 10^{1000} parallel universes in the so-called multiverse and these universes are the same size and age as ours. Will this at least give us the Gettysburg Address? No. $B = 10^{1244}$ bits gives us only $L = 869$ characters.[n] We need 1422.

To get the Gettysburg Address, we require 10^{792} multiverses.

This simple exercise illustrates conclusively that, in the absence of information, a blind random search is not sufficient to perform successfully

---

[m] A millionth of one millionth of a second.
[n] † As L becomes large, we conclude from Equation (5.2) that, asymptotically, $\log B$ becomes proportional to the message length. Specifically, $\log B \to L \log N$. Thus

$$L(\log[B/\log[N = 1244/\log_{10}[27 = 869.]]])$$

on even intermediately sized problems. Knowledge about the search space and/or the target location is essential for success.

5.4 Measuring Search Difficulty in Bits

The measure of a search problem's difficulty in the absence of any information is called *endogenous information*.[38] The degree to which the information is reduced is dubbed the *active information* and quantitatively measures the degree to which the additional knowledge has assisted in the performance of the search.[o]

Here is a more detailed discussion of this idea.

5.4.1 *Endogenous information*

We denote the endogenous information using the notation I_Ω.

The 10-bit lock in Fig. 5.8 shows another view of search difficulty measured in bits. There are 10 up-down switches, all of which need to be situated in the correct position to open a lock. An up position is one and a down position is zero. If there is only one working combination, the difficulty of the search is ten bits. The chance of choosing the correct combination is $p = \left(\frac{1}{2}\right)^{10}$ and $I_\Omega = -\log_2 p = 10$ bits.

In the search for the perfect pancake, assume there are 10 billion recipes. If only one of these recipes is acceptable, then the endogenous information of the search is

$$I = \log_2 10,000,000,000 = 33.2 \text{ bits.}$$

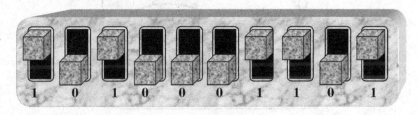

Fig. 5.8. A 10-bit lock.

---

[o]For given knowledge about a search, the search difficulty in bits can be reduced by varying amounts depending on the cleverness of the search programmer.

The difficulty of the search is therefore about the same as successfully predicting the outcome of 33 sequential flips of a fair coin. There are about 2×10^{184} Planck volumes[p] in the visible universe. Identifying a single Planck volume target in the visible universe then corresponds to an endogenous information of $I = \log_2 2 \times 10^{184} = 612$ bits.

The endogenous information is a measure of the difficulty of a search problem. The larger the endogenous information, the more difficult the problem.

Using interval halving and an assumption of Bernoulli's PrOIR, we are able to specify the target of a problem with B bits of endogenous information using B questions that can be answered with a "yes" or a "no". But this fails for almost all searches. Someone needs to know the target location and answer questions like "It is this half or the other half?" For the pancake problem, for example, there is no way to divide the 10 billion recipes into two halves and determine in which half the good recipe lies. Interval halving requires an enormous amount of knowledge about the target sought.

A search can be visualized as illustrated in Fig. 5.9. We have a search space, Ω, that consists of all of the possible outcomes. For the pancake search, Ω contains each of the 10 billion recipes. The notation $|\Omega|$ is commonly used to denote the number of elements in the set.[q]

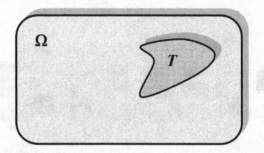

Fig. 5.9. A target, T, is imbedded in a search space, Ω.

---

[p]Planck volume $= 17.692\,55\,69946 \times 10^{-105}\,\mathrm{m}^3$.
[q]The number of elements in a set is referred to as the *cardinality* of the set.

There is a subset T (for target) in the search space which consists of all acceptable solutions in the search. For the pancake recipe, T consists of the set of all of the recipes that Bob the Taster deems acceptable. The number of elements in the target is $|T|$. If all of the elements in the search space are equally likely, then the probability of choosing an element in the target subset is simply

$$p = \frac{|T|}{|\Omega|}. \tag{5.3}$$

If, for example, we have seven white marbles and three black, then for choosing a black marble, $|\Omega| = 10$, $|T| = 3$ and $p = 0.3$. This probability measured in coin flips is the endogenous information of the search problem. The endogenous information of the search is

$$I_\Omega = -\log_2 p. \tag{5.4}$$

†5.4.1.1 *Two special cases*

Here are two special cases of endogenous information.
1. **A Target of One**. A special case of the endogenous information occurs when there is a single target within the search space, i.e. $|T| = 1$. Then $p = \frac{1}{|\Omega|}$ and

$$I_\Omega = -\log_2 |\Omega|. \tag{5.5}$$

2. **A Target Phrase**. What about choosing a specific phrase from an alphabet of characters? In English, for example, we might choose the phrase

$$\textbf{METHINKS*IT*IS*LIKE*A*WEASEL}. \tag{5.6}$$

There are two important parameters: (a) The length of the phrase, L, in characters and (b) the number of characters, N, in the alphabet. For English phrases, we can choose $N = 27$ for the 26 letters of the alphabet plus a space. For binary strings, $N = 2$ and, for a DNA sequence, $N = 4$ corresponding to the four nucleotides A, C, G and T. If we restrict ourselves to phrases of length L, then the total possible number of phrases in the search space is

$$|\Omega| = N^L \qquad (5.7)$$

corresponding, from Equation (5.5), to an endogenous information of

$$I_\Omega = L \log_2 N. \qquad (5.8)$$

For the WEASEL phrase in Equation (5.6) we have an alphabet of size $N = 27$ (26 letters and a space) and a target phrase of length $L = 28$ corresponding to an endogenous information of $I_\Omega = 28 \log_2 27 = 133$ bits. This is a measure of the difficulty of finding the phrase in the absence of any external knowledge.

5.4.1.2 *Endogenous information of the Cracker Barrel puzzle*

If you have visited one of the chain of Cracker Barrell restaurants, you have seen the Cracker Barrell puzzle shown in Fig. 5.10[39] that sits with the salt and pepper shakers at every dining table. The goal of the puzzle is to skip adjacent pieces, like checkers, and remove the skipped peg. One wins when there is only a single peg left at the end of the game. As

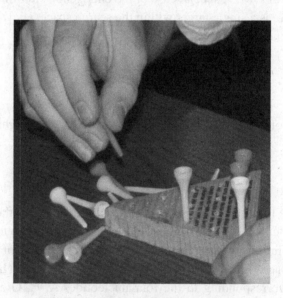

Fig. 5.10. The Cracker Barrel puzzle.

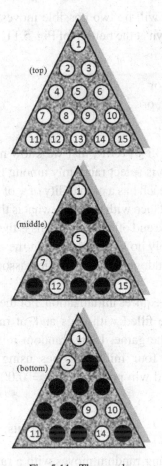

Fig. 5.11. The puzzle.

measured by endogenous information, how difficult is the Cracker Barrel puzzle?

The holes in the puzzle can be numbered from 1 to 15, as shown at the top of Fig. 5.11. After some play, the board might be as shown in the middle of Fig. 5.11. The black holes denote the absence of a peg. As is shown in the middle, there are no more moves. No peg can jump another peg and five pegs are left. Since there are no more possible jumps, the game is over and the player did not win.

In the process of playing the Cracker Barrel game, each turn presents a small number of different possible plays. The number of the plays can vary. Sometimes there will be two possible moves, sometimes six moves and, sometimes as shown at the bottom of Fig. 5.11, there are three possible moves. They are

1. Peg 1 jumps peg 2, or
2. Peg 10 jumps peg 9, or
3. Peg 14 jumps peg 9.

Assume, under Bernoulli's PrOIR, that we know nothing about the game and the best we can do is select randomly among the allowable moves. If there are three moves, each has a probability of $\frac{1}{3}$ of being selected. If every move is taken in accordance with this rule, what is the probability there will be a single peg left at the end of the game? This is the probability of winning the game with absolutely no knowledge about the game. The logarithm of this probability is the endogenous information associated with the Cracker Barrel puzzle.

A search typically requires initialization. For the Cracker Barrel puzzle, all of the 15 holes are filled with pegs and, at random, a single peg is removed. This starts the game. Using random initialization and random moves, simulation of four million games using a computer program resulted in an estimated win probability $p = 0.0070$ and an endogenous information of

$$I_\Omega = -\log_2 p = 7.15 \text{ bits.}$$

Winning the puzzle using random moves with a randomly chosen initialization (the choice of the empty hole at the start of the game) is thus a bit more difficult than flipping a coin seven times and getting seven heads in a row. An example of a sequence of moves that solves the Cracker Barrel puzzle is shown in Fig. 5.12.

The Cracker Barrel game will be revisited later when we talk about exogenous and active information.

5.4.2 *Active information*

Conservation of information dictates the need for domain expertise in search. Active information measures the amount of information added by external sources.

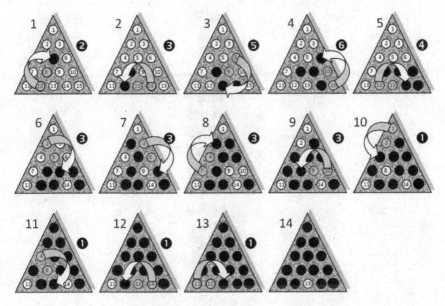

Fig. 5.12. A winning sequence of moves.

The endogenous information measures the difficulty of a search when nothing is known about the location of the target or the structure of the search space. It is based on a single query to the space. If the query is a success, we can then say that the occurrence of the success has given us I_Ω bits of information in a single query.

In Figure 5.8, we pictured a 10-bit lock of up-down flip flops. To open the lock, each switch must be in the correct position. Searching for the correct combination therefore has a difficulty, as measured by endogenous information, of 10 bits. Suppose Larry the Lockmaker approaches you and says "These locks are a lot more simple than they look. The first four bits are always down-up-down-up (0101)." If he's telling you the truth, Larry the Lockmaker has just given you four bits of *active information* which we denote by $I_+ = 4$ bits. The active information makes the search easier. We now have a search problem with a difficulty of only $10 - 4 = 6$ bits.

Active information is the degree to which a search is simplified, in bits, when applying knowledge about the search. This knowledge can be about the target being sought or the structure of the search space.

Fig. 5.13. A thumbwheel combination lock.

A more realistic lock is the thumbwheel combination lock shown in Fig. 5.13. There are 10 wheels, each of which go from 0 to 9. Thus there are $|\Omega| = 10^{10} = 10$ billion possible combinations. If there is only one combination that works, the endogenous information corresponding to searching for the correct answer is, from Equation (5.4), $I_\Omega = \log_2 10^{10} = 33.2$ bits. If Larry the Lockmaker tells us that the combination uses only 1's, 2's and 3's, there are no longer 10^{10} possible combinations. There are now only $3^{10} = 59{,}049$ possibilities, corresponding to a probability of success of $q = 3^{-10} = 1.7 \times 10^{-5}$. Since the search has been assisted by external knowledge about the target, we dub the new search an *assisted search*. The information associated with the assisted search is the exogenous information,

$$I_S = -\log_2 q. \tag{5.9}$$

For our problem, $I_S = \log_2 3^{10} = 15.8$ bits. The *active information* is the reduction of difficulty in solving the search when external knowledge is applied.

$$I_+ = I_\Omega - I_S = \log_2 p - (-\log_2 q) = -\log_2\left(\frac{p}{q}\right). \tag{5.10}$$

For the thumbwheel lock example in Fig. 5.13, the active information is $I_+ = 33.2 - 15.8 = 16.4$ bits. The active information dictates the degree to which the search's difficulty has been reduced. The difference of the unassisted search, $I_\Omega = 33.2$ coin flips, has been reduced to $I_S = 15.8$ coin flips. We therefore save a total of $I_+ = 16.4$ coin flips.

Active information is defined with respect to the reference p equal to the probability of success of a single query under the assumption of Bernoulli's PrOIR. Like any log ratio measure, such as dB, the reference probability can be placed at another level to compare relative performance.

When a mathematical model is proposed, we like to see if the model applies to cases we know are transparently obvious. Let's do this for the active information model in three cases.

1. **No knowledge:** $I_+ = 0$: If the active information is zero ($p = q$), the search performs the same as a single blind query. No information has been added to the search and, as we would expect, $I_+ = \log\left(\frac{p}{p}\right) = 0$.
2. **A perfect search:** $I_+ = I_\Omega$: For a perfect search, $q = 1$. Then the active information is equal to the endogenous information ($I_+ = I_\Omega$) and we have extracted all of the available endogenous information from the search.
3. **Poor information:** $I_+ < 0$: We might apply incorrect knowledge. For the thumb wheel combination lock, for example, we can be told that the combination consists of only 3's, 4's and 5's when, in fact, it uses only 1's, 2's and 3's. In such a case, no attention will be given during the search to a query that can be correct. The (incorrectly) assisted search will do worse that a random query ($q < p$) in which case the active information will be negative. Indeed, if $q = 0$, then the active information is negative infinity.[r]

We now have a better understanding of the waterbed analogy in Fig. 5.1. If we have no knowledge about a search and choose a search at random,

---

[r]In general, $-\infty \le I_+ \le I_\Omega$.

Table 5.3. A summary of search information measures.

	Probability	Information	
Unassisted Search	$p = \frac{|T|}{|\Omega|}$	Endogenous:	$I_\Omega = -\log_2 p$
Assisted Search	q	Exogenous:	$I_s = -\log_2 q$
		Active:	$I_+ = -\log_2\left(\frac{p}{q}\right) = I_\Omega - I_s$

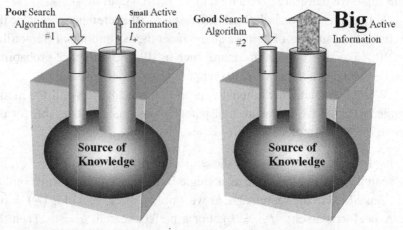

Fig. 5.14. Poor and good search algorithms for mining active information from an information source. For a given information source, the amount of active information can be viewed as a mining exercise. A good search algorithm, shown on the right, will mine more active information than the poor algorithm on the left. An evolutionary algorithm is one of a number of possible search algorithms.

there is a possibility that either negative or positive active information can result. A summary of the information measures of assisted and unassisted search is summarized in Table 5.3.

5.4.2.1 *Examples of sources of knowledge*

As illustrated in Fig. 5.14, active information is mined from a source of knowledge. Having knowledge is not the same as using it. There are good ways to mine active information from sources of knowledge and better ways. Consider, for example, the thumb wheel lock problem illustrated in Fig. 5.13. Our source of information was Larry the Lockmaker, who told us the combination, uses only 1's, 2's and 3's. A reasonable and probably optimal way to mine this information source is to proceed with a blind search of combinations, using only 1's, 2's and 3's. But this is not the only way to mine this knowledge source for active information. We could, alternately, only try 1's, 2's and 3's on the first five thumb wheels and any number on the thumb wheels remaining. This (unreasonable) algorithm also uses the source of information, but mines active information much less efficiently.

In some examples, extraction of active information from an information source is intuitive and obvious. Such is the case for the example of the thumb wheel, given that only 1's, 2's and 3's appear in the combination. In other search designs, like the evolutionary search design of antennas,[s] the best use of the information source is not obvious. NASA's evolutionary design software of an X-band antenna,[40] for example, used evaluation of fitness during its search process using *The Numerical Electromagnetics Code*[41] (NEC-4) software that simulates the physics encountered in antenna performance. NASA engineers used an evolutionary program to mine active information from NEC-4. In the sense of computer design time, is an evolutionary search the best way to extract active information from this software? Could another search have done better? Searching for a good search is addressed later in this chapter.

5.4.2.2 *Active information per query*

The best use of an information source depends on how one defines *efficiency*. If a programmer's time is the most important quantity, then an inefficient search algorithm hastily written that takes days to run on a computer might be better than a carefully crafted one-minute program whose design requires three days. Another metric is query count. Given unlimited time, even uninformed searches such as blind search will eventually find the target. If we write a program that will ultimately find the correct solution, then the performance of the program can be measured in terms of *active information per query*.

---

[s] Of the type in Chapter 3.4.1.

If all of the endogenous information, I_Ω, is extracted in Q queries, then the active information per query, $I_\oplus$, is[t]

$$I_\oplus = \frac{I_\Omega}{Q}. \qquad (5.11)$$

The measure of algorithm efficiency can be altered relative to other measures such as active information per CPU second or per programmer hourly salary.

†5.4.2.2.1 A subtle distinction[u]

When there is any stochastic component of a search, the active information, I_+, and therefore the active information per query in Equation (5.11), is a random variable. If the same search is repeated, the number of queries required for success can change. Random variables are often characterized by their means which, in turn, are estimated by averages of numerous trials. If there is a random component to the search, the mean active information can be estimated by averaging the results of numerous trials. The average number of queries from N runs of the same search algorithm is

$$\langle Q \rangle = \frac{1}{N} \sum_{n=1}^{N} Q_n,$$

where Q_n is the number of queries used on the nth trial to achieve success. This average approximates the mean $\bar{Q}$

$$\bar{Q} \approx \langle Q \rangle$$

and, according to the law of large numbers,,[42] becomes more accurate as the number of trials, N, increases. We are tempted to estimate the mean of the random variable, $I_\oplus$, denoted with an over bar by $\bar{I}_\oplus$, as $\frac{I_\Omega}{\langle Q \rangle}$ but, as is

---

[t]If the search is not perfect (i.e. does not always succeed), the active information per query is $I_\oplus = \frac{I_+}{Q}$.

[u]† Those not interested in math details may skip this section and henceforth assume $\bar{I}_\oplus \approx I_⊞ = \frac{I_\Omega}{\langle Q \rangle}$. There is no ambiguity in doing so as long as, in comparisons, the same metric is used consistently.

†Table 5.4. When there is a stochastic component to measure, repeated trials are performed and the mean value of the measure is estimated by the average of the outcomes. This is how active information per query is measured. But, as illustrated in the table below, there are different ways to do this resulting in different answers. Two searches are performed on a problem with endogenous information of $I_\Omega = 24$ bits. As shown in the table, the first search is successful after two queries and in the second search after six queries.

Two observers, Melodie and Merrick, like to keep score in different ways. Melodie likes to count queries for each search and Merrick likes to keep a tally of the active information for each search. Their short tally sheets are shown in the table. Both Melodie and Merrick average their numbers. Melodie has an average of four queries and Merrick has an average of eight bits per query. Melodie therefore gives her estimation of active information per query by dividing four queries into the endogenous information of 24 bits, giving a result of six bits per query. Merrick's estimate is eight bits per query. Both have used valid techniques but they come up with different answers. For this reason we have to be careful in our definitions. Merrick has computed the average active information per query which, due to the Law of Large Numbers, will approach the mean active information per query if a larger number of experiments are performed. Melodie, on the other hand, has estimated the active information per average query.

Trial	QUERIES (Melodie)	ACTIVE INFO (Merrick)
#1	2	12
#2	6	4
Average	4	8
Estimate	6	8

illustrated in the Table 5.4, they are not the same. Indeed, due to Jensen's inequality,[43]

$$\bar{I}_\oplus \geq \frac{I_\Omega}{\bar{Q}}.$$

For purpose of preciseness, we dub

$$I_+ = \frac{I_\Omega}{\bar{Q}} \approx \frac{I_\Omega}{\langle Q \rangle}$$

the *active information per mean query*. It is always less than $\bar{I}_\oplus$.

In the next section, we explore some subtle sources of information and show cases where an evolutionary approach mines active information poorly in comparison with some other popular algorithms. Chapter 6 is dedicated to identifying sources of active information in published software models purporting to simulate Darwinian evolution and to showing that other search algorithms mine this source much more efficiently than evolutionary search.

5.4.2.3 *Examples of active information*

In the thumbwheel lock example, the active information came in the form of a reduction in the search space size. Instead of looking for the combination in the big search space, we need to only look in a corner of the search space. Here are some other less obvious examples of sources of active information.

5.4.2.3.1 The Cracker Barrel puzzle

We return now to the Cracker Barrel puzzle. We showed that the endogenous information for solution of the Cracker Barrel puzzle by purely random choices is $I_\Omega = 7.4$ bits. Suppose an expert in the game, Puzzle Pete, tells you

"When you have a choice, don't jump into a corner."

In the puzzle shown in Fig. 5.15, the corners are numbered 1, 11 and 15.

How much active information has Puzzle Pete given you? Based on 4 million simulations with random initialization of the location of the empty hole, it turns out Pete has given you $I_+ = 2.1$ bits of active information. The problem has thus been roughly reduced in difficulty from forecasting the outcomes of 7 fair coins to that of 5 fair coins.

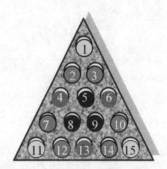

Fig. 5.15. For the Cracker Barrel puzzle, some empty peg starts will give the same results as others.

Next, Puzzle Pete whispers

"Also, always start with hole number #1 empty."[v]

This is an example of active information gained from initialization of the search process.

"But Pete," you respond after examining the board in Fig. 5.15, "If I start with hole #1 empty, my first move makes me jump into a corner. You said not to jump into a corner."

Pete smiles knowingly.

"Trust me."

And you are right to trust Pete. If you always start with hole #1 empty and, when there is a choice, avoid jumping into corners, then the active information is raised from 2.1 to $I_+ = 2.6$ bits.

But all advice is not good advice. Suppose contrarian Tony Two Toes tells you, "Ignore all of Puzzle Pete's advice. Puzzle Pete first told you to not jump into a corner. Then he told you to start with hole #1 empty. This forces you to jump into a corner on your first move. The man can't make up his mind! So don't listen to him. Listen to me. Doesn't it make better sense to start with hole #5 empty?"

Applying Tony Two Toes's advice with otherwise random moves worsens your chance of winning and results in an active information of $I_+ = -1.7$ bits. The difficulty of the problem has thus increased almost two coin flips.

Suppose Tony Two Toes then tells you, "Start with hole #5 empty and, when you can, *always* jump into a corner. Trust me."

In a million random simulations, not a single game was won using Tony Two Toes's advice. From these simulations, the active information is then estimated to be $I_+ = -\infty$. Although not yet proven to a mathematical certainty, it looks like Tony Two Toes's two rules make winning impossible.

Table 5.5 contains the active information for numerous scenarios including those discussed. Active information resulted from the domain expertise of Puzzle Pete. The advice must be accurate in order to work.

---

[v]With reference to Fig. 5.15, the symmetry of the puzzle board says starting with hole #1 empty is the same as hole #11 or hole #15 empty. Likewise, holes #2, 3, 7, 10, 12 and 14 will yield identical results. Holes #4, 6 and 13 form still another group and holes #5, 8 and 9 another.

Table 5.5. Active information for different "HINTS" for winning the Cracker Barrell puzzle. All values are in bits. The ①, for example, indicates that hole number one is initially empty.

Endogenous Information = I_Ω = 7.4 bits					
Initialization → Rule ↓	Random	①	②	④	⑤
Random	0.0	0.2	0.3	0.5	−1.7
Away from corners	2.1	2.6	2.3	2.4	−0.6
Into corners	−11.9	−11.0	−11.6	−12.6	−∞

Tony Two Toes's advice resulted in negative active information, i.e. the search performs worse than blind random search.

This example demonstrates again the validity of conservation of information illustrated by the waterbed analogy in Fig. 5.1. Guidelines for search cannot be assigned arbitrarily. Doing so can give either worse or better results. Knowledge about a search must be accurate in order to create positive active information.

5.4.2.3.2　The Monte Hall problem

Here's another more subtle example of active information. *Let's Make a Deal* was a television game show first hosted by Monty Hall. There are three curtains and the contestant's job is to barter with Monty to get the most valuable prize. The Monty Hall problem, loosely based on the show, was popularized by Marilyn vos Savant in her *Parade Magazine* column, *Ask Marilyn*, in 1990.

> "Suppose you're on a game show, and you're given the choice of three doors[w]: Behind one door is a car; behind the others, goats. You pick a door, say No. 1, and the host, who knows what's behind the doors, opens another door, say No. 3, which has a goat. He then says to you, 'Do you want to pick door No. 2?' Is it to your advantage to switch your choice?"

Untutored intuition often says it doesn't matter — you have a 50–50 chance no matter what. This is wrong. When a goat curtain is identified, we

---

[w]Monty used curtains. Marilyn used doors.

are given additional knowledge that can be mined for active information. Indeed, switching your choice from your initial pick gives you a two-thirds probability of winning. If you keep your original choice, your chance of winning is only 1/3. To see this, suppose that the car is behind door No. 1. Your first pick can be door #1, #2 or #3. Here are the possibilities.

a. If you choose door #1 and switch, you lose.
b. If you choose door #2 and switch, you win the car.
c. If you choose door #3 and switch, you win the car.

Thus, if you switch, your chances of winning are two out of three. If we repeat this exercise with the car behind door No. 2 and then No. 3, we get the same $\frac{2}{3}$ answer. Overall, using Bernoulli's PrOIR, the probability of winning is two thirds if you switch your choice and $\frac{1}{3}$ if you don't.

Let's then interpret the Monty Hall problem in the parlance of endogenous and active information. The search space consists of $|\Omega| = 3$ doors with $|T| = 1$ successful targets. Bernoulli's PrOIR says you therefore have a probability of $p = \frac{|T|}{|\Omega|} = \frac{1}{3}$ of choosing the car. The endogenous information of the search for the car is thus $I_\Omega = -\log_2 p = 1.585$ bits. When you choose a door and Monty Hall shows you another door behind which is a goat, he is giving you information that can be used to improve the odds of the search. By switching your choice, we have shown that the assisted search now has a probability of $q = \frac{2}{3}$ of succeeding. The active information we mined from Monty Hall's actions is thus $I_+ = -\log_2 \frac{p}{q} = -\log_2 \left(\frac{1}{3}/\frac{2}{3}\right) = 1$ bit thereby reducing the difficulty of the search to one with exogenous information $I_S = -\log_2 q = 0.585$ bits.

5.4.2.3.3 A sibling problem[44]

Here is another interesting example whose results are often initially counterintuitive. Tammy is hosting the annual "Men With Exactly Two Kids Club" convention next week where fathers come with their two children to spend a week together doing activities and bonding with their kids. Tammy needs to choose a father to hand out towels in the men's shower and wants to engage a man who has two sons for the task. What is the chance a randomly chosen man at the convention has two male children? Assuming a 50–50 chance of having a girl or a boy, the four equally probable possibilities of the children are ♀♀, ♂♀, ♀♂, and ♂♂. If a random father is chosen from the list of fathers, the probability they are both boys (♂♂) is thus $p = \frac{1}{4}$ corresponding to an endogenous information of $I_\Omega = 2$ bits.

Question 1: To narrow down the pool of choices for a father to hand out towels, Tammy accesses the data base of registrants. Each father answered a list of questions. For example, the "Men With Exactly Two Kids Club" is hosting a gala father–son retreat next year. To make a mailing list from the participants in the current convention, the following question is asked on the registration form:

> **Question 1:** *"Is at least one of your children a male?"*

Tammy discards from the pool every father who answered "no" to the question since they must have two girls. How much active information results from knowing the answer to this question?

Of the four possible pairings of boy and girl, the answer to the question has narrowed possibilities to three: ♂♀, ♀♂, and ♂♂. Only one has both males. Applying Bernoulli's PrOIR, the added information that one is a boy results in $q = \frac{1}{3}$. That is, if Tammy chooses a father at random from the reduced pool, her chance of choosing a father with two boys increases from $p = \frac{1}{4}$ to $q = \frac{1}{3}$ and Tammy has obtained $I_+ = -\log_2\left(\frac{1}{4}/\frac{1}{3}\right) = 0.415$ bits of active information.[x]

Tammy reads another question to glean even more active information in her search for a father with two sons. There is a follow-up question to the first from which even more active information can be mined.

> **Question 2:** *"If you answered "yes" to Question 1, Was your son born in an even year? (Or if both your children are male, was at least one of them born in an even year?)"*

---

[x]Initial intuition often suggests that, if a man has two children and at least one is male, then the chance that the other child is male is 50–50. But the analysis here shows that the correct answer is one third. There is a subtle distinction between this knowledge and knowing the *oldest* child is a male. In this case, the chance the other child is male is 50–50. When *oldest* is included in the knowledge, the active information is $I_+ = -\log_2\left(\frac{1}{4}/\frac{1}{2}\right) = 1$ bit compared to $I_+ = 0.415$ bits of when the phrase *at least one* is used. The word *oldest* therefore introduces over a half bit more of active information to the search.

If Tammy now chooses only from those who responded "yes" to **Question 2**, will it further improve her chances of choosing a father with two male children? In other words, does the knowledge about the evenness of the birth year provide additional active information? Remarkably, yes. Here is the reasoning using Bernoulli's PrOIR. Before we know anything, there are 16 equally probable possibilities. Even and odd are denoted by E and O. Thus $\male$ E is a male born in an even year.

$$(\male E, \male E) \qquad (\male E, \male O) \qquad (\male E, \female E) \qquad (\male E, \female O)$$
$$(\male O, \male E) \qquad (\male O, \male O) \qquad (\male O, \female E) \qquad (\male O, \female O)$$
$$(\female E, \male E) \qquad (\female E, \male O) \qquad (\female E, \male E) \qquad (\female E, \male O)$$
$$(\female O, \male E) \qquad (\female O, \male O) \qquad (\female O, \male E) \qquad (\female O, \male O)$$

Question 1 ("Is at least one of your children a male?") removes four entries from the table and leaves a dozen possibilities.

$$(\male E, \male E) \qquad (\male E, \male O) \qquad (\male E, \female E) \qquad (\male E, \female O)$$
$$(\male O, \male E) \qquad (\male O, \male O) \qquad (\male O, \female E) \qquad (\male O, \female O)$$
$$(\female E, \male E) \qquad (\female E, \male O) \qquad (\male O, \male E) \qquad (\male O, \male O)$$
$$(\female O, \male E) \qquad (\female O, \male O) \qquad (\male O, \male E) \qquad (\male O, \male O)$$

Of those remaining, there are seven cases where at least one of the sons was born in an even year. This leaves only seven possibilities when **Question 2** is answered yes.

$$(\male E, \male E) \qquad (\male E, \male O) \qquad (\male E, \female E) \qquad (\male E, \female O)$$
$$(\male O, \male E) \qquad (\male O, \male O) \qquad (\male O, \female E) \qquad (\male O, \female O)$$
$$(\female E, \male E) \qquad (\female E, \male O) \qquad (\male O, \male E) \qquad (\male O, \male O)$$
$$(\female O, \male E) \qquad (\female O, \male O) \qquad (\male O, \male E) \qquad (\male O, \male O)$$

Of the seven, there are three cases where there are two sons. Let's draw boxes around them.

(♂E, ♂E)	(♂E, ♂O)	(♂E, ♀E)	(♂E, ♀O)
(♂O, ♂E)	(♂O, ♂O)	(♂O, ♀E)	(♂O, ♀O)
(♀E, ♂E)	(♀E, ♂O)	(♂O, ♂E)	(♂O, ♂O)
(♀O, ♂E)	(♀O, ♂O)	(♂O, ♂E)	(♂O, ♂O)

If Tammy chooses randomly from those who answer "yes" to **Question 2**, the chances of her choosing man with two sons is[y] $q = \frac{3}{7}$ instead of $p = \frac{1}{4}$. The knowledge from **Question 2** has thus purchased us $I_+ = -\log_2\left(\frac{1}{4}/\frac{3}{7}\right) = 0.778$ bits of active information. The additional knowledge of the evenness of the birth year has increased the active information by 0.363 bits over that from **Question 1** alone.[z] Knowledge, that a son is born in an even year does not intuitively seem to be a potential source of active information for our problem. But it is. This illustrates that sources of active information can be subtle.

5.4.2.3.4 Multiple queries

Multiple queries clearly give a greater chance of success than a single query. Multiple queries can be done with replacement or without replacement. If the size of the search space is big and, in relation, the number of queries is small, then the two procedures are about the same. For Q

---

[y]Studies have purported to show that "the gender distribution in human families with two children . . . do not conform to any binomial distribution" and therefore do not follow Bernoulli's PrIOR. (Matthew A. Carlton and William D. Stansfield "Making Babies by the Flip of a Coin?" *The American Statistician*. (2005)). Bernoulli's PrIOR in our example, however, gives the best available estimate of active information. Had Tammy had access to the data used by Carlton and Stansfield, she could further increase the accuracy of the active information in her search even more.

[z]Suppose, instead of the evenness of the year, one asked, *in lieu* of **Question 2**, the following question: "If you answered "yes" to Question 1, was your son named John? (If both your children are male, was at least one of them named John?)" Detractors of Bernoulli's PrOIR might claim the active information computed using the original **Question 2** would be the same. It would not for an obvious reason: the chance a male has the name of John is not 50–50. This knowledge would translate into active information in excess of that obtained from the evenness or oddness of the birth year. To make the calculation, however, one must include the chance that a male is named John.

queries, the remarkable result for sampling with replacement is that active information is[aa]

$$I_+ \approx \log_2 Q. \tag{5.12}$$

This relationship dictates a diminished return for active information as a function of query count. For two queries, we obtain one bit of active information. Four queries give two bits of active information, a query gives three bits and 16 queries gives four bits. 1,024 queries gives $I_+ = 10$ bits and $2^{30} \approx 1$ billion queries gives only about 30 bits of active information. No matter how many queries you've made, you have to double the query count to get a single bit more of active information. In general, $Q = 2^n$ queries gives about n bits of active information.

5.4.3 *Mining active information from oracles*

A *needle-in-a-haystack* oracle announces the success or failure of a sample used in finding, for example, the ace of spades in a deck of 52 cards a special case of a fitness oracle. The fitness is either one ("we found the target!") or zero ("we didn't").

More typical of fitness oracles is the computer model used to design the antenna for NASA's evolutionary design of an X-band antenna. As discussed in Chapter 3.4.1,[45] designs are submitted to antenna simulation software oracle[46] that crunches the design numbers presented and, as was the case for Bob the Taster, presents the score or fitness assigned to the design.

5.4.3.1 *The Hamming oracle*

A simple easily understood oracle is the *Hamming oracle*. Assume we have a target phrase of L letters from an alphabet of N characters like the $L = 28$, $N = 27$ phrase in Equation (5.13). We offer the following phrase to the Hamming oracle:

[aa]† For Q queries with replacement, the probability of success is $q = Qp$. Thus,

$$I_S = -\log_2 Qp = -\log_2 Q + \log_2 p.$$

Since $I_\Omega = -\log_2 p$ and $I_+ = I_\Omega - I_S$, we get Equation (5.12). See Fig. 5.16 for details.

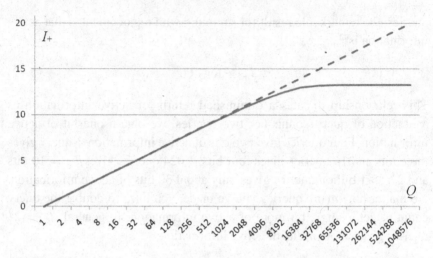

†Fig. 5.16. Active information for multiple blind queries. The dashed line is sampling with replacement and the solid line without replacement.

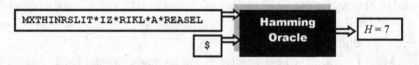

Fig. 5.17. The Hamming oracle.

MXTHINRSLIT*IZ*RIKL*A*REASEL.

Comparing this to the target phrase[bb]

METHINKS*IT*IS*LIKE*A*WEASEL,   (5.13)

we see that the two phrases differ in $H = 7$ places. This is the *Hamming distance* between the target phrase and the guess. When the Hamming distance is zero, there are no differences and we have found the target phrase.

The Hamming oracle does not tell us the locations where the letters differ, only the number of letters that differ. This can be visualized as pictured in Fig. 5.17. A phrase is entered, the oracle is paid ($) and the oracle announces the Hamming distance. How can we best spend our money? If

---

[bb]Repeated here from Equation (5.6).

we assume a message of length L with N members in the alphabet, the endogenous information of the search for the phrase is

$$I_\Omega = L \log_2 N$$

In terms of query count, here are four of many possible ways to use a Hamming oracle in a search in order of effectiveness.[47] We'll start with a poor algorithm to extract active information from the Hamming oracle.

1. *Poor*: **Needle-in-a-haystack oracle**. The Hamming oracle has the ability to specify whether or not a randomly chosen phrase is the correct phrase, i.e. it can be used inefficiently as a needle-in-a-haystack oracle. We choose a random phrase and see if the Hamming distance is zero. If it is, we have found the phrase. If it isn't, another phrase is chosen. The process is repeated until there is a success.

   There are two possibilities here: sampling with replacement and without. When sampling with replacement, $p = \frac{1}{|\Omega|}$. The sampling process is a geometric random variable[48] with an expected number of queries equal to $\bar{Q} = |\Omega| = N^L$.

2. *Good:* **Ratchet search (stochastic hill climbing)**. The needle-in-a-haystack makes no use of Hamming distance changes. The ratchet search does and performs better on the average. The basic ratchet search begins with an initialization. The Hamming distance is determined. A single character of the phrase is changed and the Hamming distance is recomputed.

   a. If the Hamming distance is larger, then a correct letter has been replaced by an incorrect letter. The position of the change is tagged and the original letter in the position must be the correct letter. The letter is tagged and remains unchanged for the rest of the search.

   b. If the Hamming distance is smaller, then a correct letter has been found. The changed letter is tagged and ratcheted into place for the remainder of the search.

   c. If the Hamming distance is the same, choose another untagged letter to change.

   The process is repeated until the Hamming distance goes to zero. The search is dubbed *ratchet* because once a Hamming distance is achieved in the search, it never gets worse.

Table 5.6. Illustration of the ratchet search for a three letter search using a Hamming Oracle and the *Good* search method (#2). The initial guess, randomly chosen, is ADF. Since the Hamming Oracle outputs a Hamming distance of three, all three letters are wrong. So we change F to a G and still get a Hamming distance of three. We keep changing to different letters until we chance on the correct letter I. We know it is correct because the Hamming distance is reduced to two. The letter I is ratcheted into the third position for the remainder of the search. The process is then repeated on the second letter, D, until the correct letter O is identified. The Hamming distance is now one. The remaining letter is then determined in a like manner. In this example, 30 queries are used to obtain the right answer. If we query with replacement (the same letter can be guessed more than once for a position), the expected number of queries is $Q = NL = 27 \times 3 = 81$. Using the blind needle-in-a-haystack approach, i.e. the *Poor* search method, the expected number of queries with replacement is $N^L = 27^3 = 19,683$. Ratchet search adds $I_+ = \log_2 \left(\frac{27^3}{27 \times 3} \right) \approx 8$ bits of active information, reducing the search difficulty from an endogenous information of $I_\Omega = \log_2 27^3 \approx 14$ bits to an exogenous information of $I_S = \log_2 27 \times 3 \approx 6$ bits.

#	Input			Hamming Distance
1	A	D	F	→ 3
2	A	D	G	→ 3
3	A	D	A	→ 3
4	A	D	I	→ 2
5	A	X	I	→ 2
6	A	Z	I	→ 2
7	A	A	I	→ 2
8	A	D	I	→ 2
9	A	T	I	→ 2
10	A	P	I	→ 2
11	A	L	I	→ 2
12	A	W	I	→ 2
13	A	R	I	→ 2
14	A	O	I	→ 1
15	R	O	I	→ 1
16	T	O	I	→ 1
17	Q	O	I	→ 1
18	W	O	I	→ 1
19	U	O	I	→ 1
20	U	O	I	→ 1
21	P	O	I	→ 1
22	I	O	I	→ 1
23	K	O	I	→ 1
24	M	O	I	→ 1

(Continued)

Table 5.6. (*Continued*)

#		Input		Hamming Distance
25	T	O	I	→ 1
26	P	O	I	→ 1
27	Y	O	I	→ 1
28	I	O	I	→ 1
29	G	O	I	→ 1
30	C	O	I	→ 0

An example of a simple ratchet search is illustrated in Table 5.6.

3. *Better:* **Ewert's**[cc] **FOOHOA.** The ratchet search uses only the current state to determine the next step in the search. No attempt is made to use the history of the search. The FOO Hamming oracle algorithm (FOOHOA) does use the history. The more knowledge a search procedure can effectively use, the greater the resulting active information per query.

If a string containing all A's is submitted to a Hamming oracle, the oracle's response will tell us how many A's are in the hidden string. By repeating this process with all of the letters in the chosen alphabet, the FOO is found for all of the letters. If there are N characters in the alphabet, establishment of the FOO requires, at most, $N - 1$ queries. The remainder of the FOOHOA is best explained by example. Consider a Hamming oracle using the English letters as its alphabet and having a message length of 5. Under this algorithm, we will already know the oracle's response to AAAAA, because we have already established the FOO for all letters. Consider the query ABAAA.

- If the second letter in the hidden string is A, the distance will increase.
- If the second letter in the hidden string is B, the distance will decrease.
- Otherwise, the distance will remain the same.

The query in question will actually test the second position for the presence of both A and B. The algorithm starts on the left side of the string and works through the string, querying each letter in order from the FOO list until it discovers the correct letter. Letters are tested starting with the

---

[cc]Winston Ewert is one of your humble authors.

most frequent because they have the largest probability of being in any unfilled position. When the correct value of a letter has been established, the FOO table is updated.

The results using Ewert's FOOHOA are significantly better than the ratchet search in the extraction of information from the Hamming oracle, as measured by query count.

4. *Best:* **Searching for the Best Search.** For a given oracle, there exists an algorithm that, on average, extracts the maximum active information per query. For the Hamming oracle, we are able to search for the optimal algorithm for easy searches. In general, a search for a search (S4S) is exponentially more computationally demanding than a search itself.[dd] Ewert composed an S4S in the case of the Hamming oracle. Using an exhaustive inspection of all possible search trees, Ewert's algorithm generates an optimal tree search in the sense of maximum extraction of per query active information from the oracle. The results are summarized

Table 5.7. The best possible use of a Hamming oracle in extracting active information using a minimum query count. N is the number of characters in the alphabet and L is the number of letters in the message. On top is the minimum average number of queries, $\langle Q \rangle$ to achieve success. The bottom table is the corresponding numerical value of $I_\boxplus$.

$\downarrow LN \rightarrow$	1	2	3	4	5	6
1	0	1.000	1.667	2.250	2.800	3.333
2	0	1.500	2.337	3.125	3.281	4.611
3	0	2.250	2.889	3.822	—	—
4	0	2.750	3.469	→	—	—
5	0	3.375	—	—	—	—
6	0	3.875	—	—	—	—

$\downarrow LN \rightarrow$	2	3	4	5	6
1	1.000	0.951	0.889	0.829	0.775
2	1.333	1.359	1.280	1.415	1.121
3	1.333	1.646	1.570	—	—
4	1.454	1.827	—	—	—
5	1.481	—	—	—	—
6	1.548	—	—	—	—

[dd]The S4S is examined in depth later in Chapter 5.8.

in Table 5.7.[49] At each iteration of a search algorithm, there is some set of possible hidden strings that have not been ruled out by previous queries. The algorithm selects a query as some function of this set. The resulting query and the response will produce a new subset containing only the strings that are compatible with the new query result. Ewert's algorithm finds the function mapping these sets to queries that will result in the lowest average number of queries to determine the target. It does so by searching every possible function to find the optimal one. This is an exhaustive S4S performed on the original search space. It should not be surprising, therefore, that the search is very expensive and can only be run for very small problems.

5. **Evolutionary Search.** These Hamming oracle examples illustrate that, given a source of information, different search algorithms mine the information source with different efficiencies. What happens when an evolutionary strategy is applied to extraction of information from a Hamming oracle? This is discussed next.

5.4.3.2   *Weasel ware and variations of information mining*

How does evolutionary search using a Hamming oracle compare with other search algorithms? A user-friendly graphical user interface (GUI) dubbed Weasel Ware 2.0, available at the *Evolutionary Informatics Lab* web (http://evoinfo.org/), allows us to explore this question.[ee]

In the example in Fig. 5.18, Weasel Ware searches for a target phrase using three different search algorithms: unassisted random search, proximity reward (evolutionary) search and Ewert's FOOHOA. We again use the target phrase METHINKS*IT*IS*LIKE*A*WEASEL in (3.12). *Unassisted Random Search* is equivalent to blind search. The blind search chooses 28 letters randomly from a library of 27 characters and asks a needle-in-a-haystack (NIAH) Oracle "Is this it?" If not, 28 new letters are chosen. The count in Fig. 5.18, 5,03,274, is nowhere near the expected 10^{40} query count expected before success. The second search, an evolutionary strategy, is labeled *Proximity Reward Search*. The evolutionary algorithm, as is shown in the search block in Fig. 5.18, has a population of 15 offspring. Each letter in each offspring has a 4% chance of being mutated to a randomly

---

[ee]Go to http://evoinfo.org/ Click on "Research Tools" and then "Weasel Ware." Other searches, described in detail, are considered on the web page, but are not considered here.

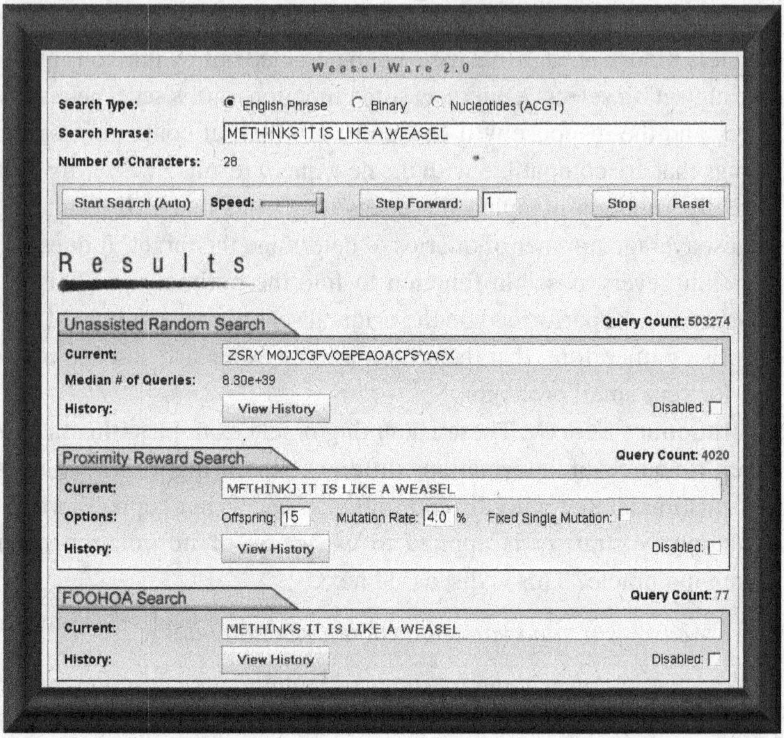

Fig. 5.18. Three searches using a Hamming oracle using Weasel Ware 2.0 available online at http://evoinfo.org/.

chosen letter in the 27-character alphabet. As identified by a Hamming Oracle, the fittest of the offspring survives and gives birth to 15 more offspring. We see the phrase is almost complete, lacking one letter, so the search is still in progress. Results are shown after 68 generations. Since there are 15 queries to the Hamming oracle for each generation, that's a total of $15 \times 68 = 4020$ queries, as is reported in Fig. 5.18. The bottom search in Fig. 5.18 is Ewert's FOOHOA search which has converged using only 77 queries.

For the Proximity Reward Search (evolutionary) algorithm, there are two parameters to tune: population size and degree of mutation.[ff] It is not readily obvious which choice of parameters will give, on average, the best result. The results of some different parameters are shown in Fig. 5.19.

[ff]Crossover is not used.

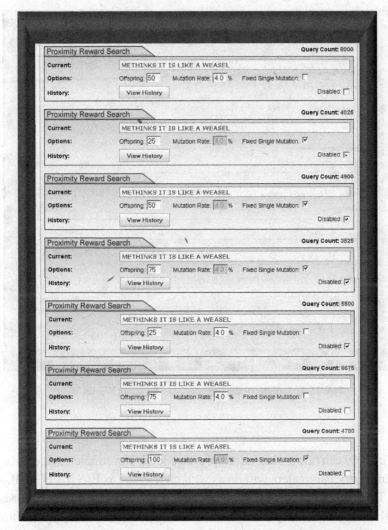

Fig. 5.19. Results from various choices of parameters in the evolutionary search for the WEASEL phrase using Weasel Ware.

The best in terms of query count is 3,523 queries for 75 offspring and one letter mutation per child. Repeating a search algorithm can give widely varying query counts. Rigorous comparison among parameters requires averaging numerous results from runs with the same parameters. The results

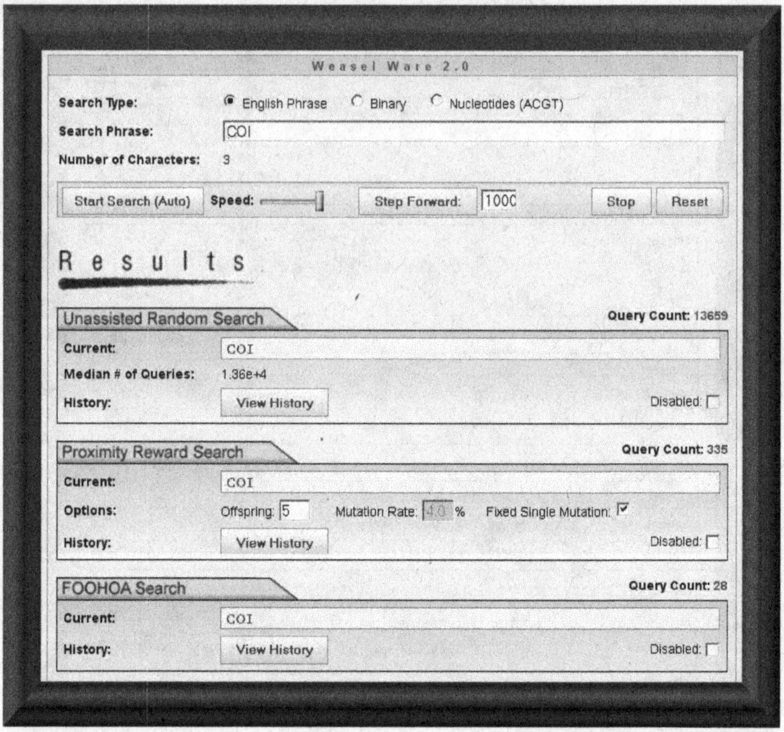

Fig. 5.20.   Search for the three letters COI using Weasel Wear.

in Fig. 5.19 can be considered simply anecdotal. Nevertheless, no choice of evolutionary parameters will do as well on average as Ewert's FOOHOA.

To assure success in all three searches, let's shorten the target phrase to the three letters: COI.[gg] The Weasel Ware result for this acronym is shown in Fig. 5.20. Unassisted blind search using an NIAH Oracle required about 14,000 queries. This is below the 20,000 queries we expect on average. Using five offspring, the Proximity Random (evolutionary) Search took 67 generations or $5 \times 67 = 335$ queries. Ewert's FOOHOA search required only 28 queries.

[gg]This is the same target phrase used for ratchet search in Table 5.6.

5.5 Sources of Information in Evolutionary Search

Sources of information embedded in any evolutionary search are mined for active information. The Hamming oracle, a source of information, can be mined with different degrees of efficiency by different search algorithms.[hh] Evolutionary search mines information rather poorly.

The sources of information in the fundamental Darwinian evolutionary model include (1) a large population of agents, (2) beneficial mutation, (3) survival of the fittest and (4) initialization.

5.5.1 *Population*

Evolutionary processes invariably start with a population of candidates — the larger, the better. The point is clarified by considering an extreme case. If we have a population consisting of all $|\Omega|$ candidates in the search space Ω then the problem is solved. The candidate with the largest fitness is the best answer. No additional steps in evolution are even necessary.

We have seen that Q blind queries produce an active information of about $I_+ \approx \log_2 Q$ bits. An evolutionary search starting with a population of Q candidates is performing Q queries all at once — in parallel if you will. Active information of $\log_2 Q$ bits is therefore generated by the first generation of the evolutionary search.

Large populations also increase the chance that mutations will produce an incrementally better result. With the guiding hand of fitness, we get better results more quickly.

Large populations in evolutionary search accelerate convergence in time. Computational requirements, however, are concentrated in space rather than time. If the count in queries is the measure of the cost in search, then a more sequential search might be advised. In Chapter 6, we see this is the case with both the EV and Avida models of Darwinian evolution. Large populations in conventional evolutionary computing quickly tally an expensive query cost.

[hh]As discussed in Chapter 5.4.3.1.

5.5.2   *Mutation rate*

Mutation is, on average, not beneficial. If it were, expectant mothers might gamble and take medication to mutate their babies. This, of course, is a repugnant idea. Nevertheless, we see fictional accounts in the movie series *X-Men* and the television series *Heroes* where humans have undergone beneficial mutation to obtain super powers.[ii]

Cornell University geneticist John C. Sanford documents the chance of a beneficial mutation in a complicated organism is essentially zero and that mutation has a greater chance of extinguishing a species than of advancing it.[50] If mutation is generally beneficial in an evolutionary program, there must be a resident source of information that guides mutation away from being a detriment.

In a single generation, the probability of improvement by mutation increases as the number of children increase. The number of children, K, has a role similar to that in blind query count in sequential blind search. We have seen that diminishing returns in active information resulted from multiple queries. Instead of the queries being performed sequentially in a generation of children, they are made in parallel with the simultaneous births of the children. Since there is no learning from mutation to mutation in a single generation, the cases are statistically identical. Let π be the probability that a single child is more fit than its parent. When K is big and π is small, the probability that at least one child is better than its parent is $1-(1-\pi)^K \approx K\pi$. The chance therefore grows only linearly with respect to the brood count. Each child makes the same contribution to overall success independent of its sibling count.

5.5.3   *Fitness landscapes*

To apply the idea of "survival of the fittest," there must be a concept of "fitness." We visited the idea of fitness landscape in Chapter 3.3.1 where a landscape is given for how well a pancake tastes. A commonly used source of information in evolutionary search is the fitness landscape. But a fitness landscape is not necessarily a source of readily accessible information. This would be contrary to the law of conservation of information and the No

---

[ii]"Darwinists should quit believing what they read in comic books."

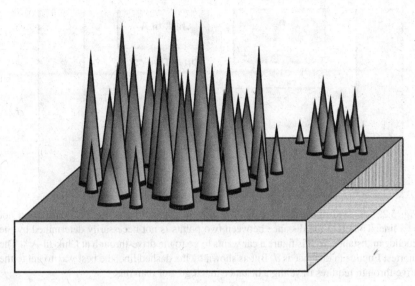

Fig. 5.21. A fitness landscape that is not smooth.

Free Lunch Theorem. To be a source of information, the fitness landscape must have a useful and exploitable structure. But arbitrarily chosen fitness landscapes of the sort illustrated in Fig. 5.21 can be difficult information sources from which to extract active information. Steepest ascent (hill climbing) search algorithms become ineffective. This is also true in the version of evolution where numerous small perturbations are required to find a suitable solution. There are many instances where a search space is not smooth. In examining the functional sensitivity to amino acid changes on enzyme exteriors, biochemist Douglas D. Axe found that unfriendly looking fitness landscapes of the type in Fig. 5.21 are encountered.[51]

How is fitness decided and who gets to say what is more fit than something else? In computer programs, an oracle is often used. We've already seen that the existence of an oracle is not sufficient to assure success in a search. Active information must be cleverly mined by the computer programmer.

As is illustrated in Fig. 5.22, the existence of high fitness at a point in a search space does not necessarily require that a small perturbation around that point will produce fitness of incremental value. Fitness functions can have unanticipated undesirable properties. Consider, for example, the

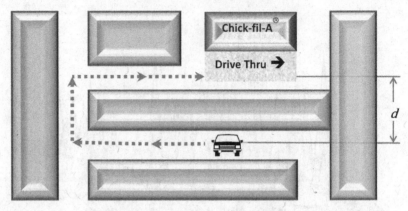

Fig. 5.22. As with the Rubik's cube, the closest distance between two points need not be a line. Therefore the distance between two points is not necessarily determined by the Euclidean distance. In this figure a car wants to go to the drive-through at Chik-fil-A®. The shortest Euclidean distance is d. But as shown by the dashed line, the best way to get to the drive-through requires traveling a distance much greater than this.

common Rubik's cube puzzle.[52] The goal (target) is to get each of the 9 squares on each of the six sides to be the same color. An obvious choice of fitness is the sum of the percents of same color on each of the 6 sides. When there is a single misplaced color on only two sides, the fitness will be as good as possible without being the solution. But to get to the solution, the fitness must be made worse. Use of a Euclidean fitness function is a poor choice in the case of the Rubik's cube. A more useful fitness is the number of steps required from a current state to solution.

A similar illustration of functional versus Euclidean fitness is a trip to Chik-fil-A® drive-through to get a Deluxe Chicken Sandwich. Curbs and buildings may block your access to the drive-through window even though you are close in a Euclidean sense. To get to the window, you might have to take a significant detour that takes you farther away from the window but eventually presents the best available path to allow you access to your Deluxe Chicken Sandwich.[53] This is shown in Fig. 5.22.

Therefore, fitness functions exist that are not conducive to slow incremental changes. There are evolutionary algorithms, specifically genetic algorithms, that do not make incremental steps in the fitness landscape. A coordinate in binary $(000100)_2 = 8$ can change with a single bit mutation to $(100100)_2 = 72$. Depending on the manner the binary string is encoded, the

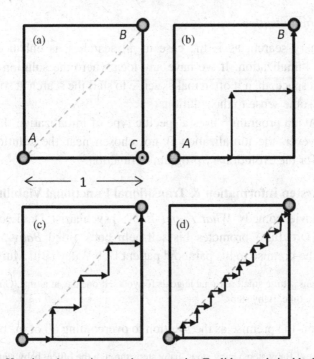

†Fig. 5.23. Here is an interesting paradox concerning Euclidean and city block distances. Shown are four squares, each one mile on each side. In (a) we see the distance between A and B shown by the dashed line is $\sqrt{2} = 1.414$ miles. Suppose we are constrained however to only move horizontally and vertically. No diagonals are allowed. Equivalently, we can only make 90° right and left hand turns. If we go from A to C in (a), make a left-hand turn and go to B we have traveled 2 miles. If as shown in (b) we make two left turns and one right, to get from A to B, we are still traveling a total of 2 miles. In the route in (c) where more turns are taken, we still are traveling a total of 2 miles. If we make numerous turns we began to hug the 45° dashed line connecting A to B as shown in (d), we still are traveling 2 miles. In the limit, we approach the dashed line but curiously are still traveling 2 miles. But the dashed line is $\sqrt{2}$ miles! It looks as though we've shown $2 = \sqrt{2}$. This is obviously incorrect. What's the resolution and what does this reveal about the assumption of Euclidean distance? (The solution can be found in Marks, *Handbook of Fourier Analysis*, Oxford University Press, 2009.)

location in the search space can jump drastically. Mutations have enormous effects on Euclidean distance and might, for example, be more useful in solving the Chik-fil-A® problem than a gradient descent method. We see again the importance of choosing the search algorithm that best matches the problem being solved. Another interesting non-Euclidean distance problem is shown in Fig. 5.23.

5.5.3.1 *Initialization*

Evolutionary search, as is the case in all searches, is enhanced by an informed initialization. If we have any idea where the solution exists in the search space, then it often makes sense to start the search at some place close[jj] in some sense to the solution.

The Avida program[kk] uses a specific type of initialization. In Avida's case, however, the initialization is not chosen near the solution but is required for the evolutionary program to function.

5.6 Stairstep Information & Transitional Functional Viability

In the movie comedy *What About Bob?*, psychiatrist Dr. Leo Marvin (Richard Dreyfuss) promotes his self-help book titled *Baby Steps*. He explains the premise to his paranoid patient Bob Wiley (Bill Murray):

> "It means setting small reasonable goals for yourself one day at a time. One tiny step at a time. Baby steps."

Bob accepts the premise as the solution to overcoming all of his problems.

> " Oh boy! Baby steps, baby steps, baby steps through the office, baby steps out the door, it works it works! All I have to do .. just take one little step at a time, and I can do anything!"

Dawkins' mountain in *Climbing Mount Improbable* uses Bob's logic. Incredibly complex design sits perched on the top of a steep cliff of endogenous information. How could this have occurred? According to Dawkins, the answer is akin to baby steps. On the other side of the mountain, is a long staircase with closely spaced steps that allows us to climb, one baby step at a time, to the mountain top. Or so Dawkins claims.

"It is the slow, cumulative, one-step-at-a-time, non-random survival of random variants that Darwin called natural selection." And, like Bob, the explanation is deemed to provide an explanation for all of the functionally complex organisms we see. And as Bob said, relying on this explanation, some claim Darwinism "can do anything!"

What, however, does evolutionary informatics tell us about stair steps?

[jj]"Close" in whatever makes sense from knowledge of the fitness landscape.
[kk] In Chapter 6.2.

5.6.1 *Baby steps*

Baby steps can work. Suppose we have 30 coins and we want them all, by chance, to show heads. The endogenous information difficulty of this problem is $I_\Omega = 30$ bits. We throw all 30 coins up in the air. They come down, bounce noisily on the title floor and eventually all show either heads or tails. We announced a success if they all show up heads. On average we would need to repeat this experiment about 1 billion times before we achieved a success.[ll] This translates to about 30 billion total coin flips.

Now let's take baby steps.

We flip the first coin until we get a heads. Then, the second. The process is repeated until all 30 coins show heads. Each coin takes, on average, two flips to get a heads.[mm] Thus, on average, it takes 60 flips to get 30 heads. That's a lot less than 60 billion flips!

In this example, climbing *Mount Improbable* works quite well. But this is a toy problem that ignores the crucial issues of functional viability and irreducible complexity.

5.6.2 *Developmental functionality and irreducible complexity*

In the emergence of complex organisms, Darwinian evolution purports to climb "*Mount Improbable.*"[54] Small perturbations accumulate to create higher life forms. In evolutionary programs on computers, there is no need to assign agent function at intermediate steps in the process. For any physical evolution that involves climbing the stair steps of *Mount Improbable*, however, every step must be a viable entity. If a worm evolves into a whale, every intermediate organism along the way must be a viable creature. There can be no intermediate step along the way that is a glob of lifeless tissue. The paths for evolution of any physical entity are therefore more highly restricted than for the general evolutionary computer program. In an evolutionary process, we can think of numerous paths for getting from an initialization point to a target. In computer simulations, the path is

---

[ll]† $I_\Omega = 30$ bits corresponds to $p \approx 10^{-9}$. The experiment is a geometric random variable with expected value of about $\frac{1}{p} \approx 1$ billion trials.

[mm]† For a single coin, the number of coin flips prior to obtaining a heads is a geometric random variable with a probability of $p = \frac{1}{2}$ and an expected value of $\frac{1}{p} = 2$ coin flips.

generally not important. For physical evolution, only those paths allowing functional viability at each step can be used.

In the evolution of natural language phrases where many champions of Darwinian evolution choose to illustrate baby steps,[55] functional viability rarely considered. Suppose we wish to evolve the phrase

ALL_THE_WORLD_IS_A_STAGE____

into

METHINKS_IT_IS_LIKE_A_WEASEL.

What phrase do we get if we simply alternate letters from the two phrases?

MLT_IHK__OTLI__SIAESAAW_A_E_

From the viewpoint of the English language, this phrase and most all phrases between the two reference phrases are nonsense and not functionally viable.

There are other examples using English where baby steps evolves a single letter into greater complexity. Consider the stair step construction of the word STRINGIER, one letter at a time. One possibility would be the stair steps

R→SR→STR→STRN→STRNR→STRNIR→STRNGIR→STRNGIER→STRINGIER.

None of the intermediate steps is a word. There is no transitional viability. A sequence with transitional viability is

I→IN→SIN→SINE→SINGE→SINGER→STINGER→STINGIER→STRINGIER.

Each entry in the sequence is a viable word that will pass a spellchecker. The viability criterion makes the search much more difficult. Another nine letter word that can be "evolved" from the letter I using viable words is STARTLING. The longest ten letter word of which we are aware that can be viably evolved is SPLITTINGS.[nn] We are aware of no other words of similar length to which this baby step process can be applied while, at each step, maintaining functional viability. Evolving words in this way is certainly limiting.

[nn]Doing so is left as an exercise for the reader.

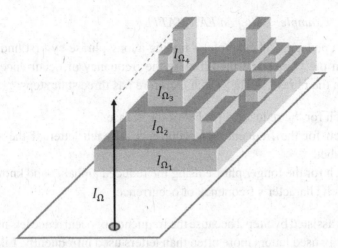

Fig. 5.24. For stair step information sources, the intermediate forms at each step must be viable.

Evolutionary computing can be guided to complex results if intermediate steps are viable. To go from a Bernoulli's PrOIR initialization to the first target requires a sufficiently small endogenous information if the search is not assisted. Likewise, the distance from the first to the second step must be sufficiently easy to allow success. Numerous stages can be used. But a search mechanism that allows small functional steps must itself be constructed from active information. Establishing these states requires *stair step* active information. This is illustrated in Fig. 5.24. The overall endogenous information of the search is I_Ω. It is broken into a number of small steps the n h of which has endogenous information of I_{Ω_n}.[oo] Requiring each stair step to display functional viability necessitates a very carefully designed staircase.

Generalization to expatiation allows construction of more complicated words. For example,

⬈ IP → RIP → RIPE → TRIPE → STRIPE ⬊

I　　　　　　　　　　　　　　　　　　　　　　　　PINSTRIPE

⬊ → 　　　IN 　　　　　→ 　　PIN 　　　→ ⬈

Such synthesis must also be carefully designed.

[oo]In his book *Proving Darwin*, Gregory Chaitin refers to the height of a stairstep, I_{Ω_n}, as a "mutation distance." We will be spending more time with Chaitin's model in Chapter 6.3.

5.6.2.1 *Example: Using an EAR_TATTER_*

Here is a pedagogical example of finding a long phrase by first finding the letters in the phrase and then finding the frequency of occurrence of the letters in the phrase.[56] The search therefore has three stair steps.

1. Search for the reduced alphabet of the phrase.
2. Search for the frequency of occurrence of each letter of the smaller alphabet.
3. Search for the longer phrase using the reduced alphabet and knowledge of each character's frequency of occurrence.

Step 3 is assisted by Step 2 because the frequency of occurrence lets us guess commonly used letters more often than letters used infrequently. Likewise, Step 2 is achieved more easily with the active information available from Step 1. The size of the alphabet has been reduced. The size of the search space is thereby reduced.

Here's an example.

1. MY_TEARS
2. EAR_TATTER_
3. _ERATTA_RETREAT _TREAT_   (5.14)

Step 1 is a search for a reduced alphabet of $L_1 = 8$ characters, MY_TEARS, from the larger alphabet of $N = 27$. We'll assume the oracle for Step 1 tells us "yes!" if we guess the eight letters in any order. To go to Step 2 from Step 1, a blind unassisted search is assumed with a needle-in-a-haystack oracle telling us "yes!" only when all of the letters are announced in order. Knowing the frequency of occurrence for each letter in Step 2 and the length of the message in Step 3 lets us know how many and which letters are used in Step 3. We simply have to shuffle the cards until the oracle at the third level gives us the answer.

Here is the result. Using the three stair steps, we will use about

$$B_{SS} = 3.58 \times 10^{14} \text{ bits.} \tag{5.15}$$

Using an unassisted search without the stair step requires about

$$B_\Omega = 3.23 \times 10^{33} \text{ bits.} \tag{5.16}$$

The difference of about nineteen orders of magnitude is astonishing! A millimeter, or 10^{-3} meters, when increased 19 orders of magnitude, is about a light year, or $\approx 10^{16}$ meters.

†5.6.2.2 *Analysis*

We now present the analysis that gives rise to the answers given in the previous section. Those uninterested in the details may want to skip this.

Step 1 requires finding the phrase MY_TEARS from an alphabet of 27 characters (26 letters and a space). The phrase contains $L_1 = 8$ letters. We assume the letters can be found in any order. The chance of attaining the first step is thus

$$\Pr[1|0] = \frac{8}{27} \times \frac{7}{26} \times \frac{6}{25} \times \cdots \times \frac{1}{20} = 4.50 \times 10^{-7}.$$

The expected number of queries for the underlying random variable is

$$Q_1 = \frac{1}{\Pr[1|0]} = 2.22 \times 10^6 \text{ queries.}$$

Each query expends $L_1 \log_2 N = 38$ bits. The total number of bits expended in getting to step one is thus

$$B_1 = Q_1 L_1 \log_2 N = 8.44 \times 10^7 \text{ bits.}$$

To go from Step 1 to Step 2, the phrase EAR_TATTER_ must be found using the $L_1 = 8$ member alphabet found in Step 1. Note that all of the letters in Step 1 are not used in Step 2. Since there are $L_2 = 11$ characters in the phrase in Step 2, the probability of going from Step 1 to Step 2 is

$$\Pr[2|1] = L_1^{-L_2} = 1.16 \times 10^{-10}.$$

Using the same reasoning as before, the total number of bits expended in this step is then

$$B_2 = \frac{L_2 \log_2 L_1}{\Pr[2|1]} = 8.54 \times 10^{10} \text{ bits.}$$

We now know that the letters in EAR_TATTER_ are used twice in the final phrase in Step 3. We simply need to arrange the code until we get the correct answer. The number of codes is a multinomial random variable. If there are k_1 green balls, k_2 blue balls, k_3 yellow balls, etc., so that

$$L = \sum_{m=1}^{M} k_m,$$

where M is the number of colors, then the number of ways these balls can be arranged is

$$\frac{L!}{k_1! k_2! k_3! \ldots k_K!}.$$

The chance of randomly arranging the balls to a single target value is the reciprocal of this value. For our problem, $L = L_3 = 22$ and the frequency of occurrence of the $M = 5$ letters is $k_E = k_R = k_A = k_- = 4$, and $k_T = 6$. Thus

$$\Pr[3|2] = \frac{k_E! k_R! k_A! k_-! k_T!}{L!} = 2.13 \times 10^{-13}$$

and

$$B_3 = \frac{L_3 \log_2 L_2}{\Pr[3|2]} = 3.581 \times 10^{14} \text{ bits.}$$

The total number of bits expended in the stair step search is then

$$B_{SS} = B_1 + B_2 + B_3 = 3.582 \times 10^{14} \text{ bits,}$$

which is the value reported in Equation (5.15).

For the unassisted search, the probability of success is

$$p = N^{-L} = 3.24 \times 10^{-32}$$

requiring a bit expenditure of

$$B_\Omega = \frac{L}{p} \log_2 N = 3.23 \times 10^{33} \text{ bits,}$$

which is the value reported in Equation (5.16).

The stair steps in this example add *a lot* of active information.

5.6.3 *Irreducible complexity*

The concept of irreducible complexity is introduced in Michael Behe's classic *Darwin's Black Box*. Many biological systems do not appear to have a functionally viable predecessor from which they could have evolved. This means that there are no stairs on *Mount Improbable*. The only way to the top is one big information step whose occurrence by chance is impossibly small.

5.7 Coevolution[57]

Techniques inspired by biological coevolution have been widely used in search algorithms. Examples include sorting networks,[58] the morphology and performance of competing agents,[59] backgammon,[60] checkers[61] and chess.[62] While traditional searches require the expertise of penalty function artists to craft a fitness function that guides the algorithm, coevolution is viewed as not requiring this prior expertise. Rather[63]

"Coevolutionary algorithms require little *a priori* knowledge about the domain."

Coevolutionary searches have been claimed to be able to violate the law of Conservation of Information[64] [15]–[18]. When the law is properly interpreted, we'll see this is not the case.

For conservation of information to apply in the case of classical search but not in the case of coevolution is odd. What is different about these co-evolutionary searches that allows them to not require prior information?

Before the analysis that shows coevolutionary search is still constrained by conservation of information, let's consider the simple example shown in Fig. 5.25. Our job is to test insecticides. We have eight candidate bug-killing formulas labeled A through H. In order to be acceptable, the insecticide must kill roaches, ants, spiders, termites, wasps, hornets, flies, mosquitoes and centipedes. We will assume that the cost of testing any one formula on any bug is the same. As you can see from the table, some tests have already been performed. Formula A, for example, kills roaches but fails to kill ants. The letter P entered in the table stands for pass. And we use the letter F for fail. With an eye to minimizing overall test cost, what should be our next experiment? In order to be acceptable, a formula must kill all of the bugs on the list. Since formula A has already failed on ants, there is no reason to

	Roaches	Ants	Spiders	Termites	Wasps	Hornets	Flies	Mosquitoes	Centipedes		Grade
A	P	F	-	-	-	-	-	-	P		F
B	P	-	-	-	P	F	P	-	-		F
C	P	-	-	F	-	-	-	-	-		F
D	F	-	-	-	-	-	-	-	-		F
E	P	P	P	P	P	P	P	P	-		P
F	F	-	-	-	-	-	-	-	-		F
G	P	P	P	P	P	-	-	-	-		P
H	P	-	-	-	-	P	-	-	-		P

Fig. 5.25. An example of coevolution.

try it on spiders. The same is true for formula B which failed to kill hornets. Formula C failed to kill termites and D made roaches sick but didn't kill them. All it takes is one failure in order to disqualify a formula. In the Grade column on the right in Fig. 5.25, we enter F if a formula has failed on one or more bugs and a P for "pass" otherwise. Further testing of formulas that have experienced a failure is a waste of time and money. Formulas E, G and H have so far passed all of the tests. It is on these formulas that we wish to spend our money.

Here is the point. Not all of the remaining possible queries in Fig. 5.25 are useful. Some queries are more valuable than others. Thus, Bernoulli's PrOIR does not apply and, apparently neither does conservation of information.

But wait a minute. Isn't the true answer we seek in the Grade column? Each element in the matrix simply provides information for the entry in the Grade column. Indeed, conservation of information becomes applicable when we consider the Grade column as a query result rather than the individual entries in the matrix. The entries in the matrix are like inferior queries — or *subjacent queries*. Subjacent queries, combined, form a total query. Total queries are still constrained by conservation of information. Subjacent queries are not.

Generalization of the coevolutionary search is illustrated in Fig. 5.26.[65] A list of candidate solutions is shown on the left side. Each row of the

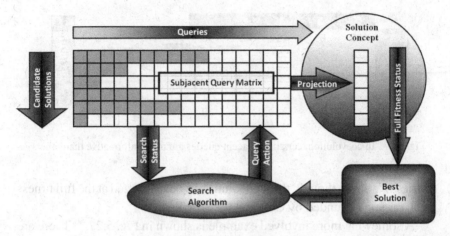

Fig. 5.26. The coevolution process.

subjacent query matrix corresponds to a candidate. As subjacent queries are made, the results are projected into a *solution concept*. This is a fancy way of saying the queries are summarized by a single number. This number is written in the right hand column labeled "Solution Concept." We next need to look at the entries in the Solution Concept column to determine the full fitness status. This tells us the best solution that we have thus far. Here's where the coevolutionary search comes into play. From the best solution we decide the next subjacent query location in order to advance our search in some appropriate manner. In the insecticide example in Fig. 5.25, for example, only insecticides with grade P are considered for further queries.

Coevolution queries inferior subjacent fitnesses that are combined into estimates of full fitness queries. The analysis of coevolution by others demonstrates that there is the appearance of a free lunch when the space of subjacent fitness values is analyzed in the same way conventional NFLT's are derived. This subjacent space, however, contains inferior information. In this sense, the NFLT is applicable to coevolution.

In engineering design coevolution has been shown effective in numerous cases and our analysis should no way be construed to discredit coevolution as a viable approach to optimization. Multiple subjacent queries, for example, can come at a cheaper cost when compared to full queries. Full queries in some cases appear only to be accessible via subjacent

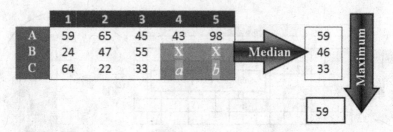

Fig. 5.27. In coevolution, certain subjacent queries are more informative than others.

queries. We show, though, that coevolution, when analyzed at the full fitness level, remains bounded by COI and the NFLT.

A somewhat more involved example is shown in Fig. 5.27.[66] There are three classrooms, A, B and C, and each has five students. Which classroom has the oldest students? For the row projection, we choose the median operation. Every time we perform a query, we pay a fixed fee to the student for their age information. Assume our study is that shown in Fig. 5.27. All five students have been queried in Classroom A and the median age is 59. Classrooms B and C each have three queries to the subjacent fitness matrix resulting in the full query estimates of 46 and 33 respectively. Since our goal is to find the largest median, the full fitness status estimate is equal to the maximum of the current median estimates, which gives the best solution of 59.

There are four students remaining to be queried. How do we best spend our money? A simple calculation shows that the largest median possible for Classroom B is 55. This would happen even if the remaining two students were each 100 years old. Thus, any additional query in Classroom B is a waste of money because there exists no outcome that will exceed the median age in Classroom A. Classroom C, on the other hand, could be the winner or tied if both of the remaining students are 59 or older. The path to finding the best solution is now clear. We first query a student in Classroom C. If the age is less than 59, we are done, Classroom A wins, no matter how old the fifth student in Classroom C is. However, if the queried student is 59 or older, the winner (Classroom A or Classroom C) will be decided by the fifth and final query in Classroom C.

In terms of conventional queries, there are the three median ages — one for each classroom. Using subjacent queries, we only have an estimate of these values. Conservation of information applies to the conventional full query.

In summary, the two unanswered queries in the boxes marked X in Fig. 5.27 are useless. The queries A and possibly B, on the other hand, will determine the winner. Not all subjacent queries are created equal.

5.8   The Search for the Search

Those who are proponents of undirected Darwinian evolution often invoke the biological equivalent of the Anthropic Principle. Specifically, they assert that we are very fortunate to have the environment and the biology necessary for us to be here. And if we didn't have the environment and the biology, we wouldn't be here to notice it.

But to what degree are we fortunate? What is the chance of choosing the environment and biology that purportedly allows Darwinian evolution? If we view evolution as a search, then we are asking how difficult it is to identify a successful search. To do so, we are undertaking a search for identifying a successful search. The difficulty of the *search for a search* (S4S) as measured in endogenous information, always exceeds the acceptable active information of the original search that serves as a fitness threshold for the S4S. More significantly, under reasonable assumptions, a successful search for a search turns out to be exponentially more difficult than the search itself.

5.8.1   *An example*

A simple example for a search for a search is shown in Fig. 5.28. There are 16 squares. On the left, the target is shown in the bottom right corner. We will consider three searches. Search (a) uses the all 16 squares. They

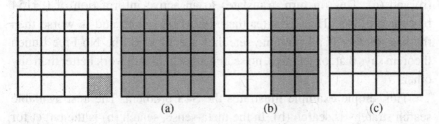

(a)   (b)   (c)

Fig. 5.28. An example of a search for a search.

Table 5.8. Outcomes of an example search for a search.

	Probability of success, q	Endogenous information, I_S	Active information, I_+
(a)	1/16	4	0
(b)	1/8	3	1
(c)	0	$-\infty$	$-\infty$
S4S	1/12	3.585	0.415

are all shaded. Search (b) only uses the eight rightmost squares. These are also shaded. Search (c) constrains the search to be only in the top eight shaded squares. Search (c), as you can see, is a poor choice for a search because there is a zero probability we will find the target in the lower right corner.

If blind search is chosen, the probability of randomly choosing the target is equal to $\frac{1}{16}$. The endogenous information for the search is four bits. The active information for search (a) is therefore zero. The probability of successfully identifying the target in one query for search (b) is $\frac{1}{8}$. This corresponds to active information of one bit. Using search (c), the probability of finding the target is zero. The target for search (c) is not in the shaded area. The active information for search (c) is therefore negative infinity. These results are summarized in Table 5.8.

A search for the search requires choosing from a number of available searches. Let's assume that searches (a), (b) and (c) are the available searches. If we have no idea which of these three searches is best, the best we can do is choose one at random with equal probability. As is seen Table 5.8, the total probability of choosing the target becomes $\frac{1}{12}$. Since the chance of choosing any of the searches is equally probable, this value is equal to the average of the probability of success for searches (a), (b) and (c). This, in turn, translates to an active information of 0.4154 bits for the S4S. This is better than the worst search and is worse than the best search. If all possible searches are allowed, the No Free Lunch theorem says that, on average, no search algorithm will work better than any other.

This simple example illustrates the S4S problem. The best available search strategy is search (b). In the meta-sense, search (b) is the target for the S4S. Once search (b) is identified, the search can proceed.

5.8.2 *The problem*

In the S4S, our job is to choose a search from a space of all possible searches. But what is our search target? We want to choose a successful search, but how do we set a fitness criterion for a successful search? The answer is a target value for the active information of the search being sought. We would like to choose a search that equals or exceeds some active information threshold. Let's denote that threshold by I_+^*. Any search with active information equal to or greater than I_+^* is deemed to be a successful search. We can write

$$I_+^* = \log_2 \left(\frac{q^*}{p} \right), \tag{5.17}$$

where q^* is the probability of success corresponding to the active information threshold I_+^*. Since the unassisted probability of success, p, is the same for all searches, requiring the active information to exceed I_+^* is equivalent to finding a search where the assisted probability exceeds the threshold q^*.

We have our search criterion defined, but must now define our search space. We consider two cases: the weak case and the strict case.

We have earlier looked at the curious case dubbed Bertrand's paradox.[PP] Bernoulli's principle of insufficient reason (PrOIR) applying a uniform distribution gave three different results. Bertrand's paradox is resolved, however, when the exact meaning of "random" is defined. When the specific nature of randomness is defined, Bertrand's paradox disappears. In the analysis of the strict version of the S4S, we must be vigilant in specifying our definition of "random" selection of a search.

One's first inclination is to use an S4S search space populated by different search algorithms such as particle swarm, conjugate gradient descent or Levenberg–Marquardt search. Every search algorithm, in turn, has parameters. Search would not only need to be performed among the algorithms, but within the algorithms over a range of different parameters and initializations. Performing an S4S using this approach looks to be intractable. We note, however, the choice of an algorithm along with its parameters and initialization imposes a probability distribution over the search space. Searching among these probability distributions is tractable

---

[PP]In Chapter 4.1.2.2.2.

and is the model we will use. Our S4S search space is therefore populated by a large number of probability distributions imposed on the search space.

5.8.2.1 *The weak case*

We will now show that the better the search we want to search for, the harder the S4S. In other words, the endogenous information for the S4S will increase as a function of the target active information. Let the endogenous information for the S4S be $\tilde{I}_\Omega$. (For all variables associated with the S4S space, we will use a $\sim$.) For the weak case, we will show

$$\tilde{I}_\Omega \geq I_+^*. \tag{5.18}$$

In other words, the endogenous information for the S4S always equals or exceeds the active information of the search itself. The S4S is thus at least as difficult as the active information we wish to add to the search.

5.8.2.2 *The strict case*

When the negative log base two of the probability is taken, the unit of information is bits. When the natural log is used, the unit of information is nats.[qq] One nat is $\log_2 e \approx 1.443$ bits. For the strict case of the S4S, we find it convenient to use information measured in nats. Under the condition that (1) the number of probability bins is large, i.e. $N \gg 1$, and (2) the threshold for the probability of success is very very small ($q^\uparrow * \ll 1$), then the endogenous information for the S4S is approximately, in nats,

$$\tilde{I}_\Omega \approx e^{I_+^*}. \tag{5.19}$$

The S4S is thus exponentially more difficult than the active information it seeks!

In both cases we see that conservation of information cannot be violated by passing the difficulty to a higher level search. The higher level search becomes more and more difficult as the required search's active information is increased. And the endogenous information of the S4S always equals or exceeds the active information threshold set for the S4S.

[qq]This was addressed in Chapter 2.2.2.

†5.8.3 *Proofs*

We will keep the derivation of these two results at as high a level as possible. The use of some math probability theory, however, is unavoidable. For an even more rigorous derivation, see our paper.[67] Those who are squeamish about math may want to take us at our word and skip the rest of this section.

†5.8.3.1 *Preliminaries*

We will make use of a probability mass function as illustrated in Fig. 5.29. The height of each of the bars, $\pi_1 \pi_2 \pi_3 \ldots \pi_N$ corresponds to the probability of an event in the search space happening. The target is chosen to be a single event and in Fig. 5.29 this event is the one with the highest bar. The probability of finding the target is $\pi T = q$. Since, these are all probabilities, all of the bars stacked on top of each other must add up to one.

$$\sum_{n=1}^{N} \pi_n = 1. \tag{5.20}$$

We note in particular that, for a uniform distribution, each then has a probability of

$$p = \frac{1}{N}.$$

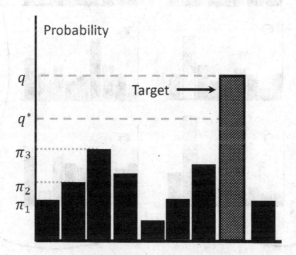

†Fig. 5.29. Event probabilities.

The endogenous information of the original search is therefore

$$I_\Omega = \log N. \tag{5.21}$$

Requiring the active information to exceed the threshold I_+^* is equivalent to requiring the probability of the assisted search exceed the threshold q^*.

$$q \geq q^*.$$

This is our search success criterion. When we choose a probability distribution from those available, we declare success when the probability of success exceeds q^*.

An example of a portion of the space from which we choose probability distributions is illustrated in Fig. 5.30. Continuing with the notation used in

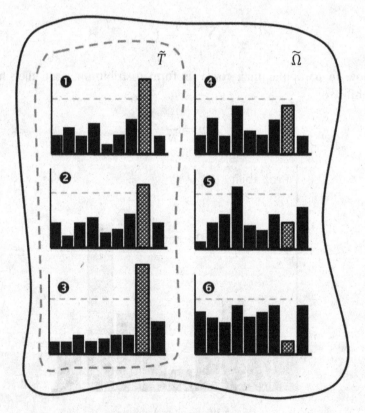

†Fig. 5.30. S4S targets.

Chapter 5, the search space is labeled $\tilde{\Omega}$. There are $|\tilde{\Omega}| = 6$ probability distributions in the S4S search space. The target, $\tilde{T}$, contains all the distributions where the probability of success exceeds the threshold. These solutions are encircled by a dashed line in Fig. 5.30. There are $|\tilde{T}| = 3$ distributions in the target.

†5.8.3.2 *The weak case*

For the distributions in the target in the S4S search space, let's take the average of all of the probabilities of success. Since each of the probabilities of success equals or exceeds the threshold, we know that this average must be larger than the threshold.

A weaker inequality results if we sum up over the entire S4S space of distributions:

$$\sum_{n \in \tilde{\Omega}} q_n \geq \sum_{n \in \tilde{T}} q_n \geq |\tilde{T}| q^*.$$

We now divide both sides by the cardinality of the S4S search space

$$\frac{1}{|\tilde{\Omega}|} \sum_{n \in \tilde{\Omega}} q_n \geq \frac{|\tilde{T}|}{|\tilde{\Omega}|} q^* = \tilde{p} q^*.$$

But the probability of choosing a successful distribution is $\tilde{p} = \frac{|\tilde{T}|}{|\tilde{\Omega}|}$ and the probability of the success of the search is the average of all of the probabilities of success. That is,

$$p = \frac{1}{|\tilde{\Omega}|} \sum_{n \in \tilde{\Omega}} q_n.$$

There is an assumption here: The average probability of success in the S4S space, $\tilde{\Omega}$, is equal to the uniform probability of success resulting from the application of Bernoulli's PrOIR in the original search space.[π] It follows that

$$p \geq \tilde{p} q^*,$$

[π]† This assumption, for example, is not met in the sparse S4S sample space in Fig. 5.29. The entire search of spaces is required.

or

$$\frac{q}{p} \leq \frac{1}{\tilde{p}}.$$

Taking the base two logarithms of both sides gives us our desired result as promised in Equation (5.18).

$$\tilde{I}_\Omega \geq I_+^*.$$

This is the promised weak form of the difficulty of the S4S. The difficulty of the search for a search surpasses the search being sought.

†5.8.3.3   *The strict case*

For the strict S4S case, we make use of a *simplex*. The simplex is the locus of all positive numbers that add to one. In other words it's the plane that obeys Equation (5.20). When there are two probability masses, π_1 and π_2, the simplex is simply a line in the first quadrant that intersects the π_1 and π_2 axes at $\pi_1 = 1$ and $\pi_2 = 1$. In three dimensions the simplex is a triangle in the first octant that intersects all the axes at one. This is illustrated in Fig. 5.31. From this surface we will choose a probability distribution function at random. On the triangular simplex, we assume that distributions are uniformly distributed. The surface of the simplex triangle is our $\tilde{\Omega}$ = the search space for the S4S.

With reference to Fig. 5.31, we will assume that the target is associated with probability $q = \pi_3$. Recall that a successful search consists of all values of $q \geq q^*$ where q^* defines the smallest active information deemed acceptable. This threshold is shown in Fig. 5.31. The threshold defines the region on the simplex on the triangle *abc*. The area of this triangle then corresponds to the S4S target, $\tilde{T}$. A little bit of geometry shows that the probability of success for this three-dimensional example, equal to the ratio of the area of the small equilateral triangle to the large simplex, is

$$\tilde{p} = \frac{\tilde{T}}{\tilde{\Omega}} = (1 - q^*)^2.$$

Area scales exponentially with dimension. For example, if we were to work this problem with two probabilities instead of three, we would find that

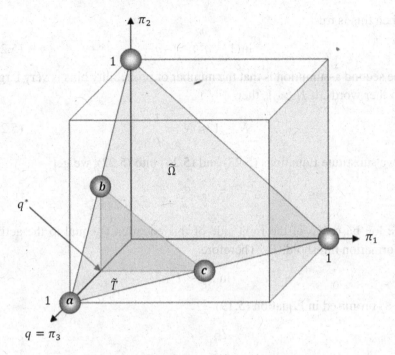

†Fig. 5.31. The strict case S4S search geometry.

$\tilde{p} = (1 - q^*)$. If we have N dimensions, the ratio is

$$\tilde{p} = (1 - q^*)^{N-1},$$

where N is the number of probability bins in the distribution. Taking the natural logarithm of both sides gives

$$\ln \tilde{p} = (N - 1) \ln(1 - q^*).$$

Since $\tilde{I}_\Omega = -\ln \tilde{p}$ nats, this can be written as

$$\tilde{I}_\Omega = -(N - 1) \ln(1 - q^*). \tag{5.22}$$

Now we will make two (very realistic) assumptions. The first assumption is that our probability of success threshold is a very small number:

$$q^* \ll 1.$$

When this is true

$$\ln(1 - q^*) \approx -q^*. \tag{5.23}$$

The second assumption is that the number of probability bins is very large. In other words, if $N \gg 1$, then

$$N - 1 \approx N = \frac{1}{p}. \tag{5.24}$$

If we substitute Equations (5.23) and (5.24) into (5.22), we get

$$\tilde{I}_\Omega \approx \frac{q^*}{p}.$$

The log base two of the right side of this equation is equal to the active information threshold, I_+^*. Therefore

$$\ln \tilde{I}_\Omega \approx I_+^*$$

or, as promised in Equation (5.19),

$$\tilde{I}_\Omega \approx e^{I_+^*}.$$

Thus ends our derivation of the strict form of the S4S search. A second derivations of the identical result, generated from a completely different point of view, has also been published.[68]

5.9   Conclusion

In evolutionary computation, the Darwinian "survival of the fittest/mutation" mechanism creates no information. There is an information source already resident in the search algorithm. Evolutionary search merely mines the information from that source. Indeed, other search techniques can often be applied to mine the information source more efficiently as measured with the currency of queries. With no information source, conservation of information, as manifest in Mitchell's observation that bias is required for learning,[69] Schaffer's conservation law for generalization performance,[70] and Wolpert and Macready's No Free Lunch Theorem,[71] dictates that, on average, one search algorithm will perform as well as any other.

The evolutionary approach may be biologically well-suited to extract information from the environment. A query is, in a sense, a life form asking whether or not it is worthy of survival. And the more offspring, the more queries. Evolution itself, however, can produce no information. It is rather a finely tuned process that extracts information from a source of knowledge. And it generally does so poorly.

If evolution cannot produce information, but rather only extracts information from sources of knowledge in the environment, from where do those sources of knowledge come? In the case of a computer model, the answer is clear: the source of knowledge was placed there by the intelligent design of a programmer. Non-teleological evolutionary processes must have another explanation for their sources of knowledge. Any appeal to an Anthropic Principle explanation of "that's just the way it is — exactly right for us" is problematic. The search-for-the-search analysis establishes that the "just right" Goldilocks condition is, itself, exponentially more difficult to establish than the actual evolutionary process itself. The efficacy of evolutionary theory depends on the ability to offer an account of the source of knowledge that Darwinian evolution depends on.

In the next chapter, a number of simulations of evolution from the literature are presented. Each purports to demonstrate Darwinian evolution. We will show, however, that they suffer from the same problems and that the evolutionary process creates no information. Success is always traceable to active information mined from a source of knowledge.

Notes

1. C. Darwin, *The Autobiography of Charles Darwin*, available at the Gutenberg Project Online (1887).
2. David H. Wolpert and William G. Macready, "No free lunch theorems for optimization." *IEEE Trans. Evolutionary Computation*, 1(1), pp. 67–82 (1997).
3. Jie Li and Jianbing Chen, *Stochastic Dynamics of Structures* (Wiley, 2009).
4. R.J. Marks II, *Handbook of Fourier Analysis and Its Applications* (Oxford University Press, 2009).
5. A. Jerri, "The Shannon Sampling Theorem — Its Various Extensions and Applications: A Tutorial Review." *Proceedings of the IEEE*, 65, 1565–1595 (1977).
6. S. Bringsjord, P. Bello, and D. Ferrucci, "Creativity, the Turing test. and the (better) Lovelace test," *Minds and Machines*, 11(1), pp. 3–27 (2001).
7. L. Brillouin, *Science and Information Theory* (Academic Press, New York, 1956).

8. T.M. Mitchell, "The need for biases in learning generalizations." Technical Report CBM-TR-117, Department of Computer Science, Rutgers University, p. ·59 (1980). Reprinted in *Readings in Machine Learning* edited by J.W. Shavlik and T.G. Dietterich (Morgan Kauffmann, 1990), pp. 184–190.

9. C. Schaffer, "A conservation law for generalization performance." In *Proc. Eleventh International Conference on Machine Learning*, H. Willian and W. Cohen (Morgan Kaufmann, San Francisco, 1994), pp. 295–265.

10. *References are given in*: William A. Dembski and R.J. Marks II, "Bernoulli's Principle of Insufficient Reason and Conservation of Information in Computer Search." *Proceedings of the 2009 IEEE International Conference on Systems, Man, and Cybernetics.* San Antonio, TX, USA — October 2009, pp. 647–2652.

11. David H. Wolpert and William G. Macready, *op. cit.*

12. Yu-Chi Ho and D.L. Pepyne, "Simple explanation of the no free lunch theorem of optimization." *Proceedings of the 40th IEEE Conference on Decision and Control*, pp. 4409–4414 (2001).
    Yu-Chi Ho, Qian-Chuan Zhao, D.L., Pepyne, "The no free lunch theorems: complexity and security." *IEEE Transactions on Automatic Control*, 48(5), pp. 783–793 (2003).

13. *Ibid.*

14. O. Häggström, *Biology and Philosophy* 22, pp. 217–230 (2007).

15. C. Schaffer (1994), *op. cit.*

16. Richard O. Duda, Peter E. Hart and David G. Stork, *Pattern Classification*, 2nd edition (Wiley-Interscience 2000).

17. L.J. Fogel and W.S. McCulloch, "Natural automata and prosthetic devices." *Aids to Biological/Communications: Prosthesis and Synthesis*, Vol. 2, D.M. Ramsey-Klee (ed.) 2, pp. 221–262. Reprinted in David B. Fogel, *Evolutionary Computation: the Fossil Record* (Wiley-IEEE Press, 1998).

18. T.C. Service and D.R. Tauritz, "Free lunches in pareto coevolution." *Proceedings of the 11th Annual conference on Genetic and Evolutionary Computation* — GECCO '09, pp. 1721–1727 (2009).
    And "A No-Free-Lunch Framework for Coevolution." in *Proceedings of the 10th annual conference on Genetic and Evolutionary Computation* — GECCO '08 (ACM Press, New York, USA, 2008), pp. 371–378.
    D.H. Wolpert and W.G. Macready, "Coevolutionary free lunches." *IEEE Transactions on Evolutionary Computation*, 9(6), pp. 721–735 (2005).
    D.W. Corne and J.D. Knowles, "Some multiobjective optimizers are better than others." In *The 2003 Congress on Evolutionary Computation*, 2003. CEC '03, 4. IEEE, pp. 2506–2512 (2003).

S. Droste, T. Jansen, and I. Wegener, "Perhaps Not A Free Lunch But At Least A Free Appetizer." University of Dortmund, Dortmund, Germany, Tech. Rep. (1998).

19. Winston Ewert, William A. Dembski, and Robert J. Marks II, "Conservation of information in relative search performance." *Proceedings of the 2013 IEEE 45th Southeastern Symposium on Systems Theory* (SSST), Baylor University, pp. 41–50 (2013).

20. M. Koppen, D.H. Wolpert, and W.G. Macready, "Remarks on a recent paper on the "no free lunch" theorems." *IEEE Transactions on Evolutionary Computation*, 5(3), 295–296 (2001).

21. *Ibid.*

22. Unsupervised learning is typically performed using clustering. For example, see R. Xu and D. Wunsch, *Clustering* (Wiley-IEEE Press, 2008).

23. Commonly used criteria for training such as use of test and validation data to avoid needless complexity, are not addressed here. Interested readers are referred to Duda *op. cit.*

24. C.A. Jensen, R.D. Reed, R.J. Marks II, M.A. El-Sharkawi, Jae-Byung Jung, R.T. Miyamoto, G.M. Anderson, and C.J. Eggen, "Inversion of feedforward neural networks: algorithms and applications." *Proceedings of the IEEE*, 87, pp. 1536–1549 (1999).

25. M. Minsky and S. Papert, *Perceptrons: An Introduction to Computational Geometry* (MIT Press, 1969). Later editions of the book were also published.

26. *Ibid.*

27. R.J. Marks II, "CIFEr: Exchange and Synthesis." *Proceedings of the IEEE/IAFE Conference on Computational Intelligence for Financial Engineering* (CIFEr), p. 7, April 9–11, 1995; New York, New York at http://robertmarks.org/REPRINTS/1995_CIFEr_ExchangeAndSynthesis.pdf (URL date May 2, 2016).

   R.J. Marks II and John Marshall, "Message from CIFEr '96 General Chairs." *Proceedings of the IEEE/IAFE 1996 International Conference on Computational Intelligence for Financial Engineering*, March 24–26, New York City, p. 6 (1996).

   J.F. Marshall & R.J. Marks II, "Message from the CIFEr '97 General Chairs." *Proceedings of the IEEE/IAFE 1997 International Conference on Computational Intelligence for Financial Engineering*, March 23–26, New York City, pp. 6–7 (1997).

28. Russell D. Reed, and Robert J. Marks, *Neural Smithing: Supervised Learning in Feedforward Artificial Neural Networks* (MIT Press, 1999).

29. John F. Marshall and Vipul K. Bansal, *Financial Engineering* (Kolb Publishing Company, 1993).
    John F. Marshall and Kenneth R. Kapner, *Understanding Swaps* (Wiley, New York, 1993).
    John F. Marshall, *Dictionary of Financial Engineering*. (John Wiley & Sons, 2001).
30. CIFEr, *op.cit.* Personal communication with Marks at the first CIFEr.
31. D. Thomas, "War of the Weasels: An Evolutionary Algorithm Beats Intelligent Design." *Skeptical Inquirer*, 43, pp. 42–46 (2010).
32. D. Thomas, "Target? TARGET? We don't need no stinkin' Target!." http://pandasthumb.org/archives/2006/07/target-target-w-1.html (2006) (URL date May 2, 2016).
33. W. Ewert, William A. Dembski, and Robert J. Marks II, "Climbing the Steiner Tree—Sources of Active Information in a Genetic Algorithm for Solving the Euclidean Steiner Tree Problem." *Bio-complexity*, 2012(1), pp. 1–14 (2012).
34. D. Thomas, "Steiner Genetic Algorithm — C++ Code." http://pandasthumb. org/archives/2006/07/steiner-genetic.html. (2006) (URL date May 2, 2016).
35. *Ibid.*
36. L. J. Fogel and W. S. McCulloch, *op. cit.*
37. Garry Wills, *Lincoln at Gettysburg: The Words That Remade America*, (Simon & Schuster (1993)).
38. William A. Dembski and Robert J. Marks II, "Conservation of information in search: measuring the cost of success." *Systems, Man and Cybernetics, Part A: Systems and Humans, IEEE Transactions on*, 39(5), pp. 1051–1061, (2009).
39. "PegSolitaire" by Jonathunder — Own work. Licensed under GFDL 1.2 via Wikimedia Commons — https://commons.wikimedia.org/wiki/File:Peg Solitaire.jpg#/media/File:PegSolitaire.jpg (URL date May 2, 2016).
40. J.D. Lohn, D.S. Linden, G.S. Hornby, A. Rodriguez-Arroyo, S.E. Seufert, B. Blevins, and T. Greenling, "Evolutionary design of an X-band antenna for NASA's Space Technology 5 mission." *2004 IEEE Antennas and Propagation Society International Symposium*, 3(20–25), pp. 2313–2316 (2004).
    J.D. Lohn, D.S. Linden, G.S. Hornby, and W.F. Kraus, "Evolutionary design of a single-wire circularly-polarized X-band antenna for NASA's Space Technology 5 mission." *2005 IEEE International Symposium Antennas and Propagation Society*, 2B (3–8) (2005).
41. Gerald J. Burke, *Numerical Electromagnetics Code NEC-4, Method of Moments, Part I: Users Manual*, Lawrence Livermore National Laboratory.

See also Gerald J. Burke, *Numerical Electromagnetics Code NEC-4, Method of Moments, Part II: Program Description Theory*, Lawrence Livermore National Laboratory (1992).

42. R.J. Marks II, *op. cit.*
43. Thomas M. Cover, and Joy A. Thomas, *Elements of Information Theory* (John Wiley & Sons, 2012).
44. This problem was apparently first proposed as *The Two Child Problem* in Martin Gardner, *The Second Scientific American Book of Mathematical Puzzles and Diversions* (Simon & Schuster, 1954).
45. J.D. Lohn, *op. cit.*
46. Gerald J. Burke, *op. cit.*
47. Detailed analysis of extraction of information from a Hamming oracle from which this discussion is taken, including a discussion of Ewert's algorithm, may be found in Winston Ewert, George Montañez, William A. Dembski and Robert J. Marks II, "Efficient Per Query Information Extraction from a Hamming Oracle." *Proceedings of the 42nd Meeting of the Southeastern Symposium on System Theory*, IEEE, University of Texas at Tyler, March 7–9, 2010, pp. 290–297. (Available at www.EvoInfo.org).
48. R.J. Marks II, *Handbook, ibid* .
49. Ewert, Montañez *et al. ibid*. Table 5.7 is from this paper.
50. John C. Sanford, *Genetic Entropy & the Mystery of the Genome*, ILN (2005).
51. Douglas D. Axe, "Extreme functional sensitivity to conservative amino acid changes on enzyme exteriors." *J. Mol. Biol.* 301, pp. 585–595 (2000).
52. J. Slocum, D. Singmaster, W.-H. Huang, D. Gebhardt, G. Hellings, and E. Rubik, *The Cube: The Ultimate Guide to the World's Bestselling Puzzle — Secrets, Stories, Solutions* (Black Dog & Leventhal Publishers, 2009).
53. The authors thank George Montañez for the Rubik's cube and Chik-fil-A examples.
54. R. Dawkins, *Climbing Mount Improbable* (W.W. Norton & Company, 1997).
55. H.S. Wilf and W.J. Ewens, "There's plenty of time for evolution." *P Natl Acad Sci*, 107, pp. 22454–22456 (2010).
   R. Dawkins. *The Blind Watchmaker: Why the Evidence of Evolution Reveals a Universe Without Design* (Norton, New York, 1996).
56. William A. Dembski and Robert J. Marks II, "Conservation of Information in Search: Measuring the Cost of Success." *IEEE Transactions on Systems, Man and Cybernetics A, Systems and Humans*, 39(5), pp. 1051–1061 (2009).
57. A version of this section previously appeared as W. Ewert, William A. Dembski, Robert J. Marks II, "Conservation of Information in Coevolutionary Searches." *BIO-Complexity* (2017).

58. W. D. Hillis, "Co-evolving Parasites Improve Simulated Evolution as an Optimization Procedure." *Physica D: Nonlinear Phenomena*, 42(1–3), pp. 228–234 (1990).

59. K. Sims, "Evolving 3D morphology and behavior by competition." *Artif Life*, 1(4), pp. 353–372 (1994).

60. P.J. Darwen, "Why Co-evolution beats temporal difference learning at Backgammon for a linear architecture, but not a non-linear architecture." in *Proceedings of the 2001 Congress on Evolutionary Computation* (IEEE Cat. No.01TH8546), 2. IEEE, pp. 1003–1010 (2001).

61. K. Chellapilla and D. B. Fogel, "Evolving an Expert Checkers Playing Program without Using Human Expertise." *IEEE Transactions on Evolutionary Computation*, 5(4), pp. 422–428 (2001).

62. D.B. Fogel, T.J. Hays, S.L. Hahn, and J. Quon, "A self-learning evolutionary chess program." *Proceedings of the IEEE*, 92(12), pp. 1947–1954 (2004).

63. S. G. Ficici, "Solution Concepts in Coevolutionary Algorithms." Dissertation, Brandeis University (2004).

64. T.C. Service *op. cit.*

65. This figure is from Ewert *et al. op. cit.*

66. *Ibid.*

67. William A. Dembski. and Robert J. Marks II, "The Search for a Search: Measuring the Information Cost of Higher Level Search." *J Adv Comp Intel, Intel Informatics*, 14(5), pp. 475–486 (2010).

68. *Ibid.*

69. T. M. Mitchell (1980) *op. cit.*

70. Cullen Schaffer (1994) *op. cit.*

71. Wolpert and Macready (1997) *op. cit.*

6

ANALYSIS OF SOME BIOLOGICALLY MOTIVATED
EVOLUTIONARY MODELS

"[T]he preservation of the complex, improbable organization of the living creature needs more than energy for the work. It calls for information or instructions on how the energy should be expended to maintain the improbable organization. The idea of information necessary for the maintenance and, as we shall see, creation of living systems is of great utility in approaching the biological problems of reproduction."

George Gaylord Simpson and William S. Beck[1]

When software engineers perform a computer search, they are always looking for ways to improve the results of the search and how to better incorporate knowledge about the problem being solved into the search algorithm. Evolution computer programs written by Darwinists, on the other hand, are aimed at demonstrating the Darwinian evolutionary process. The efficiency of the search is of secondary importance.

Despite these differences, the fundamentals of evolutionary models offered by Darwinists and those used by engineers and computer scientists are the same. There is always a teleological goal imposed by an omnipotent programmer, a fitness associated with the goal, a source of active information (e.g. an oracle), and stochastic updates.

Having established the background for conservation of information[2] for evolutionary processes, we are now ready to examine some of the more publicized biological computer models of Darwinian evolution. In each of the cases examined, information sources are tapped resulting in sufficient active information to allow the models to work. We suspect the authors of the software, possibly numbed by familiarity with the evolutionary paradigm, had no hidden agenda when infusing the information into the algorithm. In any case, for the computer simulations, we can specifically identify the sources of the active information.

The first program we analyze is dubbed EV.

6.1   EV: A Software Model of Evolution

Thomas Schneider designed software simulation to demonstrate Darwinian evolution. He called it EV and wrote a paper describing its performance.[3] In the paper, Schneider made the following claims:

- "The [EV] simulation [of evolution] begins with zero information and, as in naturally occurring genetic systems, the information measured in the fully evolved binding sites is close to that needed to locate the sites in the genome."
- "The [evolutionary] transition is rapid, demonstrating that information gain can occur by punctuated equilibrium."
- "The EV model quantitatively addresses the question of how life gains information."
- "[The] EV program also clearly demonstrates that biological information, measured in the strict Shannon sense, can rapidly appear in genetic control systems subjected to replication, mutation and selection."

In the light of the mathematics of conservation of information, these statements are irrefutably wrong. There is no "information gain by natural selection" as claimed by Schneider. Information sources are included in the program. Using an evolutionary process, this information source is mined for active information that guides the search to the desired result. The evolutionary search, in fact, does a rather poor job in extracting active information from information sources. Other algorithms do better. We saw this property in the previous chapter where different algorithms extracted active information from Hamming oracles with different efficiencies. This also applies to EV.

6.1.1   *EV structure*

Cartoonist Rube Goldberg was famous for drawing cartoons of complicated machinery that perform simple tasks.

- A small steal ball rolls down two closely spaced parallel rods and then falls three feet and hits one side of a small see-saw.
- On the other side of the see-saw's fulcrum is a spoonful of dry dirt, that is launched into the air as a cloud of dust.
- The dust is inhaled by a tethered dog, who sneezes and blows out a lit candle that has been keeping a small mouse warm.
- As it moves through a tube to a warm blanket, the mouse triggers a trip wire that launches a marshmallow towards a delicately balanced paperback book positioned above the light switch.
- The book falls and flips the switch from the upward on position to off.

This overly complicated Rube Goldberg machine has just successfully turned off the light. A simple task is performed with a high overhead of expensive complexity. EV is not unlike this.

Stripping away the Rube Goldberg structure of EV leaves the search problem illustrated in Fig. 6.1. There are four nucleotides: A, C, G and T. Two bits are assigned to each to them as follows:

$$A = 00 \qquad C = 01 \qquad G = 10 \qquad T = 11.$$

A string of nucleotides, interpreted as a binary string, is fed into a mechanistic number cruncher that outputs another string of bits. The output is compared to the target and the Hamming distance between the output and the target is announced by a Hamming oracle. Evolution is said to have successfully occurred when the Hamming distance is zero and the target has been identified.

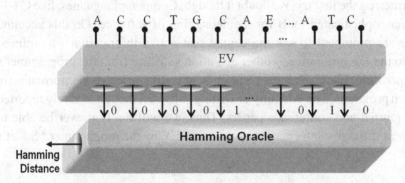

Fig. 6.1. The digital organism used in EV.

Sixty-four of the "digital organisms" shown in Fig. 6.1 are used to find the target. This is shown in Fig. 6.2. The Hamming distance is used as the fitness. During evolution, a copy is made of the 32 organisms with the highest fitness. They replace the discarded organisms with the worst Hamming distances. The population is then mutated by replacing a randomly chosen nucleotide location with a randomly chosen A, C, G or T. There is therefore a 25% chance that the replaced nucleotide is the same as the replacement. Each cycle is referred to as a generation. A different target is chosen for each initialization of EV, but remains fixed throughout the search. All organisms seek the same target. The target is said to represent nucleotide binding sites. On the nucleotide strand, a one is assigned to a binding site. Otherwise, a zero is assigned. Since a number of nucleotides must be situated between adjacent binding sites, the targets chosen by EV all consist of a sea of zeros with a sparse sprinkling of ones. As we will see, this is one of many contributing factors to the success of EV.

In the literature, only positive research results are typically published. When programs like EV appear, there is a requirement that successful evolution has been demonstrated by the software. Programs that are not successful won't be published. As is the case with Edison designing the light bulb or the 409 trials needed for the successful invention of Formula 409™, one must ask how many trials were needed to design the EV program? How much effort was taken in the debugging of the initial program? And if the original idea didn't work, how many times was the program rewritten trying different scenarios? Writers of software know that original programs rarely work the first, second, or the tenth time. The EV program could have been written on the first try. We doubt it though. Computer languages, like C++, offer sophisticated tools for the debugging of software. On this account, we are prompted to ask the degree that active information was infused into the EV program and other evolution software from the programmer's experience. The programmer's brain is, of course, a source of information in such programs. The difficulty of writing software, though, is rarely reported in journal and conference papers. Thus, we will rarely if ever be able to assess the active information infused into EV by the programmer.[a] So let's

---

[a]This is the man-in-the-loop source of active information discussed in Chapter 3.7.3.

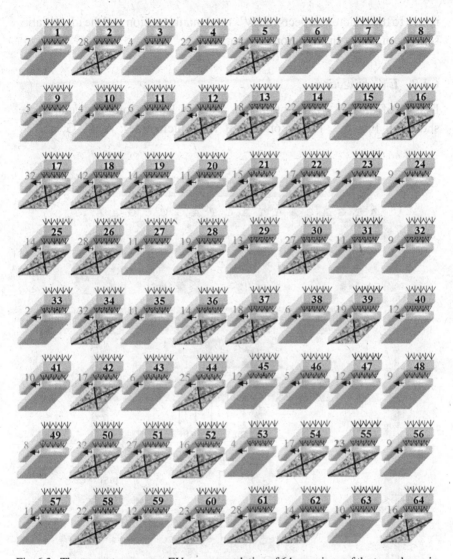

Fig. 6.2. The computer program EV uses a population of 64 organisms of the type shown in Fig. 6.1. Each seeks the same target. A Hamming oracle provides a measure of how close the organism is to the target. In each generation, the 32 organisms with the smallest Hamming distance are duplicated and replace those organisms with the largest, In the new population, a single nucleotide is replaced in the input, the Hamming distances are recalculated, and the process is repeated.

return to the concrete aspects of EV's final manifestation and the identifiable sources of active information therein.

6.1.2 *EV vivisection*

Details of the EV digital organism, with its Rube Goldberg details, are shown in Fig. 6.3. DNA consists of four nucleotides: A, C, G, and T.

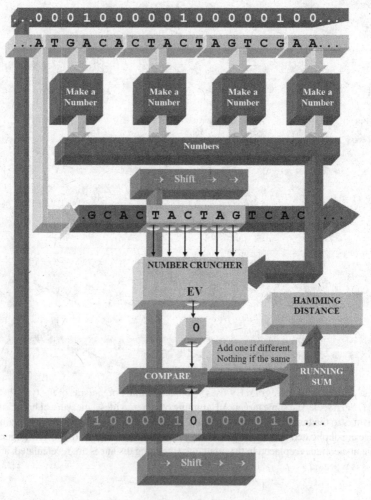

Fig. 6.3. Details of the EV digital organism.

At the top of Fig. 6.3, there is a sequence of 256 nucleotides.[b] Since there are four nucleotides, assuming Bernoulli's PrOIR, each has $I = \log_2 4 = 2$ bits of information each. We assign two bits each to them as follows

$$A = 00 \qquad C = 01 \qquad G = 10 \qquad T = 11.$$

This way, any string of N bits can be interpreted uniquely as a string of nucleotides when N is even, and *vice versa*. The nucleotide sequence CTAAGC becomes the bit string 011100001001 and the bit string 000111110010 becomes the nucleotide sequence ACTTAG. The EV simulation of evolution uses a string of 256 nucleotides (512 bits) in each of its digital organisms.

Accompanying the nucleotide string at the top of Fig. 6.3 are a sequence of ones and zeros shown at the bottom of the figure. A "1" denotes that the nucleotide is a *binding site*. A "0" means that it is not. The EV program assigns the binary string at the program's start. Although the assignments have a random component, the binding sites must be separated. This requires that most of the bits in the binary string are "0's" and that "1's" are padded on both sides by zeros. The goal of the search is to find a set of nucleotides that generate the specified binding sites.

The manner that the nucleotides determine the binding sites is determined by the EV program diagramed with the flow graph in Fig. 6.3. First, nucleotides are used to "Make a Number." They are used in groups of five. Since each nucleotide has two bits of information, each number has ten bits of accuracy. Since $4^5 = 2^{10} = 1024$ and negative numbers are desired, EV interprets each of these numbers between -512 and $+511$. These numbers are fed into the "EV Number Cruncher." The number cruncher allows input of six nucleotides and outputs a zero or a one. The nucleotide sequence at the top of Fig. 6.3 is shifted across the number cruncher one nucleotide at a time. The first output of the number cruncher is determined by the first six nucleotides. The second bit output of the number cruncher is determined

---

[b]There are five additional nucleotides for a total of 261. The extra five are needed to accommodate a sliding six nucleotide window. In Fig. 6.3, the window occurs in the synchronized "Shift".

by nucleotides 2 through 7. The shifting is continued until 256 bits are generated by the number cruncher.[c]

Each time the number cruncher spits out a bit, it is compared to the target bit stream. The shifting nucleotide string shifts with the target bit string.[d] If the number cruncher output differs from the target bit, a running sum is incremented by one. If they match, the running sum is not incremented. After the shifting is complete, the running sum contains the Hamming distance between the 265 bit target and the output of the number cruncher. Only the Hamming distance is used as the fitness of the digital organism. The specific locations along the genome where the number cruncher and target bits agree and differ are not used in the search. Nor will we use them in any of the searches we propose. Recording the total Hamming distance between an output and a target constitutes use of a *Hamming oracle*. The Hamming oracle can be a rich source of information.[e] Indeed, if our goal is to find the 265 bit target in EV, we could do so in no more than 256 queries using the Hamming oracle. This is not, however, a very interesting evolution problem. Our task, rather, is finding the target filtered through the mechanistic Rube Goldberg EV number cruncher.

The workings of the number cruncher are shown in Fig. 6.4. The "Make a Number" blocks in Fig. 6.3 are used to place numbers between -512 and 511 in a 4×6 matrix in Fig. 6.4 and to set a threshold. The width of four in the matrix allows the four nucleotides to shift through. Six is the length of the window. Each nucleotide activates one of four numbers depending on whether the nucleotide is A, C, T or G. The six activated numbers are added together and compared to a threshold generated from "Make a Number." Whether the sum exceeds the threshold determines whether the number cruncher outputs a zero or a one.

6.1.3 *Information sources resident in EV*

The goal of EV is to find a set of nucleotides that gives a resulting Hamming distance of zero. It is a search problem to which a number

---

[c]The need for the additional five nucleotides is now evident. To generate the final output, for example, the final nucleotide is needed, as are five additional nucleotides to fill the needed six input locations in the number cruncher.

[d]As is shown in Fig. 6.3.

[e]We saw this in Chapter 5.4.3.1.

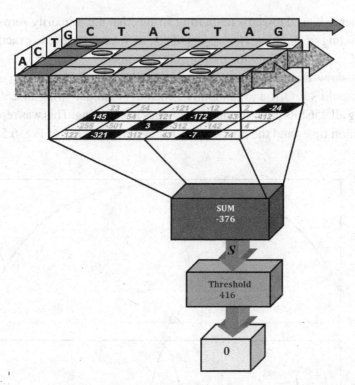

Fig. 6.4. The EV number cruncher. As the nucleotides shift across the top, selected numbers in the matrix are added and compared to a threshold to determine whether the output is one or zero. The nucleotides are shifted one to the right and the process is repeated for the next bit.

of search algorithms other than evolutionary search can be applied. It is not the evolutionary program that is responsible for generation of active information. There are already rich sources of active information in EV. Even though accessed through the EV number cruncher, the Hamming oracle is one such source. We are accurately being told how close we are to the desired result of a zero Hamming distance. And, as always, the large number of digital organisms examined as in Fig. 6.2 is a minor source of information.

The number cruncher is a rich source of information. The EV programmer probably did not purposefully design the number cruncher to be a source of information. But, then again, had the EV program not worked using the number cruncher, no publication would have resulted. The number

cruncher is biased towards outputting strings that are primarily zeros with
a sprinkling of ones (or *vice versa*). This, as we have seen, is exactly the
type of target describing the binding site locations.

To show this, we chose a string of nucleotides uniformly according
to Bernoulli's PrOIR and randomly generate an output string of 256 bits.
Adding all 256 bits gives the number of ones in the string. This was repeated
10 million times and the normalized[f] histogram at the top of Fig. 6.5[4] was

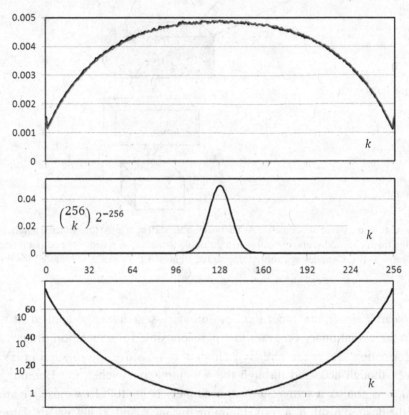

Fig. 6.5. The top plot is a histogram of the number of ones generated by the EV number
cruncher. The middle plot is the normalized histogram we would expect. The bottom plot
is the ratio of the two plots.

---

[f]The histogram is normalized to give it a unit area. Such histograms can be viewed as
empirical estimates of probability density functions.

generated. If you look closely at the top graph, you'll see that there is a second plot. That's 10 million additional trials except that the number of zeros are added at the output. The histograms are graphically nearly indistinguishable.

There are $2^{256} = 1.15792 \times 10^{77}$ possible bit strings of length 256. Only one of these strings contains all zeros. On the other hand, there are $\binom{256}{128} = 5.76866 \times 10^{75}$ strings that contain exactly 128 ones. Thus, the bulge in the middle of the histogram in the top plot in Fig. 6.5 is reasonable. But it isn't a big enough bulge. If we assume that each bit in a string is generated with a 50–50 coin flip, the normalized histogram should be close to the bell-shaped curve[g] in the middle of Fig. 6.5. The bottom curve in Fig. 6.5 is the top curve divided by the middle curve. It shows the degree of deviation amplification of what we would expect to see if each binary string were determined by a sequence of fair coin flips. The number cruncher is seen to drastically prefer binary strings with either a preponderance of zeros or a preponderance of ones.

The biased nature of the number cruncher is illustrated if we examine how the number cruncher can generate an output of all zeros. There is only one way to generate an output of all zeros, so the endogenous information of this problem is $I_\Omega = 256$ bits. The 10 million queries of the number cruncher, however, show that the probability of a single query generating all zeros is an astonishingly large $q = 0.00155$. This is an exogenous information of $I_S = 9$ bits corresponding to an astounding $I_+ = 247$ bits of active information generated by the number cruncher.

There is another interesting insight we can glean from this all-zeros experiment. Since there are $|\Omega| = 4^{261} = 1.37 \times 10^{157}$ distinct nucleotide sequences, and since the probability of choosing a sequence that produces an output of all zeros is $q = 0.00155$, we are left to conclude that there are an astonishing $q|\Omega| = 2 \times 10^{154}$ nucleotide sequences that will generate an output of all zeros!

Although the goal of EV is not to generate a string of all zeros, the plots in Fig. 6.5 illustrate conclusively that the EV number cruncher is

---

[g]† From the Laplace–Demoivre Theorem, the plot of $\binom{256}{k} 2^{-256}$ in the middle of Fig. 6.5 is a Gaussian or normal curve often referred to as a bell-shaped distribution. With $n = 256$ and $p = \frac{1}{2}$, its mean is $np = 128$ and its variance is $np(1 - p) = 64$.

predisposed to generating a sequence of zeros peppered with ones or a sequence of ones peppered with zeros. In this manner, the number cruncher is a rich source of active information for the type of targets chosen in EV.

6.1.4   *The search*

We have identified a number of sources of information resident in EV. How can we best exploit them to search for a set of nucleotides that give us a match to the binding sites?

6.1.4.1   *Search using the number cruncher*

EV's number cruncher provides active information when it generates target-like bit strings. Using the number cruncher alone, the exogenous information has been upper bounded as $I_S < 90$ bits.[2] Forecasting the outcome of 90 flips of a fair coin is highly improbable. Therefore, the Hamming oracle or some other information source is required to work with the number cruncher to yield a successful search.

6.1.4.2   *Evolutionary search*

EV's evolutionary approach uses 64 copies of the organisms.[h] The 32 organisms with the largest Hamming distances are discarded and replaced with duplicates of the organisms with the lowest Hamming distance. Then one nucleotide in each organism is chosen at random and replaced with another nucleotide. The process is then repeated. The original EV paper reports convergence in 704 cycles or generations. That's $704 \times 64 = 45,056$ Hamming distances measured. We score each Hamming distance measurement as a query. We ran a total of 100,000 EV simulations[i] and 9,115 were successful. Each simulation was limited to a maximum of one hundred thousand queries. Our simulations of EV averaged 993 generations for success or, on average, 63,552 queries. Although larger than the 45,056 queries reported in the EV paper, the resulting comparisons are not unreasonable.

---

[h]As we see in Fig. 6.2.
[i]That's about 1,563 generations since $64 \times 1,563 \approx 100,000$ queries.

Using a query count, how does this performance compare to a simpler search algorithm that uses the same source of knowledge?

6.1.4.3 *EV and stochastic hill climbing*[j]

We can do better than multi-agent evolutionary search using a single organism. We start with a single randomly chosen nucleotide string as an input and note the Hamming distance between the output and the target. Then one of the input nucleotides is changed and the new output Hamming distance is noted. If the Hamming is larger, the change is discarded and another nucleotide is randomly chosen and changed. Otherwise, the change is kept and the process repeated. Ten thousand searches were performed using the stochastic hill climbing search[6] and, even though the same upper bound of 100,000 queries was imposed on the search, every search was successful. The average query count for success using this algorithm is 10,601. This average was found from 10,000 separate searches.

The evolutionary algorithm used in EV requires *six times* the number of queries as compared to the stochastic hill-climbing approach. Both searches used the same information sources. The hill-climbing search used them six times more efficiently as measured by average query count.

The source of success in the EV program is not the evolutionary program. It is the information sources embedded in the program by the programmer, most notably the EV number cruncher and the Hamming oracle.

6.1.4.4 *Mutation rate*

Search algorithms have parameters that can be tuned to make the search more efficient. Both the evolutionary search algorithm and the stochastic hill-climbing algorithm assume the mutation of a single nucleotide per query. Is this the best mutation rate? As can be seen in Fig. 6.6,[7] the answer is no. Two mutations per iteration give better results. As was the case in the original run, each point in Fig. 6.6 makes use of 10,000 runs using a population size of 64 and a query cutoff of 100,000 queries. The plot is the fraction of times the search succeeded prior to cutoff. Fractional

---

[j]Also known as an *evolutionary strategy*.

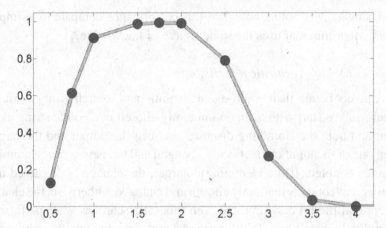

Fig. 6.6. Success rate as a function of mutation for the evolution algorithm search applied to EV.

mutations are generated by randomizing the mutation number. To achieve 1.75 mutations per child, for example, each organism receives at least one mutation and has a 75% chance of receiving another.

To increase the probability of success, the mutation rate in EV using the evolutionary search must be tuned. If the rate exceeds four mutations out of 261 nucleotides, there will be close to zero chance of success in the search using the limited resources allotted.

6.1.5   *EV ware*

An interactive GUI, available on the EvoInfo.org web site,[k] is capable of demonstrating EV and its variations. The control panel for EV Ware, shown in Fig. 6.7, allows a wide choice for implementing variations of the EV algorithm.

Figures 6.8–6.10 shows three different runs using the EV structure. The target (labeled "What you want") is shown with the darker gray in the lower portion of each row. The result of the latest query (labeled "What you got") is on top. The output corresponds to the bit stream shown at the bottom of Fig. 6.3. The input, not shown, is the bit stream on the top of Fig. 6.3.

---

[k]http://www.evoinfo.org/ev.html.

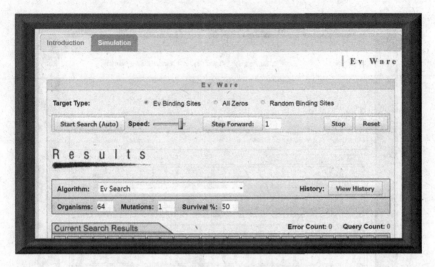

Fig. 6.7. The control panel for EV Ware.

The futility of the blind search is illustrated in Fig. 6.8. An EV organism was queried randomly over 900,000 times without a success.

A sample run of the EV algorithm in Fig. 6.9 found success after 50,048 queries. Since the evolutionary program used 64 organisms per generation, this is equivalent to 782 generations. Fewer queries are required when using a single EV organism and applying stochastic hill climbing. The example in Fig. 6.10 found success in a few more than 9,000 queries and therefore mines the knowledge source more efficiently than does the EV evolutionary algorithm.

6.1.6 *The diagnosis*

With the analysis, simulations and understanding of the conservation of information, we are now in a position to revisit the claims made by EV and comment on them:

- "The [EV] simulation [of evolution] begins with zero information and, as in naturally occurring genetic systems, the information measured in the fully evolved binding sites is close to that needed to locate the sites in the genome."

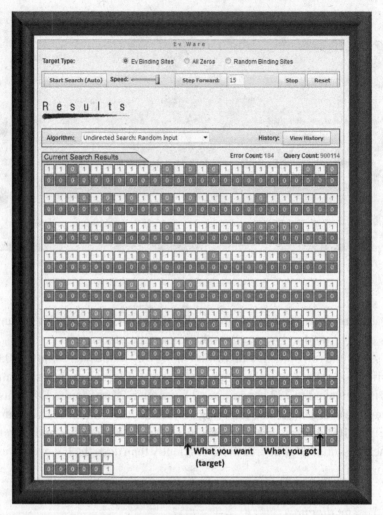

Fig. 6.8. EV Ware for "Undirected (Blind) Search" generated no solution after over 900,000 queries.

The EV program starts with rich sources of information the most prominent of which are the Hamming oracle and the EV number cruncher. These sources of active information are resident in the program before the search begins.

- "The [evolutionary] transition is rapid, demonstrating that information gain can occur by punctuated equilibrium."

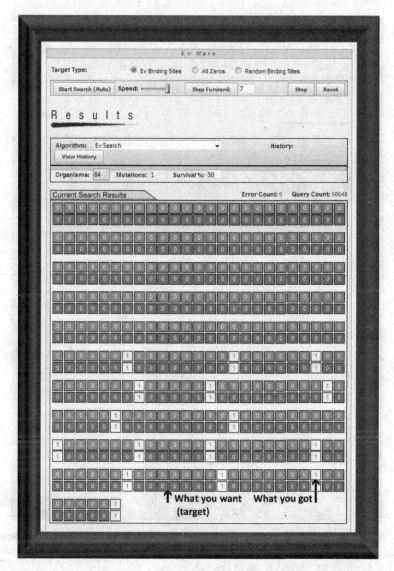

Fig. 6.9. In this run, EV evolutionary search succeeded in a bit over 50,000 queries.

The rapidness of the transition is due only to the mining of active information in the sources resident in EV.

- "The EV model quantitatively addresses the question of how life gains information."

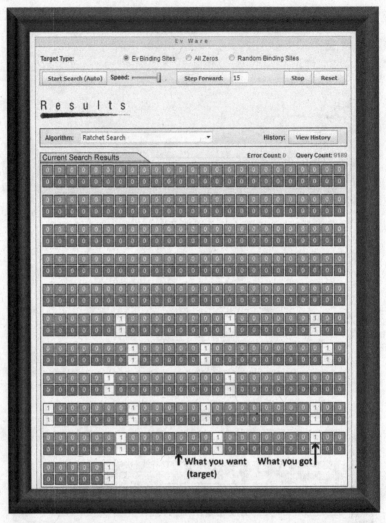

Fig. 6.10. Stochastic hill-climbing, discussed in Chapter 6.1.4.3, is called Ratchet Search in this figure. Success here was achieved in 9,189 queries. This is far fewer than is required by EV's evolutionary search result in Fig. 6.9.

The implication is that the evolutionary program generates the information. It does not. The evolutionary algorithm, rather, mines information sources resident in the program and, as has been demonstrated conclusively, does so rather poorly.

- "[The] EV program also clearly demonstrates that biological information, measured in the strict Shannon sense, can rapidly appear in genetic control systems subjected to replication, mutation and selection."

Any information gained is not due to "replication, mutation and selection." It is due to the information sources designed by the programmer and placed in the simulation program. The same results are obtained more quickly using stochastic hill climbing.

When the stochastic hill-climbing search was applied to EV, we saw a successful search in every case. A nucleotide sequence was always found that generated the target string of 256 bits. We are reminded of the law of large numbers as demonstrated through Buffon's needle experiment.[1] Numerous implementations of Buffon's needle problem converged to the unexpected fixed point of $1/\pi$. Each convergence followed a different path but they all ended at $1/\pi$. This also appears to be the case in the simulations we see of EV using stochastic hill-climbing. The target was achieved even though there are different initializations and different mutations.

Most simulations claiming to illustrate Darwinian evolution are similar to EV. The programmer writes a stochastic program with the goal in mind of achieving some fixed point. When the program is run, we should not be surprised that a fixed result is reached by different paths.

6.2 Avida: Stair Steps to Complexity Using NAND Logic

Like EV, Avida[2] is a computer program which, its creators say, "show[s] how complex functions can originate by random mutation and natural selection." Also like EV, contrary to the claims of the authors, the source of the success of Avida is not due to the evolutionary algorithm, but to sources of information embedded in the computer program.[3] A strong contribution to the success of Avida is stairstep information source embedded in the computer program. Also like EV, the sources of information can be mined more efficiently using other search algorithms.

Like EV, the Avida program is a complex Rube Goldberg algorithm. Its goal is to generate a complex logic function called EQU. The pinball

---

[1] In Chapter 4.2.1.

machine analogy is appropriate. As with the steel ball bouncing around in a pinball machine, there are numerous possible paths, but the steel ball eventually falls down the little hole behind the flippers. Well, almost always. Sometimes the ball gets stuck between two bumpers and sometimes searches get stuck in local minima.

6.2.1   *Kitzmiller et al. versus Dover area school district*

Avida has a legal history in the intelligent design debate. We'll give a short overview before getting into the technical aspects of the program.

The Dover Area School District in Pennsylvania wanted intelligent design recognized as a viable alternative to Darwinian evolution. Controversy built, some parents sued, and in stepped the ACLU to the defend the Darwinists.

Even though there was no mention of a creator, and even though the Dover statement to students could be used to defend agnostic Francis Crick's directed panspermia,[m] the ACLU claimed that such actions were a violation of the Establishment Clause of the United States Constitution. The first amendment in the Bill of Rights reads

> "*Congress shall make no law respecting an establishment of religion, or prohibiting the free exercise thereof*; or abridging the freedom of speech, or of the press; or the right of the people peaceably to assemble, and to petition the Government for a redress of grievances."

The italicized portion is the Establishment Clause. Since the ACLU claimed Dover violated the US Constitution and since Congress made a law about the establishment of intelligent design as a religion (we're still not clear when the US Congress did this), the challenge by the ACLU was made in federal court. The ACLU therefore needed to prove the Dover Area School District in Pennsylvania was involved in the establishment of a religion.

In a federal bench trial, the Dover Area School District was found in violation of the Establishment Clause. In the words of the ACLU[4]

> "On December 20, 2006, Judge John E. Jones II issued a blistering 139-page opinion in which he found intelligent design to be a religious view and not a scientific theory"

---

[m]The belief that life was purposely planted on planet Earth by an alien intelligence.

Intelligent design was therefore tagged as a veil hiding religion.

The Dover trial included testimony from Robert Pennock,[5] a coauthor of the original Avida paper. Avida was presented as evidence that evolution was a scientific fact. Pennock was asked

"[Avida is] designed to instantiate Darwin's law, correct?"

Interestingly, the need for the evolutionary program to require design was an explicit component of the question. In his answer, Pennock testified that[n]

"In the [Avida] system we're not simulating evolution. Evolution is actually happening."

When this testimony was given, Avida had not yet been illuminated in the light of COI. We'll show that, like EV, the source of information required for Avida to succeed was written into the program and the program was fine-tuned to succeed. Before discussing the details, we need to establish a background in Boolean logic which is the mathematics around which Avida is designed.

6.2.2 *Boolean logic*

Avida is based on elementary Boolean logic and NAND gate synthesis.

AND and OR logic operations are used in everyday communication. Another logic operation is NOT. In the 1992 movie *Wayne's World*, Wayne's buddy, Garth, when stranded, says

"I'm having a good time... NOT!"

Putting a NOT at the end of a statement reverses its meaning. If a statement is true, putting a NOT afterwards makes it false. The opposite is also true.

---

[n]The court reporter in the Dover trial typed Avida as "Evita". In quotes from the transcript, we insert "AVIDA" in place of "Evida".

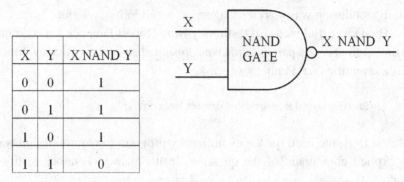

X	Y	X NAND Y
0	0	1
0	1	1
1	0	1
1	1	0

Fig. 6.11. The NAND truth table and the schematic for a NAND gate. The output is the bit flip of the AND. The little circle of the output of the gate denotes the NOT operation.

A false statement followed by a NOT is true. In logic, NOT is an operation that operates on a single bit. If the input is a 0, the output is 1 and if the input is 1 the output is 0. In other words, the NOT operation is a "bit flip."

In terms of notation, NOT X is written as $\bar{X}$. If X is one, then $\bar{X}$ is zero and if X is 0, then $\bar{X}$ is 1. The NOT operation is often placed at the output of a logic operation. The term NOT AND is contracted to NAND.

The NAND truth table is shown in Fig. 6.11. The consequent in each row is the complement of the consequent of the AND logic operation. A schematic of the *NAND gate* is also shown on the right in Fig. 6.11. The inputs to the gate are X and Y, either of which can be a 0 or a 1. The output is a 0 or a 1 depending on the entry on the truth table.

We can likewise put a NOT after the OR operation and get a NOR, and a NOT after the XOR to get an XNOR. There are many options. Some of them are shown in truth tables in Table 6.1.

Table 6.1. Truth tables for some common logic operations.

X	Y	$\bar{X}$	$\bar{Y}$	AND	NAND	OR	NOR	XOR	XNOR	$\bar{X}$ OR $\bar{Y}$	X OR $\bar{Y}$	$\bar{X}$ AND Y	X AND $\bar{Y}$
0	0	1	1	0	1	0	1	0	1	1	1	0	0
0	1	1	0	0	1	1	0	1	0	1	0	1	0
1	0	0	1	0	1	1	0	1	0	0	1	0	1
1	1	0	0	1	0	1	0	0	1	1	1	0	0

6.2.3   NAND logic

Here is a theorem from Boolean algebra that is important in Avida software: All logic operations, including those in Table 6.1, can be realized by connecting NAND gates together.[o] For a given logic operation, there can exist numerous configurations of NAND gates able to achieve the operation. This property of NAND gates is essential for the success of Avida. If Avida used, rather, both AND and OR gates without a NOT gate, the ability to characterize an arbitrary Boolean function would not be possible. The synthesis of all of the logic operations in Table 6.1 using only NAND gates is shown in Figs. 6.12–6.15. These diagrams turn out to be important for understanding Avida. As more and more NAND gates are added, note that the structures contain components of simpler operations. These are the stair steps used by Avida to achieve more complex NAND logic using simpler NAND logic. The more complex operations are built with simpler operations. A stair step information source to generate more complex operations must signify that the more complex operations are more fit than the simple operations. If this is not the case, the existence of the stair steps is not useful. As the stairs are climbed, we must be informed we are getting "warmer," i.e. closer to the result we seek. When a more complex operation degrades into a simpler one, we are informed that we are getting colder. This active information source is the reason for Avida's success. As is always the case, the evolutionary program does not create any information. Indeed, other algorithms mine the information source better and achieve the results of Avida more efficiently. More on this later.

†6.2.3.1   Logic synthesis using NAND gates

Let's walk through these operations one at a time. In all cases, we will concentrate on connecting the minimum number of NAND gates to achieve

---

[o]Students of Boolean logic know that any proposition in the Boolean truth table can be expressed using AND, OR and NOT operations (e.g. prime implicants) As our treatment of Avida unfolds, we will see that AND, OR and NOT gates can be synthesized using only NAND gates. Hence the NAND gate alone is sufficient for implementation of all Boolean logic. (The NOR gate can also be used to express all Boolean logic functions.)

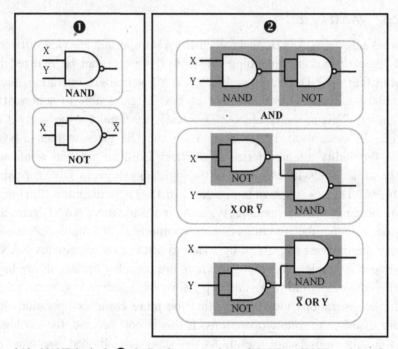

Fig. 6.12. NAND logic. In ❶, the Boolean operations of NAND and NOT can be performed with a single NAND gate. Operations possible with two NAND gates are shown in ❷. (Continued in Fig. 6.13.)

an operation. (Those not interested in the details of the Boolean operations and NAND logic may want to skip ahead.)

In Fig. 6.12 in the block marked ❶ are two operations that can be performed with a single NAND gate. Obviously, the NAND operation is possible. The NOT operation is also possible. As shown, both the inputs of the NAND gates are connected and the same value serves as the input. Since 1 NAND 1 = 0 and 0 NAND 0 = 1, an input of $X = 1$ gives and output of $\bar{X} = 0$ while an input of $X = 0$ gives and output of $\bar{X} = 1$. Thus when the same inputs are required, the NAND gate operates as a NOT gate.

Also shown in Fig. 6.12 are logic operations that can be achieved with two NAND gates. The first in the ❷ block is the AND operation which takes the NOT of a NAND gate output. Since two negatives make a positive, the composite operation is an AND. Note, significantly, how the

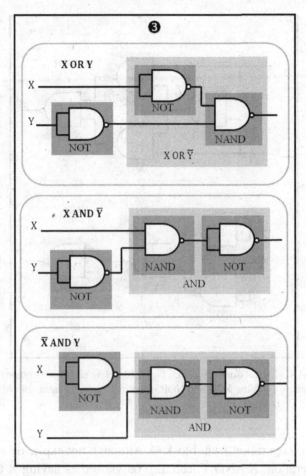

Fig. 6.13. NAND logic. In ❸ we have the logic operations achievable with three NAND gates. Each entry makes use of the operations using one NAND gate in ❶ and two NAND gates in ❷. (Continued in Fig. 6.14.)

single gate operations NAND and NOT in ❶ are used as components in the operations in ❷. This is the first case of the presence of stair step active information. Block ❸ in Fig. 6.13 shows operations achievable with three NAND gates. The first is a logical OR. Two other operations from Table 6.1, X AND Ȳ and X̄ AND Y, are also shown. Each of the logic operations uses the stair step operations in ❶ and ❷ as building blocks to synthesize the operations. On the top in block ❸ is the logic OR operation. It uses the X OR Ȳ logic in block ❷ as a component. The remaining two operations

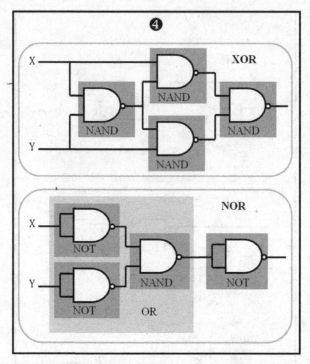

Fig. 6.14. NAND logic. (Continued from Fig. 6.13.) Here are two operations that require four NAND gates. Both the XOR and NOR operations require a minimum of four NAND gates. (Continued in Fig. 6.15.)

use the AND operation from block ❷. Although not explicitly shown, the middle operation, X AND $\bar{Y}$, can also be viewed as having $\bar{X}$ OR Y as a component. Likewise, the bottom logic operation in block ❸, $\bar{X}$ AND Y, can be construed as having the operation X OR $\bar{Y}$ in block ❷ as a component.

Both the XOR and NOR, as shown in Fig. 6.14, require a minimum of four NAND operations. The NOR operation in block ❹ contains the OR operation as a component. It can also be construed as containing the AND operation in ❷.

The XNOR operation in Fig. 6.15 requires, at minimum, five NAND gates. It is the operation sought by the Avida program. The XNOR operation is referred to as EQU in the Avida paper. With attention to the XNOR truth table in Table 6.1, note that the output is one only if both the inputs are the same, i.e. inputs are both 0 or both 1. Hence the EQU tag.

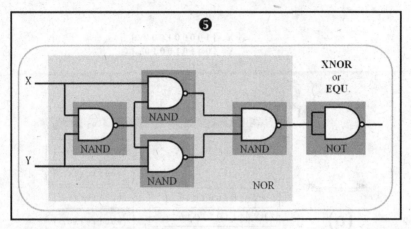

Fig. 6.15. NAND logic. (Continued from Fig. 6.14.) In ❺ we have a minimal NAND logic representation of the XNOR operation.

The EQU operation, as shown in block ❺, can be construed as having the XOR in block ❹ as a component. It also has the $\bar{X}$ AND Y operation and the X OR $\bar{Y}$ components shown in block ❸ and the AND operation in block ❷.

The NAND logic shown in Figs. 6.12–6.15 are examples of using the minimum number of NAND gates to perform the designated operation. There exist other NAND gate configurations that achieve these operations. Two cascaded NOT gates cancel each other and can be placed anywhere in the circuit. For example, one additional NOT can be cascaded at the end of the EQU in Fig. 6.15. The augmented circuit will undo the effect of the other NOT gate and the overall circuit will generate an XOR operation using six NAND gates. In the top circuit in block ❹, the XOR operation is achieved using only four NAND gates.

6.2.4 *The Avida organism and its health*

Like EV, Avida contains a digital organism. Unlike EV, Avida displays transitional functional viability in the sense that each step towards its goal corresponds to one or more logic operations. Avida is illustrated in Fig. 6.16. On the left there is a loop on which there are simple computer commands. There are a total of 26 commands in Avida and each is depicted by a lower case letter. The instruction **(q),** shown in a larger font than the other letters in

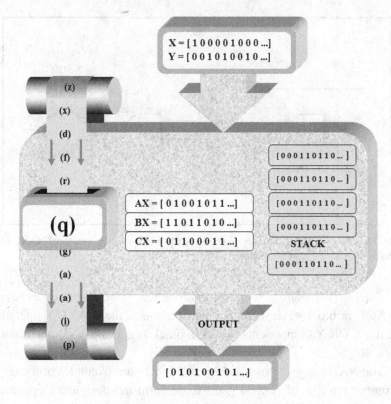

Fig. 6.16. The Avida digital organism.

Fig. 6.16, is the current instruction. The instructions manipulate the binary numbers to the right in Fig. 6.16. When there are multiple organisms, the instructions can also dictate the interaction among organisms.

Each organism is born with two strings of bits titled **X** and **Y**. These strings, shown at the top of the organism, remain the same throughout the organism's life. Internal to the Avida organism are a number of scratch pads where strings of bits can be stored. Three of these pads, as shown in Fig. 6.16, are **AX**, **BX** and **CX**. The default *target register* is **BX** unless modified by a previous instruction. There is also a **STACK** that can be used to store strings of 32 bits. An instruction might copy the string of bits in **X**, for example, into **AX**. There is also an **OUTPUT** shown on the bottom. An instruction, for example, might dictate the contents of register **CX** be copied into the **OUTPUT**.

Table 6.2. The 26 operations used by Avida.

(a) nop-A	(h) swap-stk	(o) sub	(u) h-search
(b) nop-B	(i) swap	(p) nand	(v) mov-head
(c) nop-C	(j) shift-r	(q) IO	(w) jmp-head
(d) if-n-equal	(k) shift-l	(r) h-alloc	(x) get-head
(e) if-less	(l) inc	(s) h-divide	(y) if-label
(f) push	(m) dec	(t) h-copy	(z) set-flow
(g) pop	(n) add		

Here is a description of some of the more important operations listed in Table 6.2.

- **(p) nand** performs a **nand** operation on BX or CX and writes the result in the target register. For example, if

```
AX:  0 0 0 1 1 0 1 1 1 0 1 0 1 1 1 0 0 1 0 1 0 0 1 1 1 0 0 1 0 1 0
BX:  1 0 0 0 1 1 1 0 1 1 1 0 1 1 1 0 1 0 1 1 0 0 1 1 0 0 1 0 1 1 1
```

the bitwise **nand** operation generates

```
1 1 1 0 1 0 1 0 0 1 1 1 0 0 0 1 1 1 1 1 1 0 0 1 1 1 1 1 0 1
```

which it writes in the target register. The default target register is **BX**. If the **nand** operation is taken from the Avida list of instructions, the possibility of producing any logic operation nosedives. Avida counts on the **nand** operation to perform the NAND gate implementation and therefore all other logic operations.
- **(q) IO** places the target register into the **OUTPUT** register and reads in the next value of **X** and **Y**.
- **(f) push** and **(g) pop** inputs or outputs from the stack register.
- **(i) swap** interchanges the target register with the next register of interest.

The other operations manipulate the internal registers, facilitate the reproduction of the Avida organism, or manipulate the content and size of the program loop. Some of the operations as we will see are deleterious to the formation of logic operations by AVIDA. The **IO** operation is, however, essential for the operation of AVIDA. If removed, Avida will not work. The shuffling of bit streams by operations such as **push**, **pop** and **swap**, are likewise essential for the operation of Avida.

The fitness of Avida is determined by the relationship of the **X** and **Y** registers to the **OUTPUT** register. If, for example, each bit in the output is the logic OR of the corresponding two bits in **X** and **Y**, then Avida is credited with performing an OR operation. If **O** denotes the output, an example of a successful OR operation is as follows.

X: 1 0 1 1 0 1 0 0 1 1 0 0 1 0 1 0 0 1 1 1 0 0 1 0 1 0 0 0 0 1 1 0
Y: 1 0 0 0 1 1 0 0 1 1 1 1 0 1 0 1 1 0 0 1 1 0 0 1 0 1 1 1 0 1 1 0
O: 1 0 1 1 1 1 0 0 1 1 1 1 1 1 1 1 1 1 1 0 1 1 1 1 1 1 1 0 1 1 0

Since **X** and **Y** are assigned at the organism's creation, only **O** is changed as the program runs.

The values of **X**, **Y** and **OUTPUT** used in Fig. 6.16 illustrate the XNOR operation. This is the operation using NAND logic that minimally requires the most NAND gates.[p] Avida does not refer to the operation as an XNOR, but as an EQU.

The fitness used by Avida for performing operations is a function of the number of NAND gates needed for its minimal representation. If G is the number of gates used in a minimal representation, the fitness assigned by Avida is $f = 2^G$. The OR operation in block C at the top of Fig. 6.13 requires a minimum of $G = 3$ NAND gates and therefore has a fitness of $f = 2^3 = 8$. The fitness of the logic operations shown in Figs. 6.12–6.15 used by AVIDA is listed in Table 6.3.

The use of stair steps as an information source in AVIDA is now evident. Lower stairs for logic operations required fewer NAND gates. As we saw in the logic synthesis using NAND gates, blocks of less complicated operations can be combined to achieve more complicated operations.

Avida's search for logic operations is akin to the stair step example of finding longer phrases built on the success of finding shorter phrases. In an example of stair step information,[q] we used the 26 letters of the English alphabet plus a space to search smaller phrases so we can climb the stairs to success in a complex search. Now we are using the 26 instructions in the alphabet in Table 6.2 to find simpler logic operations to climb the stairs to obtain the more complex EQU operation. Recognizing a series of letters

---

[p]See Fig. 6.15.
[q]Presented in Chapter 5.6.

Table 6.3. Fitness, f assigned by Avida for performance of different logic operations using NAND logic.

Logic	Figure	G	f
NOT	6.12	❶	2
NAND	6.12	❶	2
AND	6.12	❷	4
($\bar{X}$ OR Y) or (X OR $\bar{Y}$)	6.12	❷	4
OR	6.13	❸	8
($\bar{X}$ AND Y) or (X AND $\bar{Y}$)	6.13	❸	8
NOR	6.14	❹	16
XOR	6.14	❹	16
EQU (XNOR)	6.15	❺	32

is more intuitive than analyzing a string of computer instructions, but the searches are conceptually the same.

Like EV, Avida uses a large population for its evolutionary search. As depicted in Fig. 6.17, for most generations of the evolutionary search, 3,600 of the organisms in Fig. 6.16 are used.

6.2.5 *Information analysis of Avida*

Avida provides a nurturing environment for the computation of the XNOR (EQU) logic operation. In comparison to the other logic operation steps on the staircase, EQU is the most complicated in the sense that it requires the most nand gates. Avida interconnects these intermediate results to generate EQU. Stairstep active information is mandatory to do this.

The authors of Avida recognize and confess to the need for the active information in allowing Avida to work. They write that when stairstep active information is available,

"... at least one population evolved EQU."

What happens when no stairstep active information is applied? Nothing.

"At the other extreme, 50 populations evolved in an environment where only EQU was rewarded, and no simpler function yielded energy. We expected that EQU would evolve much less often because selection would not preserve the simpler functions that provide foundations to build more complex features. Indeed, none

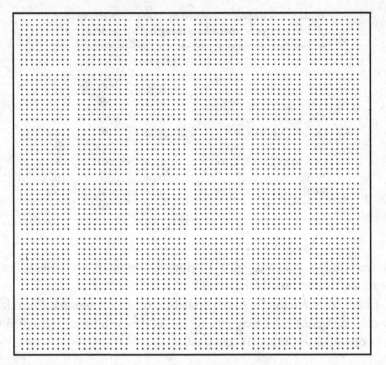

Fig. 6.17. Each of the 3,600 dots in this array represents a single Avida organism in Fig. 6.16.

of these populations evolved EQU, a highly significant difference from the fraction
that did so in the reward-all environment."

Firmly entrenched ideology can blind its proponents to the obvious. How
did the stairstep information get there to allow Avida to work? The answer
is obvious. It was put there by a designer. The writers of Avida agree in
part:

> "Some readers might suggest that we stacked the deck by studying the evolution
> of a complex feature that could be built on simpler functions that were also
> useful. However, that is precisely what evolutionary theory requires, and indeed,
> our experiments showed that the complex feature never evolved when simpler
> functions were not rewarded."

Yes, the deck is stacked. And if this is what "evolutionary theory requires,"
then evolution requires intelligent design. As we show in our discussion of

the search for the search (S4S), searching for information-rich environments is exponentially harder than performing the search being sought.

We have published a detailed critique of Avida where sources of active information are identified and measured.[6] Those interested in nitty-gritty details should examine this paper available on EvoInfo.org.

6.2.5.1 *Performance*

Here are some results from simulations using Avida software.[7]

6.2.5.1.1 The evolutionary approach

Using analysis applied to simulations using Avida, we showed that, using 85 instructions,[r] there are about 1.82×10^{108} of the possible $26^{85} = 1.87 \times 10^{120}$ programs that will compute an EQU. For a single random sequence of 85 instructions, the probability of choosing a program that generates EQU is the ratio of these two numbers which is $p = 9.71 \times 10^{-13}$. The corresponding endogenous information is the $-\log_2$ of this probability which is

$$I_\Omega \approx 39.9 \text{ bits.}$$

This means that the chance of a randomly drawn sequence of 85 instructions has more than one chance in one trillion of producing an EQU.

All of the logic operations in Table 6.3 can be used as stair steps in Avida. What happens when a stair or two is removed? Here is a comparison of different results for Avida using $I_\oplus$ = active information per instruction.[s]

---

[r]Fifteen instructions, native to the Avida organism, allow the process of replication in the evolutionary search. The 85 instructions referred to here are added for a total of 100 instructions.

[s]† The active information per instruction is $I_\oplus = \mathbf{E}[I_+ / \beth]$ where $\mathbf{E}$ denotes expectation, $\beth$ is a random variable corresponding to the number of instructions, and I_+ is the corresponding active information. We estimate this mean using K trials by

$$I_\oplus \approx \frac{I_\Omega}{K} \sum_{\text{successes}} \frac{1}{\beth_k},$$

where $\beth_k$ is the number of instructions for the case of a successful trial. Results for unsuccessful trials do not contribute to the sum.

1. Using Avida's default parameters (all 26 instructions and all steps), we find that

$$I_{\oplus}^{\text{Avida}} \approx 1.90 \times 10^{-9} I_{\Omega}.$$

2. Removing some steps from the staircase should worsen performance. If we remove rewarding the XOR and NOR stair steps in Table 6.2, we get the worse figure

$$I_{\oplus}^{\text{XOR\&NOR}} \approx 1.36 \times 10^{-9} I_{\Omega}.$$

3. Let's take away a few more steps. Besides XOR and NOR, let's remove AND_N and OR stairs. The active information per instruction becomes even smaller

$$I_{\oplus}^{\text{XOR\&NOR\&OR\&AND\&OR}} \approx 0.62 \times 10^{-9} I_{\Omega}.$$

4. What happens if, in the previous example, we took away the AND step instead of the OR step? In this case, it looks like the OR step is more important than the AND step since

$$I_{\oplus}^{\text{XOR\&NOR\&OR\&AND\&AND}} \approx 0.52 \times 10^{-9} I_{\Omega}.$$

6.2.5.1.2 The ratchet approach

The fitness available from the stair steps can be viewed as an oracle. When an Avida program is presented to the stairstep oracle, the oracle responds with a fitness value. As we saw with the Hamming oracle, there are bad and good ways to extract active information from the stairstep oracle. Remember how we were able to extract more active information from a Hamming oracle using more efficient algorithms? We can do the same with the stairstep oracle resident in the Avida program. In fact, evolutionary extraction of active information is a relatively poor method for mining information from the stairstep oracle.

The other search algorithm we analyze is a simple ratchet approach. Let's take a single Avida organism and mutate it. If the mutation gives a smaller fitness according to the stairstep oracle, we discard the mutation and try again. This way, the fitness of the single Avida organism never decreases. In terms of query count, this ratchet (or stochastic hill climbing) approach performs significantly better than Avida's evolutionary approach using 3,600 organisms. Let's go through the same scenarios as we did for the Avida search. For notation contrasts, let's call the active information per instruction $R_\oplus$ (R for *ratchet*) rather than $I_\oplus$. Here are the results:

1. Using all 26 operations and all stair steps, we get

$$R_\oplus^{\text{Avida}} \approx 25.30 \times 10^{-9} I_\Omega.$$

2. Removing the XOR and NOR steps, we get

$$R_\oplus^{\text{XOR\&NOR}} \approx 16.26 \times 10^{-9} I_\Omega.$$

3. Besides XOR and NOR, remove the AND_N and OR stairs. The active information per instruction for the ratchet search is then

$$R_\oplus^{\text{XOR\&NOR\&OR\&AND\&OR}} \approx 6.72 \times 10^{-9} I_\Omega$$

4. And lastly we remove the XOR, NOR, AND_N and AND stairs.

$$R_\oplus^{\text{XOR\&NOR\&OR\&AND\&AND}} \approx 8.05 \times 10^{-9} I_\Omega.$$

Interestingly, for the ratchet search the AND stairstep looks more important than the OR stairstep in this particular scenario. The opposite was true for evolutionary Avida.

6.2.5.1.3 Comparison

The active information results for the various searches are summarized in Table 6.4. The conclusion is inescapable. Like all evolutionary programs that work, Avida has resident in it an oracle mined by the evolutionary search program. And the evolutionary search program does a poor job of mining information in comparison to a simpler ratchet search.

6.2.5.2 *Minivida*

Minivida is a web-based simulator available on EvoInfo.org.[t] It is similar to, but not identical to, the simulation done by the main Avida program.[u]

---

[t] http://www.evoinfo.org/minivida/.

[u] In order to run efficiently in a web-based environment several elements of Avida have been simplified. All instructions relating to copying instructions are either ignored or only partially implemented. The simplifications have been done on non-critical elements of Avida's design

Table 6.4. Comparison of the endogenous information per instruction multiplier for Avida and a rachet search using the same stairstep oracles. The ratchet approach proved superior every time revealing that, on a per instruction basis, the ratchet search mines information from the stairstep oracle more efficiently than does Avida. (Each number in the table should be multiplied by 10^{-9}.)

	Avida	Ratchet
No Stairs Removed	1.90	25.30
XOR and NOR	1.36	16.26
XOR, NOR, AND_N, OR	0.62	6.72
InXOR, NOR, AND_N, AND	0.52	8.05

For those interested in details, Minivida runs on an internet browser and anyone can download and see the code.

Not only are the elements of Avida resident in Minivida, but the user can change them to see what happens.

- **Instructions.** Minivida's 26 instructions, the same as for Avida, are shown in Fig. 6.18. Minivida allows all of the instructions to be either turned off or on. Not all of the instructions available to Avida are useful. In fact a majority of them can be thrown out with affecting the ability of the programs to produce EQU. Under the instructions tab, you can control which instructions the program is allowed to do.
- **Fitness.** The fitness from the stair step finesses in Table 6.3 are represented in Minivida in Fig. 6.19. By default, in both Avida and Minivida, operations are rewarded relative to the number of NAND gates required to produce them. Minivida allows you to vary these values and even remove steps from the stairstep oracle.
- **Population Size.** Avida has a default population size of 3,600. Minivida lets you choose whatever population size you want. (See Fig. 6.20.)

(continued) so that this simulation is sufficiently similar to the original Avida program to make it helpful. An attempt has been made to maintain as much compatibility with Avida as possible, so most Avida programs should run on this simulator with the same results.

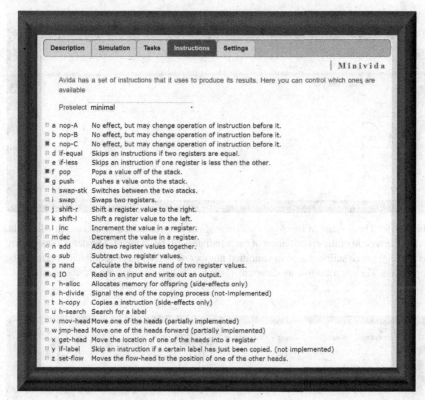

Fig. 6.18. A page from Minivida on EvoInfo.org. The 26 operations in Avida are all assigned a letter in the English alphabet.

6.2.5.2.1 The full program

For the full simulation, there are 3,600 digital organisms. All 26 instructions are used and the oracle uses all nine stairsteps.

Good Result: One outcome, shown in Fig. 6.21, converged to EQU in only 13,449,600 queries to the stairstep oracle. That's 3,736 generations of 3,600 organisms. As is seen in the figure, logic schematics are shown for each generation. For this version of EQU, six NAND gates are used.

Less Favorable Result: Another simulation with identical parameters had less favorable results. As shown in Fig. 6.20, 600,000,000 queries was not enough to create an EQU.

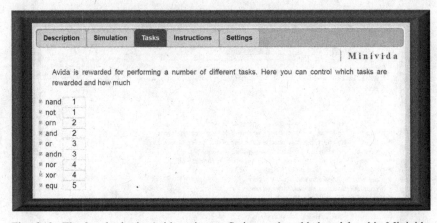

Fig. 6.19. The 9 stairs in the Avida staircase. Stairs can be added or deleted in Minivida. Also, the weight of the contribution of each stairstep can be changed. The default, as shown, is to weight each stair equal to the minimal number of NAND gates required to perform the operation. The contribution, as shown in Table 6.3, is two raised to the number of gates.

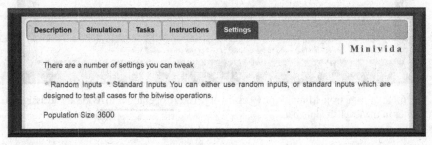

Fig. 6.20. In Minivida, you can specify the population size for your simulation. In Avida, the default value is 3,600 digital organisms.

6.2.5.2.2   Remove the staircase

If all of the Minivida parameters are kept the same except that the staircase is removed, what happens? For Avida, when there are no stairs,

> "... none of these populations evolved EQU, a highly significant difference from the fraction that did so in the reward-all environment."

The same thing happens in Minivida when only the top stair, EQU, is recognized and rewarded. In the simulation shown in Fig. 6.23, over 2 billion

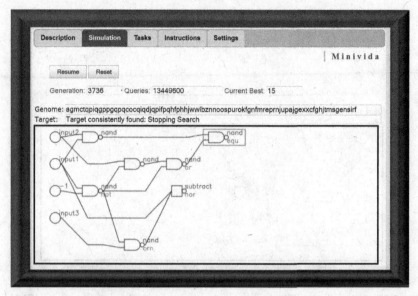

Fig. 6.21. A successful implementation of Minivida using all of Avida's default parameters. EQU is found. The evolved computer code giving rise to this result is in the block labeled Genome. Each letter is assigned an operation in Fig. 6.18. A less favorable result using the same parameters is shown in Figure 6.22.

queries produce no result. This is understandable. Jumping to the top of the building when there are no stairs is difficult.[v]

6.2.5.2.3   Minimal instructions

Not only are all 26 instructions not needed in Avida, some junk instructions actually get in the way of finding an EQU. If we strip away all of the instructions we consider obstructions, the *minimal set* of instructions remains.[w] When the junk instructions are scrapped, Minivida finds EQU very quickly.

The target EQU is now easily found. A simulation result is shown in Fig. 6.25 where EQU is found by Minivida in 11 generations using less than 40 thousand queries to the stairstep oracle.

The EQU is found using the minimal set even when the stairsteps are removed. See Fig. 6.26.

---

[v] See the cartoon in Fig. 6.24.
[w] The minimal set of instructions is shown by the checked boxes in Fig. 6.18.

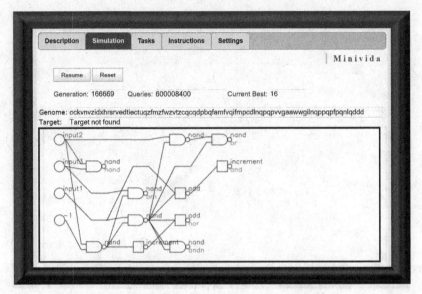

Fig. 6.22. Six hundred million instructional queries are insufficient to generate an EQU in this Minivida run.

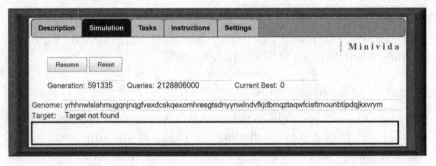

Fig. 6.23. When the staircase is removed, no EQU is found in this simulation after over 2 billion queries.

So much active information can be extracted from the oracle when using minimal instructions, even a blind search will work. Setting the population size to one in the *Minivida Settings* tab results in a blind search. For the minimal set of instructions the simulation in Fig. 6.25[x] finds EQU in less than 20,000 program queries to the full stairstep oracle. The minimal

---

[x]† The operation performed in Fig. 6.25 is $((\neg X)\bar{\cap}(Y\bar{\cap}(X\bar{\cap}Y)))\bar{\cap}(X\bar{\cap}Y) = EQU$.

Fig. 6.24. Carefully constructed stairstep active information is one of many design parameters that allows Avida to work. From the S4S, finding a design for a successful search is more difficult than performing the search itself.

number of 5 NAND gates is used but using different corrections than Fig. 6.27.

6.2.6 *Avida is intelligently designed*

The analysis of Avida *via* simulation results reveals that Avida is designed to work. We believe the authors of the original Avida paper had no goal of deceit or sneaking active information to the search. A more probable explanation is that they were numbed by their exhilaration in demonstrating Darwinian evolution and the celebration of its success. Here are some facts and one supposition supporting the claim Avida is intelligently designed.

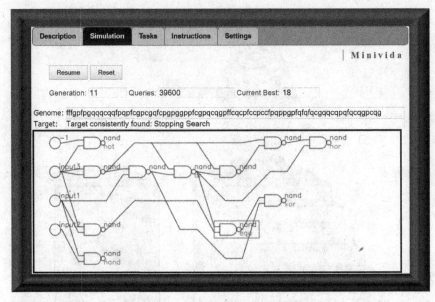

Fig. 6.25. Using the minimal set of instructions in Minivida. Three thousand six hundred digital organisms are used per generation. All stairsteps are used.

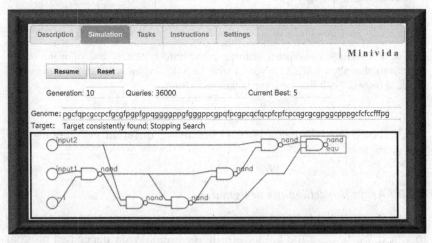

Fig. 6.26. The minimal set of instructions works in Minvida even when the stairsteps are removed and only the EQU is awarded.

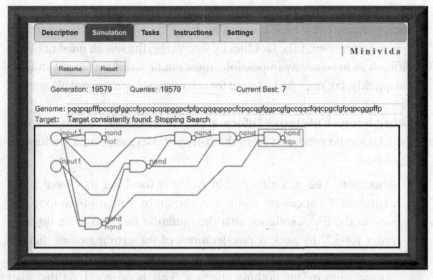

Fig. 6.27. When the junk instructions are purged from Minivida, the remaining minimal instruction set is efficient at accessing active information. Blind search in this simulation found EQU quickly.

- **Man-In-The-Loop.** First the supposition. There is no report of which we are aware that documents the iterative development of Avida. Software is written and repetitively tested, debugged, and tested again. Design by its nature is iterative and a man-in-the-loop is part of this process. We are aware of no one who writes search software of non-trivial length that works correctly on the first try.[y]

- **Stair Step Active Information.** Avida works only because of the designed staircase. Avida's designers are to be congratulated on designing a staircase where each step displays functional viability. Without a carefully designed staircase, the probability of success for a search for EQU nosedives. The unassisted endogenous information of the search, at $I_\Omega = 40$ bits is simply too large.

- **Obfuscation Tuning.** With the minimal set of instructions, EQU is found quickly. Too quickly. We could claim to prove evolution by rolling two dice until we rolled snake eyes (two ones). Avida using minimal instructions is not as easy as rolling snake eyes, but converges

---

[y] See Chapter 3.7.3.

too quickly to inspire any awe. Junk instructions, get in the way of convergence. They have allowed an EQU to evolve slowly enough to appear interesting. Like Goldilocks's porridge, the search must not be as difficult as to be nearly impossible, must not be so easy as to get an EQU too quickly, but must be just right for convergence in a reasonable amount of time.

- **Other Sources of Active Information.** Other design conditions allow the EQU to be produced from the software. Here are some we haven't discussed:

  1. **Mutation.** The mutation rate in Avida is fixed but its choice is not explained. Chances are that it was chosen by a man-in-the-loop. We saw in the EV simulation that the mutation rate had to be tuned in order for EV to work. Considerations of the extreme cases dictates that they must always be a sweet spot for mutation. At one extreme, no mutation means nothing changes. This is no good. At the other extreme, everything changes and we are performing a blind search. For Avida, this makes no sense. A sweet spot must exist between these two extremes.

  2. **Fitness.** Why are the fitness values shown in Table 6.3 chosen? The fitness of the stairstep is $f = 2^G$ where G is the number of NAND gates required for minimal representation. Why not use $f = G$ or $f = \log G$ or $f = G^{10}$? The default choice of the fitness in Avida fully crafts the staircase to allow easy accent while discouraging the search from falling down the stairs. It is the work of a *penalty function artist*.

  3. **Initialization.** For reasons we explain elsewhere,[8] the initialization of Avida is critical.

Lastly, we make note of the obvious: Avida slams into Basener's ceiling. The program will never do anything more exciting than generate an EQU. It will never learn how to play chess or solve the Cracker Barrel Puzzle.

6.2.7   *Beating a dead organism*

Despite its limitations and clear use of wired information to succeed, Avida has had a significant impact in academia. *Supply Side Academics* measure success by publications and funding. The National Science Foundation (NSF) awarded a \$25 million grant for the study of digital evolution. The grant is centered at the Digital Evolution Lab[9] (DevoLab[z]) at Michigan State University. The Lab was founded by Charles Ofria and Richard Lenski, who are two of the co-authors of the Avida paper.[10]

The Avida software platform has been embraced by numerous authors claiming to have demonstrated various aspects of Darwinian evolution.[11] Avida has even been used as a teaching tool to support Darwinian evolution.[12] Papers continued to appear even after our debunking of Avida in 2009.[13]

Some mathematical facts apparently take time to sink in.

6.3 Metabiology[14]

Metabiology is a model of Darwinian evolution grounded in the discipline of algorithmic information theory.

Gregory Chaitin developed algorithmic information theory[15] independently in parallel with Kolmogorov and Solomonov. Building on the work of Gödel and Turing, algorithmic information theory deals in part with mind-bending mathematics such as proving there are unprovable propositions and knowing there are things that can't be known.

Gregory Chaitin has embarked on the project of developing a field he calls *metabiology*.[16] The underlying impetus in Chaitin's model is to provide a solid mathematical under pinning for Darwinian evolution. Although the mathematics are beautiful, the end model sheds no light on the process of biological Darwinian evolution theory. Metabiology's approach is to consider evolution in the abstract realm of computer programs run on Turing machines. Chaitin claims, essentially, that evolution is about software and not hardware or simulations. By focusing on the software alone, Chaitin hopes to focus on the pure essence of the evolutionary process.

Chaitin evolves programs that output strange enormously large numbers dubbed *busy beaver* numbers. He shows that the programs will produce

---

[z]Ironically (or not) Devo was the name of a 1970's rock band who wore red plastic flower pots for hats and whose name is a contraction of the word "de-evolution." The title of their first 1978 album began with the question "Are We Not Men?"

large numbers very quickly.[aa] Chaitin's model uses

- *A halting oracle*: A computer program known not to exist.
- *Busy beaver numbers*: Numbers so large, making a list of them is non-computable.[17]
- *Unbounded albeit finite resources*: Both in space and time.

And despite these extraordinary tools, Chaitin's algorithm follows in nearly all respects the other models of evolution we have analyzed. The halting oracle is a source of knowledge that can be mined in numerous different ways with a varying amount of active information resulting.

Turing's halting problem[18] is taught to undergraduates in computer science. Given an arbitrary computer program X, there is no meta computer program, Y, able to analyze X to announce whether or not, when run, X will stop or not. Turing showed that writing a halting program Y is not possible. A hypothetical device capable of answering this question is dubbed a *halting oracle*. Halting oracles do not exist.[bb]

[aa]† As measured in big *O* notation.

[bb]† **The Halting Problem in a Nutshell**. All computer programs can be written as a binary string of ones and zeros. Each possible program can therefore be written as a positive integer. We arrange all these programs in a list starting with the smallest. The pth program is appropriately labeled as an integer p. Let H(p, i) be a halting oracle program that decides if a program p with input i, written p(i) halts or not. H(p, i) outputs a 1 if the program p(i) halts and 0 if it doesn't. As with programs, all possible inputs can be ordered and assigned an integer number, in this case i. Then, consider the program

```
function N(p) {
    if(H(p,p) == 1) {
        while(1 == 1) {
        }
    }
    return 0;
}
```

Given a program p, this program outputs a 0 when p(p) doesn't halt and runs forever in a while loop if the program p(p) halts. What, then, of the program N(N)? In this case, the program is analyzing itself to see whether or not it will halt. The results are contradictory. If H(N,N)=1 in the program, we get stuck in the while loop forever. But H(N,N)=1 means the program N(N) halts. This is a contradiction. Likewise, if H(N,N)=0 in the program, a zero is printed and the program stops. But H(N,N)=0 means the program

If halting oracles did exist, all open problems in that could be disproven by a single counterexample could be solved. An example is Goldbach's *conjecture* which hypothesizes that all even numbers greater than two can be written as the sum of two primes. Instances include $10 = 7+3, 56 = 51+5$, $1028 = 1021 + 7, 73200 = 73189 + 11$ and $143142 = 71429 + 71713$. A program X could be written to sequentially test each even number to see if it were the sum of two primes. If a counterexample is found, the program stops and declares "I have a counterexample!" Otherwise, the next even number would be tested. If Goldbach's conjecture were true, the program would run forever. If a halting oracle existed, we could feed it X. If the halting oracle says "this program halts" Goldbach's conjecture is disproved. If the halting oracle says "This program never halts," then Goldbach's conjecture is proved. There are numerous other open problems in mathematics that can be proved or disproved if we had a halting oracle. Examples are the question of the existence of an odd perfect number and the Riemann hypothesis. Substantial cash prizes are offered for the solution to many of these problems.

Chaitin uses the halting oracle in his model of Darwinian evolution.[19] The use of computer tools proven not to exist, like the halting oracle, is at the outset, an obvious major strike against a theory purporting to demonstrate reality.

6.3.1 *The essence of halting*

All evolutionary processes seek increased fitness. In Chaitin's metabiology, fitness is found through seeking *busy beaver numbers*.[20,21] Although not immediately apparent, there is a relationship between busy beaver numbers and the halting problem.

Here is the standard definition for busy beaver numbers: For a Turing machine with N states that utilize only zeros and ones, what program will output the largest number? This program is dubbed the busy beaver program and the number output is the busy beaver number. As N increases, the busy beaver number cannot get smaller.

(continued) N (N) doesn't halt. Another contradiction. Thus, the assumption there is a halting program H (p, i) that works for all p and i has been proven false.

Simply generating larger and larger numbers is not difficult. For example, a program can be improved by the construction of a new program that runs the original program and adds one to the result. Without imposition of any stop criterion, the search for ever-increasing numbers as N increases requires unbounded computational resources. The increase is enormous in the search for busy beaver numbers. Chaitin's metabiology programs have unbounded length and can run for an unbounded amount of time. The unboundedness undermines the creativity required to solve the large number problem. With unbounded resources and unbounded time, one can do almost anything. One can also quickly exceed the computational resources of the known universe.[22]

Chaitin uses a variation of the busy beaver number, calling $BB(K)$: the largest number of steps using a (prefix free) computer program of length K before the program halts. Here is the relationship between $BB(K)$ and the halting problem. When $BB(K)$ is reached, all programs of length K that haven't halted will never halt. And because $BB(K)$ gets larger as K increases, all programs with length less than K that haven't halted will also never halt. Achieving $BB(K)$ therefore is the same as having a halting oracle for all computer programs less than or equal to K. Since a halting oracle is not possible, it is not surprising that $BB(K)$ soon increases faster than can be computed.

6.3.2   *On with the search*

Chaitin's metabiology asks whether busy beaver programs can be found by evolving computer programs. Unlike many other proposed models of evolution, there is no artificially imposed fitness function or artificially designed fitness landscape. Rather, metabiology's landscape flows from the mathematical structure of Turing machine programs. Using the mathematical construct of busy beaver programs, Chaitin's metabiology does not undertake to deliberately assist the evolutionary process as many other evolutionary models have done. We note, though, mathematics is replete with other number theoretic landscapes, e.g. prime numbers, perfect numbers and twin primes.

Numerous properties in Chaitin's model have been critically examined earlier in this Chapter.[23] Alleged demonstrations of the power of evolution, for example, often work by extracting information from an oracle. The oracle is the source of the information and is responsible for the success of a program. Evolution is a process that merely mines this information. Often, other search approaches can mine the information more efficiently.[24] Chaitin's model is an example.

We have discussed four ways to extract information from a Hamming oracle in Chapter 5.4.3.1.[cc] When presented a binary string, the base 2 Hamming oracle returns a single number indicating the number of mismatches in 1's and 0's between a binary string of specified length, L, and an unknown target of the same length. We outlined a poor way to use the Hamming oracle to do this, and a good way and a better way. The goodness of an extraction method was measured by the number of queries required to fully identify the target string. The fewer the queries, the better. We also identified an optimal best search. The number of queries is minimized but the computational overhead of each query becomes large.

Metabiology's use of the halting oracle differs from use of a Hamming oracle, but there are compelling similarities. Both seek identification of an unknown binary string of fixed length L. In the case of metabiology, the binary string corresponds to a computer program. For both oracles, there are both efficient and inefficient ways to extract active information. Chaitin uses the halting oracle to search for busy beaver numbers in three different ways. He dubs the different algorithms

- Exhaustive Search (Poor)
- Random Evolution (Good)
- Intelligent Design (Better)

The contrast between the use of the Hamming and halting oracles is summarized in Table 6.5.[dd] For exhaustive search, both Hamming and halting oracle programs require 2^L queries on the average. The introduction of guided search in ratchet search (a.k.a. stochastic hill climbing) and metabiology's "random evolution" greatly decreases the number of expected operations. Both oracles can be used more intelligently to reduce the expected number of queries even lower.

[cc] In Chapter 5.4.3.1.
[dd] Details of the entries for the Hamming oracle are from Chapter 5.4.3.1.

Table 6.5. Comparison of three ways to use the Hamming and the halting oracles. The value given next to metabiology requires interpretation in big O notation which is read "on the order of" $O(L^2)$ means[ee] "on the order of L^2".

Oracle	Hamming Oracle Hamming		Metabiology Halting Oracle	
Poor	Needle-In-A-Haystack Oracle	2^L	"Exhaustive Search"	2^L
Good	Ratchet Search	$\leq L$	"Random Evolution"	between L^2 and L^3
Better	Ewert's FOOHOA	$\ll L$	"Intelligent Design"	L

Chaitin properly refers the halting oracle as a source of creativity in metabiology. The three different methods he uses to mine active information from the halting oracle again reveal that the evolutionary process itself does not create information. It is simply mining information from a source of information, the oracle. And it does so more poorly than other available algorithms.

†6.3.3 *The math: "intelligent design" in metabiology*

(Those impatient with math will want to skip to the next section.)

Metabiology is indirectly delated to Chaitin's number. Recall prefix-free computer programs.[ff] Let p be the index of a prefix-free code and let the length of the code be ℓ_p bits. The *Kraft inequality*[gg] is illustrated in Fig. 6.28 and requires that

$$\sum_{\text{all } p} 2^{-\ell_p} \leq 1. \tag{6.1}$$

Some of the programs at the leaves of the tree halt. Some don't. Chaitin's number,[25] illustrated in Fig. 6.29, is this sum over all of the programs that halt.

$$\Omega = \sum_{\text{all } p\text{'s that halt}} 2^{-\ell_p}. \tag{6.2}$$

[ff]† Introduced in Chapter 2.2.1.1.
[gg]† Also introduced in Chapter 2.2.1.1.

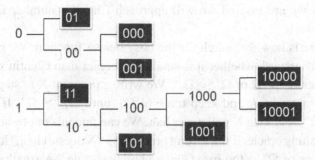

†Fig. 6.28. Illustration of the Kraft inequality in Equation (6.1). Each of leaves on the tree correspond to a prefix-free computer program. (Actual programs are, of course, much longer.) The leaves are prefix-free because one program cannot be the start or prefix of another. For example, one program is 001. None of the other programs begins with 001. There are two programs of length $\ell = 2$, three programs are of length $\ell = 3$, one of length 4 and two of length 5. Then $2 \times 2^{-2} + 3 \times 2^{-3} + 1 \times 2^{-4} + 2 \times 2^{-5} = 1$, which satisfies the Kraft equality.

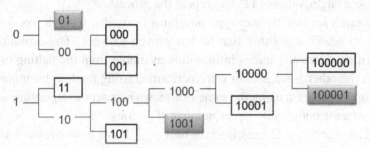

†Fig. 6.29. Illustration of Chaitin's number. The tree of programs is the same as in the previous figure. The programs in the shaded boxes halt. The others don't. Chaitin's number, Ω in Equation (6.1), is tallied like the Kraft inequality except the sum is only over programs that halt. In this example Chaitin's number is $\Omega = 2^{-2} + 2^{-4} + 2^{-6} = 0.328125$.

If we run all programs of length L or fewer for L steps, some of the programs will stop. We can look at all of these programs and compute

$$\Omega_L = \sum_{\substack{\text{all } p\text{'s not more than } L \text{ bits} \\ \text{that halt in } L \text{ or fewer steps}}} 2^{-\ell_p}.$$

Clearly, we have not yet identified all of the programs that have stopped so that $\Omega_L \leq \Omega$. But as the number of steps increases without bound

$(L \to \infty)$ we are assured we will approach Chaitin's number $\Omega_L \to \Omega$ from below.

So here is how we search for the busy beaver function: We guess at a number Ω^* and ask whether it is smaller or bigger than Chaitin's number, i.e. whether $\Omega^* > \Omega$ or $\Omega^* < \Omega$.[hh] We write a program X to step through different values of L and keep track of Ω_L until $\Omega_L \geq \Omega^*$. If we have guessed $\Omega^* > \Omega$ then X will never halt. We can find this out by submitting X to the halting oracle. If the halting oracle says "X doesn't halt," it is saying "Your guess of Ω^* is too big. Guess a smaller value." A smaller value is guessed and the process is repeated. If the halting oracle, on the other hand, says "X halts," it is telling us that $\Omega_L \leq \Omega^* < \Omega$. So we run all programs of one bit one step, 2 and 1 bit programs for two steps,[ii] ..., programs 10 bits or less for 10 steps, etc. We keep tally of $\Omega_1, \Omega_1, \ldots, \Omega_{10}, \ldots, \Omega_\ell$ at each step. We keep going until we get an L such that $\Omega_L \geq \Omega^*$ We know this will eventually happen because the halting oracle says it will. We can then choose a larger value of Ω^* and repeat the process.

Search for busy beaver type programs is similar. Chaitin has devised a clever search algorithm that he has proven to work. The evolutionary algorithm efficiently mines information available from the halting oracle. If, on the other hand, search were performed using random bit mutations within the program using the same oracle, we suspect the algorithm would require a astronomically larger number of queries.

The search for Ω uses interval halving.[jj] If we have overshot Ω, the halting oracle tells us so and we make a smaller guess. If the halting oracle says the program will halt, we keep finding Ω_ℓ for ever increasing ℓ until we find an L where $\Omega_L \geq \Omega$.

An illustration is shown in Fig. 6.30. A staircase of Ω_ℓ is shown as a function of ℓ. It asymptotically approaches Ω as $\ell \to \infty$. Our first guess of Ω is $\Omega^*[1]$. A program X[1] is written to sequentially compute Ω_ℓ for ever increasing ℓ until it equals or exceeds $\Omega^*[1]$. The halting oracle says X[1]

[hh]† We are assured equality doesn't happen when Ω^* is rational because Ω has been shown to be irrational.

[ii]† There are, of course, probably no one or two bit programs that are complete programs. This is for illustration.

[jj]† As we saw in Chapter 2.2.2.2, interval halving is an effective method of performing search when resources allow.

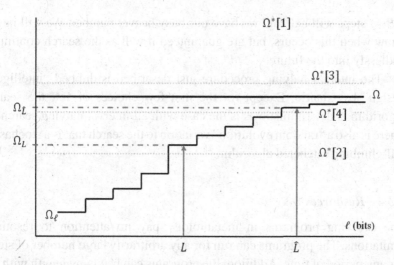

Fig. 6.30. Interval halving in the "intelligent design" version of metabiology.

will never stop. So the estimate needs to be reduced. We choose $\Omega^*[2]$ and submit X[2] to the halting oracle which says that the program will eventually stop. So we run X[2] until we get an $\ell = L$ such that $\Omega_L \geq \Omega^*[2]$.

Once Ω_L is found, we know the true value of Ω lies between Ω_L which we know is too small and $\Omega^*[1]$ which we know is too big. Using interval halving, we next test $\Omega^*[3]$ which lies between these two values. This is shown in Fig. 6.30. The program X[3] is presented to the halting oracle, which responds "This program will never halt." In other words, $\Omega^*[3]$ is too big. Now we know Ω lies between Ω_L and $\Omega^*[3]$. The intermediate value of $\Omega^*[4]$ is chosen and X[4] is presented to the halting oracle, which announces that the program will halt. Thus, as before, we sequentially evaluate Ω_ℓ's until we find an $\ell = \hat{L}$ where, for the first time, $\Omega_{\hat{L}} \geq \Omega^*[4]$. We now know that the true value of Ω lies between $\Omega_{\hat{L}}$ and $\Omega^*[3]$. This interval halving process is repeated to get estimates closer and closer to Ω.

Recall, however, that the search is not for Chaitin's number Ω, but for busy beaver numbers. The interval halving process allows us to do so. When all the programs ℓ bits long have been run for L steps ($\ell < L$), some of the programs have stopped and some have not. Of those that have halted, the program that ran the longest provides a lower bound to $BB(\ell)$. As the interval halving search progresses, more and more programs will halt giving better and better estimates to $BB(\ell)$. Eventually, the program with

$BB(\ell)$ steps will halt and we have our busy beaver number. We will never know when this occurs, but are guaranteed it will as the search continues endlessly into the future.

The interval halving procedure just described is dubbed "intelligent design" by Chaitin. Except for the first few choices of Ω^*, the search algorithm is deterministic as is the case with all interval halving searches. There is also a "random evolution" variation to the search that is a stochastic hill-climbing ratcheted algorithm.[kk]

6.3.4 *Resources*

The evolving programs in metabiology pay no attention to resource limitations. The programs can run for any arbitrarily large number of steps for any period of time. Additionally, programs can be of any length with no penalty imposed for longer programs. Running a program for the number of steps for busy beaver type numbers requires more computational resources than are universally available.

Chaitin also considers the class of all programs, not merely those limited by a certain size. As a result, there is no program which is a true busy beaver, only some programs with longer run times. It is always possible to produce a longer Turing machine program which produces a larger number. Creativity is required in attempting to solve the problem because the program must make the most out of limited resources. Unbounded resources separates metabiology from any possibility of modeling reality.

The most interesting part of Chaitin's result is that he has shown evolution amongst Turing machine programs which we would not suspect are suitable for the evolutionary process. We would think that changing a single bit of a Turing machine program can produce very large changes in the output. As any computer programmer will tell you, landscapes of computer program fitness are not smooth. Changing a single character can cause a program to crash, generate a totally different output, or transform a program that halts into one that runs forever. As a result, we would not expect evolution to fair well. Metabiology overcomes this problem by running

---

[kk]As discussed in Chapter 5.4.3.1.

all viable programs. This is very computationally expensive and is only possible in theory where there are no resource limitations.

Chaitin notes that, as his metabiology is made more biologically realistic, he will probably be unable to prove results and instead have to be content with simulation. It seems that the first step toward making it realistic would be the introduction of these limitations. However, it is the very absence of such limitations which makes the proofs work.

Even if the question of resources was not an issue, metabiology has the same characteristics as other models of Darwinian evolution such as Avida and EV. An embedded resident source of knowledge is mined for active information that allows the seeking stochastic process to perform a successful search.

6.4   Conclusion: Sweeping a Dirt Floor

Despite firm establishment of the concept of active information in our 2009 paper,[26] there are still claims being published that purport to demonstrate Darwinian evolution as a creator of information. All of the efforts we have seen so far show a lack of awareness of conservation of information, or else they misinterpret it or fail to take it into account.

Here is a quick synopsis of two more failed attempts to model Darwinian evolution.

6.4.1   *Evolving a Steiner tree*

Assume we want to build roads for a bunch of houses so that the roads connect every house with every other house. Furthermore, we want the overall length of the roads minimized. The connection that does this is called a Steiner tree.[ll] An example is shown in Fig. 6.31.

David Thomas wrote a genetic algorithm that came close to solving the Steiner tree. Wishing to discredit proponents of ID, David Thomas wrote[27]

"...two pillars of ID theory, 'irreducible complexity' and 'complex specified information' [have been] shown not to be beyond the capabilities of evolution, contrary to official ID dogma."

[ll]Steiner trees can be constructed in higher dimensions. For our purposes, two dimensions suffice.

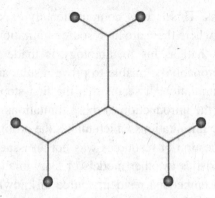

Fig. 6.31. A Steiner tree for six cities.

At the conclusion of his blog post, Thomas issued a challenge to ID advocates[28]:

> "If you contend that this algorithm works only by sneaking in the answer (the Steiner shape) into the fitness test, please identify the precise code snippet where this frontloading is being performed."

So we did.[29] One snippet is presented in Chapter 5.2.3 and it shows that Thomas tuned his algorithm to work.

Other code indicates that the mutation rate was tuned using a man-in-the-loop.

Adjusting parameters in genetic algorithms is common practice and is in fact necessary in cases, like the Steiner tree problem, where fine tuning is required to make the search work. In addition, based on knowledge of the problem being solved, a number of other sources of active information were identified in our analysis.[30]

6.4.2   *Time for evolution*

In a paper published in the prestigious *Proceedings of the National Academy of Sciences*, Wilf and Ewens[31] offer a model that they claim supports Darwinian evolution. Their model is similar to the problem of guessing letters in a word or phrase, as on the television game show *Wheel of Fortune*. A phrase 20,000 letters long is specified, with each letter in the phrase corresponding to a gene locus that can be transformed from its initial "primitive" state to a more advanced state. Finding the correct letter for a particular position in the target phrase roughly corresponds to finding a beneficial mutation in the corresponding gene. During each round of mutation all positions in the phrase are subject to mutation, and the results are selected by a *partitioned search*[32] oracle based on whether the individual positions match the final target phrase. Those that match are frozen in place for the remainder of the search.

Partitioned search oracles are loaded with active information. Consider, for example, a string of ones and zeros used as a target. We choose a random string of ones and zeros and the oracle tells us which of the bits match. We keep these locations while flipping all of the incorrect bits. We have identified the target with one query! If the binary string is L bits long, a blind search would require, on average, $Q = 2^L$ queries. Wilf and Ewens do not use the partitioned search oracle opting instead for random mutations of the incorrect characters. They mine the available source of information poorly.

The assistance of the oracle as the source of active information is undeniable.

6.4.3 *Finis*

AVIDA, EV, Dawkin's WEASEL problem, and metabiology are all written by proponents trying to demonstrate Darwinian evolution works. Each is a designed stochastic process that, like Buffon's needle[mm] or tetherball,[nn] converges to one or more fixed points. To do so, each requires sources of knowledge to generate active information to guide the search. The success of the program depends on an intelligent designer. Conservation of information requires it.

Notes

1. George Gaylord Simpson and William S. Beck, *Life: An Introduction to Biology*, 2nd ed. (London: Routledge and Kegan, 1965).
2. William A. Dembski and Robert J. Marks II, "Conservation of Information in Search: Measuring the Cost of Success." *IEEE Transactions on Systems,*

[mm] See Chapter 4.2.1.
[nn] See Chapter 4.2.3.

Man and Cybernetics A, Systems and Humans, vol. 39, #5, September 2009, pp. 1051–1061.

3. W. Ewert, William A. Dembski, and R.J. Marks II, "Evolutionary synthesis of Nand logic: dissecting a digital organism." *Proceedings of the 2009 IEEE International Conference on Systems, Man, and Cybernetics*. San Antonio, TX, USA, pp. 3047–3053, (2009).

4. American Civil Liberties Union of Pennsylvania, Kitzmiller *et al.* v. Dover Area School District, http://www.aclupa.org/our-work/legal/legaldocket/intelligentdesigncase/dovertrialtranscripts/ (URL date May 2, 2016).

5. American Civil Liberties Union of Pennsylvania, Dover Trial Transcripts, http://www.aclupa.org/our-work/legal/legaldocket/intelligentdesigncase/dovertrialtranscripts/ (URL date May 2, 2016).

6. W. Ewert, W.A. Dembski, and R.J. Marks II, "Evolutionary synthesis of Nand logic: dissecting a digital organism." *Proceedings of the 2009 IEEE International Conference on Systems, Man, and Cybernetics*. San Antonio, TX, USA, pp. 3047–3053, (2009).

7. *Ibid.*

8. *Ibid.*

9. Digital Evolution Lab: http://devolab.msu.edu/ (URL date May 2, 2016).

10. R.E. Lenski, C. Ofria, R.T. Pennock, and C. Adami, "The evolutionary origin of complex features." *Nature*, 423(6936), pp. 139–144 (2003).

11. Here are a few:

- **2003:** Bill O'Neill, "Digital evolution." *PLoS Biology* 1(1), e18 (2003). F. Tim Cooper and C. Ofria, "Evolution of stable ecosystems in populations of digital organisms." *Artificial Life*, 8. *Proceedings of the Eighth International Conference on Artificial Life*, International Society for Artificial Life: 9–13 December 2002; Sydney, Australia. (2003).

- **2004**: C. Ofria and O.C. Wilke, "Avida: A software platform for research in computational evolutionary biology." *Artif Life*, 10(2), pp. 191–229 (2004); M. Dusan, R.E. Lenski and C. Ofria, "Sexual reproduction and muller's ratchet in digital organisms." *Ninth International Conference on Artificial Life*. (2004); W. Daniel and C. Adami, "Influence of chance, history, and adaptation on digital evolution." *Artif Life*, 10(2), pp. 181–190 (2004); H. George *et al.*, "Using Avida to test the effects of natural selection on phylogenetic reconstruction methods." *Artificial Life*, 10(2), pp. 157–166 (2004); Goings, Sherri, *et al.*, "Kin selection: The rise and fall of kin-cheaters." *Proceedings of the Ninth International Conference on Artificial*

Life (2004); J. Tyler and C.O. Wilke. "Evolution of resource competition between mutually dependent digital organisms." *Artif Life* 10(2), pp. 145–156 (2004).

- **2005**: C. Ofria and O.C. Wilke, "Avida: Evolution experiments with self-replicating computer programs." *Artificial Life Models in Software* (Springer, London, 2005), pp. 3–35; Carl Zimmer, "Testing Darwin." *Discover*, 26(2), pp. 28–34 (2005); Philip Gerlee and T. Lundh, "The genetic coding style of digital organisms." *Advances in artificial life* (Springer, Berlin Heidelberg, 2005), pp. 854–863.

- **2006**: Christoph Adami, "Digital genetics: unravelling the genetic basis of evolution." *Nat Rev Genet*, 7(2), pp. 109–118 (2006); B. David Knoester *et al.*, "Evolution of leader election in populations of self-replicating digital organisms." Dept. Comput. Sci., Michigan State Univ., East Lansing, MI, Tech. Rep. MSU-CSE-06-35 (2006); C.O. Wilke and S.S. Chow, "Exploring the evolution of ecosystems with digital organisms." *Ecological Networks: Linking Structure to Dynamics in Food Webs* (Oxford University Press, New York, 2006), pp. 271–286; Terence Soule, "Resilient individuals improve evolutionary search." *Artif Life*, 12(1), pp. 17–34 (2006).

- **2007**: Robert T. Pennock, "Models, simulations, instantiations, and evidence: the case of digital evolution." *J Exp Theor Artif Intell*, 19.1, pp. 29–42 (2007); Benjamin E. Beckmann *et al.*, "Evolution of cooperative information gathering in self-replicating digital organisms." *First International Conference on Self-Adaptive and Self-Organizing Systems, 2007. SASO'07.* IEEE, 2007; Heather J. Goldsby *et al.*, "Digitally evolving models for dynamically adaptive systems." *Proceedings of the 2007 International Workshop on Software Engineering for Adaptive and Self-Managing Systems.* IEEE Computer Society (2007); B. David Knoester *et al.*, "Directed evolution of communication and cooperation in digital organisms." *Advances in Artificial Life* (Springer Berlin Heidelberg, 2007), pp. 384–394; Elena, F. Santiago *et al.*, "Effects of population size and mutation rate on the evolution of mutational robustness."*Evolution*, 61(3), pp. 666–674 (2007); J. Clune, C. Ofria, and R.T. Pennock, "Investigating the emergence of phenotypic plasticity in evolving digital organisms." *Advances in Artificial Life* (Springer, Berlin Heidelberg, 2007), pp. 74–83; Dehua Hang *et al.*, "The effect of natural selection on the performance of maximum parsimony." *BMC Evol Biol*, 7(1), p. 94 (2007).

- **2008**: J. Heather Goldsby and Betty H.C. Cheng, "Avida-MDE: a digital evolution approach to generating models of adaptive software behavior." *Proceedings of the 10th Annual Conference on Genetic and Evolutionary Computation* (ACM, 2008); Philip McKinley *et al.*, "Harnessing digital evolution." *Computer* 41(1), pp. 54–63 (2008); J. Heather Goldsby *et al.*, "Digital evolution of behavioral models for autonomic systems." *International Conference on Autonomic Computing, 2008. ICAC'08*. IEEE, 2008; E. Benjamin Beckmann *et al.*, "Autonomic Software Development Methodology Based on Darwinian Evolution." *International Conference on Autonomic Computing, 2008. ICAC'08*. IEEE, 2008; Charles Ofria, Wei Huang, and Eric Torng, "On the gradual evolution of complexity and the sudden emergence of complex features." *Artificial Life* 14(3), pp. 255–263 (2008); M. Laura Grabowski *et al.*, "On the evolution of motility and intelligent tactic response." *Proceedings of the 10th Annual Conference on Genetic and Evolutionary Computation* (ACM, 2008); Santiago F. Elena and R. Sanjuán, "The effect of genetic robustness on evolvability in digital organisms." *BMC Evolutionary Biology*, 8(1), p. 284, (2008); J. Heather Goldsby and Betty H.C. Cheng, "Automatically generating behavioral models of adaptive systems to address uncertainty." *Model Driven Engineering Languages and Systems* (Springer, Berlin Heidelberg, 2008), pp. 568–583; Philip Gerlee *et al.*, "The gene-function relationship in the metabolism of yeast and digital organisms." *ALIFE*, (2008).

- **2009**: E. Beckmann Benjamin and P.K. McKinley, "Evolving quorum sensing in digital organisms." *Proceedings of the 11th Annual Conference on Genetic and Evolutionary Computation* (ACM, 2009); David B. Knoester *et al.*, "Evolution of robust data distribution among digital organisms." *Proceedings of the 11th Annual Conference on Genetic and Evolutionary Computation* (ACM, 2009); Sherri Goings and C. Ofria, "Ecological approaches to diversity maintenance in evolutionary algorithms." *IEEE Symposium on Artificial Life* (2009). ALife'09. IEEE (2009); B. David Knoester and P.K. McKinley, "Evolution of probabilistic consensus in digital organisms." *Third IEEE International Conference on Self-Adaptive and Self-Organizing Systems, 2009. SASO'09*. IEEE, 2009; Elsberry, Wesley R. *et al.*, "Cockroaches, drunkards, and climbers: Modeling the evolution of simple movement strategies using digital organisms." *IEEE Symposium on Artificial Life, 2009. ALife'09*. IEEE, 2009; Mark A. Bedau, "The evolution of complexity." *Mapping the Future of Biology* (Springer

Netherlands, 2009), pp. 111–130; Charles Ofria, David M. Bryson, and Claus O. Wilke, "Avida: A software platform for research in computational evolutionary biology." *Artificial Life Models in Software* (2009): 1; Heather J. Goldsby *et al.*, "Problem decomposition using indirect reciprocity in evolved populations." *Proceedings of the 11th Annual conference on Genetic and evolutionary computation* (ACM, 2009); C. Ofria, David M. Bryson, and Claus O. Wilke, "Avida." *Artificial Life Models in Software* (Springer London, 2009), pp. 3–35.

12. Robert T. Pennock, "Learning evolution and the nature of science using evolutionary computing and artificial life." *McGill J Educ* 42.2 (2007), pp. 211–224.
    Elena Bray Speth *et al.*, "Using Avida-ED for teaching and learning about evolution in undergraduate introductory biology courses." *Evolution: Education and Outreach* 2.3 (2009), 415–428.
    Diane Ebert-May and Everett Weber, "OOS 17–5: Avida-ED: Learning evolution through inquiry." (2007).
    W. Johnson, "Introduction to Evolutionary Computation (lesson & activity)." *Teach Engineering Digital Library Submission Portal* (2012).

13. Here are a few:

    • **2010**: Laura M. Grabowski *et al.*, "Early Evolution of Memory Usage in Digital Organisms." ALIFE. 2010; Goldsby, Heather J., David B. Knoester, and Charles Ofria, "Evolution of division of labor in genetically homogenous groups." *Proceedings of the 12th annual conference on Genetic and evolutionary computation* (ACM, 2010); Beckmann, Benjamin E., Jeff Clune, and Charles Ofria, "Digital evolution with avida." *Proceedings of the 12th annual conference companion on genetic and evolutionary computation* (ACM, 2010); Brian D. Connelly, Benjamin E. Beckmann, and Philip K. McKinley, "Resource abundance promotes the evolution of public goods cooperation." *Proceedings of the 12th annual conference on Genetic and evolutionary computation* (ACM, 2010).

    • **2011**: B. David Knoester and P.K. McKinley, "Evolving virtual fireflies." Advances in Artificial Life. *Darwin Meets von Neumann* (Springer Berlin Heidelberg, 2011), pp. 474–481; B. David Knoester and P.K. McKinley, "Evolution of synchronization and desynchronization in digital organisms." *Artif Life*, 17(1), pp. 1–20 (2011); Heather J. Goldsby *et al.*, "Task-switching costs promote the evolution of division of labor and shifts in individuality." *Proceedings of the National Academy of*

Sciences, 109(34), pp. 13686–13691 (2012); Heather J. Goldsby *et al.*, "The evolution of division of labor." Advances in Artificial Life. *Darwin Meets von Neumann* (Springer Berlin Heidelberg, 2011), pp. 10–18; Evan D. Dorn and Christoph Adami, "Robust Monomer-Distribution Biosignatures in Evolving Digital Biota." *Astrobiology*, 11(10), pp. 959–968 (2011); J. Daniel Couvertier and P.K. McKinley, "Effects of biased group selection on cooperative predation in digital organisms." *GECCO* (Companion). 2011; Robert John Platt, "The evolutionary dynamics of biochemical networks in fluctuating environments." Diss. University of Manchester, 2011.

- **2012**: Tomonori Hasegawa and Barry McMullin, "Degeneration of a von Neumann Self-reproducer into a Self-copier within the Avida World." *From Animals to AnimaLs* 12 (Springer, Berlin, Heidelberg, 2012), pp. 230–239; L. Bess Walker and C. Ofria, "Evolutionary potential is maximized at intermediate diversity levels." *Artificial Life*, 13 (2012); B. David Knoester *et al.*, "Evolution of resistance to quorum quenching in digital organisms." *Artif Life*, 18(3), pp. 1–20 (2012); W. Arthur Covert III *et al.*, "The role of deleterious mutations in the adaptation to a novel environment." *Artificial Life*, 13 (2012).
- **2013**: Jack Hessel and S. Goings, "Using Reproductive Altruism to Evolve Multicellularity in Digital Organisms." *Advances in Artificial Life, ECAL*, 12 (2013); T. Hasegawa and B. McMullin, "Analysing the mutational pathways of a von Neumann self-reproducer within the Avida world." (2013); Hasegawa, T. and B. McMullin. "Exploring the point-mutation space of a von Neumann self-reproducer within the Avida world." *Advances in Artificial Life, ECAL*, 2 (2013).

14. Some of this section is taken from E. Winston, W.A. Dembski, and R.J. Marks II, "Active information in metabiology." *BIO-Complexity* (2013).
15. G.J. Chaitin, *The limits of mathematics*, IBM TJ Watson Research Center, (1995).
    G.J. Chaitin, *The Unknowable* (Springer-Verlag, 1999).
    G.J. Chaitin, *Exploring Randomness* (Springer-Verlag, 2001).
    G.J. Chaitin, *Conversations with a Mathematician* (Springer-Verlag, 2002).
    G.J. Chaitin, *Algorithmic Information Theory* (Cambridge University Press, 2004).
    G.J. Chaitin, *Meta math!: The Quest for Omega* (Vintage, 2006).
    G.J. Chaitin, *Thinking about Gödel and Turing: essays on complexity*, 1970–2007 (World Scientific Pub Co Inc, 2007).

16. G.J. Chaitin, *Proving Darwin: Making Biology Mathematical* (Pantheon, 2012).
17. T. Rado, "On non-computable functions." *Bell Syst Tech J*, 41(3), pp. 877–884 (1962).
18. T.M. Cover and J.A. Thomas, *Elements of Information Theory*, 2nd edition, (Wiley, 2006).
19. G.J. Chaitin, *Proving Darwin, op. cit.*
20. *Ibid.*
21. S. Aaronson, "Who Can Name the Bigger Number?" http://www.scotta aronson.com/writings/bignumbers.html (URL date May 2, 2016).
22. S. Lloyd, "Computational capacity of the universe." *Phys Rev Lett*, 88(23), (2002).
    See also W.A. Dembski, "The logical underpinnings of intelligent design." *Debating Design: From Darwin to DNA* (Cambridge University Press, 2004).
23. Dembski and Marks (2009), *op. cit.*
    See also G. Montañez, W. Ewert, W.A. Dembski, and R.J. Marks II, "Vivisection of the EV Computer Organism: Identifying Sources of Active Information." *Bio-Complexity*, 2010(3), pp. 1–6 (2010).
    See also W. Ewert, W.A. Dembski, and R.J. Marks II, "Climbing the steiner tree — sources of active information in a genetic algorithm for solving the Euclidean Steiner tree problem." *Bio-Complexity*, 2012(1), pp. 1–14, (2012).
    See also W. Ewert, W.A. Dembski, and R.J. Marks II, "Evolutionary Synthesis of NAND and Logic: Dissecting a Digital Organism." *Proceedings of the 2009 IEEE International Conference on Systems, Man, and Cybernetics*, San Antonio, TX, USA (2009), pp. 3047–3053.
    See also W.A. Dembski and R.J. Marks II, "Life's Conservation Law: Why Darwinian Evolution Cannot Create Biological Information." In B. Gordon and W.A. Dembski, editors, *The Nature of Nature* (ISI Books, Wilmington, Del, 2011), pp. 360–399.
24. W. Ewert, G. Montañez, W.A. Dembski, and R.J. Marks II, "Efficient per query information extraction from a Hamming Oracle." *Proceedings of the 42nd Meeting of the Southeastern Symposium on System Theory*, IEEE, University of Texas at Tyler, March 7–9, 2010, pp. 290–297.
25. Cover and Thomas, *op. cit.*
26. Dembski and Marks (2009), *op. cit.*
27. D. Thomas, "War of the Weasels: An Evolutionary Algorithm Beats Intelligent Design." *Skepti Inq* 43, pp. 42–46 (2010).

28. D. Thomas, "Target? TARGET? We don't need no stinkin' Target!" (2006), http://www.pandasthumb.org/archives/2006/07/target_target_w_1. html (URL date May 2, 2016).

29. W. Ewert, W.A. Dembski, and R.J. Marks II. "Climbing the Steiner Tree– Sources of Active Information in a Genetic Algorithm for Solving the Euclidean Steiner Tree Problem." *BIO-Complexity*, 2012.

30. Ewert *et al., op. cit.*

31. H.S. Wilf and W.J. Ewens, "There's plenty of time for evolution." *Proceedings of the National Academy of Sciences*, 107(52), 22454–22456 (2010).

32. Dembski and Marks (2009), *op. cit.*

7

MEASURING MEANING: ALGORITHMIC SPECIFIED COMPLEXITY

"No amount of argument, or clever epigram, can disguise the inherent improbability of orthodox [Darwinian] theory; but most biologists feel it is better to think in terms of improbable events than not to think at all"

Sir James Gray[1]

7.1 The Meaning of Meaning

Fundamentally, meaning is related to context. An image of the sunset is meaningful because the viewer experientially relates it to other remembered sunsets. Any object exhibiting contextual content rather than random noise fits some pattern known *a priori* by the observer.

The two pictures in Fig. 7.1 contain the same number of bits, but the picture on the left has more meaning than the image of noise on the right. The fundamental context on the left is recognition of people. Additional context includes a rough idea of people's age, demeanor (most are smiling) and clothing. These assessments come from experiential context. There are various degrees of meaning depending on available context. If you know the identity of the people in the left image (Ray, Monika, Bob, Marilee, Kris, Tristan, Leslie, Joshua, Jeremiah), the picture has more meaning than if you don't. The degree of meaning increases with the context in which information is interpreted.

We can use this contextual definition of meaning to develop a model by which meaning can be measured.

Both Shannon and Kolmogorov–Chaitin–Solomonoff (KCS) measures of information are famous for not being able to measure meaning.[a] Shannon

---

[a]As discussed in Chapter 2.

Fig. 7.1. Illustration of meaningful information (left) versus random noise. Uncompressed, both images require the same number of bits and therefore the same Shannon information. The picture on the left has even more meaning if you know the people. Meaning is a function of context.

information is useful in assessing the amount of active information that has been infused into a search,[b] but is not able, by itself, to assess the final meaning of that design. A Blu-ray containing the movie *Braveheart* and a Blu-ray full of correlated random noise can both require the same Shannon information, as measured in bytes. The KCS measure of information is therefore also not able to, by itself, measure informational meaning. A maximally compressed text file can either contain a classic European novel or can correspond to a sequence of random meaningless alphanumeric characters.

To have meaning, an object needs to be complex. Both of the images in Fig. 7.1 are complex because they each require thousands of bits. Only the image on the left displays specificity: there are three women and six men, all fully clothed, mostly happy, one is wearing glasses, another a hat, one of the males is very young, etc. Appropriately, complex objects with specificity are said to display *specified complexity*.[2,3]

A striking example of the reader's ability to acquire image context is in Fig. 7.2. Upon first viewing, the image seems to have no meaning. It seems, rather, to consist of a number of meaningless gray splotches. During prolonged viewing of Fig. 7.2, however, the mind scans its library of content to place the image in context and the meaning of the image

---

[b]This was the topic of Chapter 5.4.2.

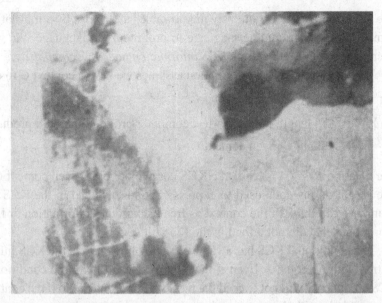

Fig. 7.2. Here is an image that initially appears to be only random splotches of gray. After prolonged viewing, however, the mind finds context by which to interpret the image. Once the context is established and the image seen, subsequent viewing will immediately revert to the contextual interpretation of the image: W.C. Stone[4] describes the image: "The object in the picture is a cow. The head of the cow is staring straight out at you from the center of the photograph, its two black ears framing the white face. The picture is widely used by the *Optometric Extension Program Foundation* to demonstrate the difference between eyesight and vision."

typically becomes clear. Interestingly, once the image is recognized by the reader, it will always be recognized. Spoiler alert: a description of the image is in the caption.

7.2 Conditional KCS Complexity

In order to discuss measuring specified complexity, a quick recap of Kolmogorov–Chaitin–Solomonov (KCS) information (or complexity) is necessary. The KCS complexity of Y is[c]

$K(Y)$ = the length of the shortest computer program that will produce output Y.

---

[c]This is covered more in detail in Chapter 2.2.1.

The KCS complexity is famously unknowable[d] and varies by a translation number from programming language to programming language. We will interchangeably use the terms *KCS information* and *KCS complexity*.

The conditional KCS information assumes we have a context C to use in compressing the string.

$K(Y|C)$ = the length of the shortest computer program that will produce

output Y given context C.

The notation $K(Y|C)$ is read "the KCS complexity of Y given context C." The length of any code used to express C is not included in the KCS bit count. We can think of the context as free background information or free subroutines that are not tallied in the KCS bit count.

The conditional KCS has a value equal to or lower than the KCS information with no context. Even if the context doesn't help, the conditional KCS complexity will not exceed the KCS without context. So if the context does not help with the compression, simply ignore it and we end up with the original KCS information without context. Thus

$$K(Y|C) \leq K(Y). \tag{7.1}$$

Let Y be the King James version of the Bible and let C be a list of batting averages for a Little League team. The batting averages have next to no useful information concerning the Bible and we would expect $K(Y|C) \approx K(Y)$.

The fact that KCS complexity $K(Y)$ is unknowable at first seems problematic. Note, however, any compression we achieve is an upper bound to the KCS complexity. Whatever compression we achieve must be equal to or greater that the maximum compression. We will call the upper bound the *observable KCS bound* and will denote it with a tilde as $\tilde{K}$. Since K is the length of the smallest program, we are assured that

$$K \leq \tilde{K}.$$

Lastly in our review, recall that the KCS complexity differs from computer to computer, at most, the length of the translation program between the

---

[d]This was proved in Chapter 2.2.1.3.

two programming languages.[e] We will assume that such additive constants are dwarfed by the other contributions to the KCS.

Those interested in these details are referred to our technical papers.[5]

7.3 Defining Algorithmic Specified Complexity (ASC)

Both of the images in Fig. 7.1 are highly improbable. The probability of choosing either by random bit selection is both identical and miniscule. Improbable events happen all the time. This probability, p, of randomly choosing either image can be expressed as the endogenous information[f] $I_\Omega = -\log_2 p$. The endogenous information, however, assume that we know nothing about the target. We might, though, know something about the target. For images, adjacent pixels change gray levels slowly. Images of faces display symmetry. For an object Y, we'll let $p(Y)$ describe the probability of choosing the target image using a specified model. There is a corresponding self-information of $I(Y) = -\log_2 p(Y)$ which we will dub the *intrinsic information*. Intrinsic information is a measure of the difficulty of constructing X using a model where the chance occurrence of X has probability $p(X)$. There is no consideration of meaning in the intrinsic information.

The *algorithmic specified complexity* (ASC), as illustrated in Fig. 7.3, is defined as:

$$A(Y, C, I) = I(Y) - K(Y|C). \tag{7.2}$$

The ASC is a function of

- $Y =$ the object to be compressed
- $C =$ the context
- $I(Y) =$ the intrinsic information of the object
- $K(Y|C) =$ the conditional KCS complexity

If context does help reduce the conditional KCS complexity, then the ACS will be small.

---

[e]As discussed in Chapter 2.2.1.
[f]Endogenous information is defined and discussed in Chapter 5.4.1.

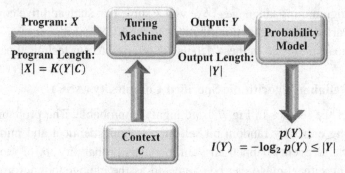

Fig. 7.3. Illustration of ASC is defined in Equation (7.2). The shortest program X to generate a given output string Y given context C is, by definition, an elegant program with length $|X| = K(Y|C)$. The probability of the occurrence of the output is determined by a probability model that evaluates the probability $p(Y)$ with corresponding self-information $I(X) = -\log_2 p(Y)$. The difference between this self-information and the length of the elegant program is the ASC.

It is simpler to write out this equation using shorter notation where arguments are assumed implicit.

$$A = I - K(Y|C). \tag{7.3}$$

If $\tilde{K}$ is used *in lieu* of K in the definition of ASC, then we are assured, since $K \leq \tilde{K}$, that

$$A = I - K(Y|C) \geq I - \tilde{K}(Y|C). \tag{7.4}$$

The observed conditional KCS complexity can thus be used to establish a lower bound for the ASC.

†7.3.1 *High ASC is rare*

Randomly generating items with meaning is highly improbable. If an object has a high ASC, the probability it occurred by chance is miniscule. The chance of getting more than 10 bits of ACS are less than chance in a thousand. Getting more than 40 bits is less than chance in a trillion. In general, for α bits,

$$\Pr[A \geq \alpha] \leq 2^{-\alpha}. \tag{7.5}$$

Proof: For those wanting to dive into the math, here we go. Using the definition in Equation (7.1)

$$\Pr[A(Y) \geq \alpha] = \Pr[I(Y) - K(Y|C) \geq \alpha] = \Pr[I(Y) \geq K(Y|C) + \alpha]$$

But $I(Y) = -\log_2 p(Y)$ so

$$\Pr[A(Y) \geq \alpha] = \Pr\left[p(Y) \leq 2^{-K(Y|C)-\alpha}\right]$$

According to the probability model, some output binary strings will be more probable than others. Define the set

$$\beta_\alpha(Y) = \left\{Y \mid p(Y) \leq 2^{-K(Y|C)-\alpha}\right\}$$

Comparing

$$\Pr[A(Y) \geq \alpha] = \Pr\left[p(Y) \leq 2^{-K(Y|C)-\alpha}\right] = \sum_{Y \in \beta_\alpha(Y)} p(Y)$$

$$\leq \sum_{Y \in \beta_\alpha(Y)} 2^{-K(Y|C)-\alpha} = 2^{-\alpha} \sum_{Y \in \beta_\alpha(Y)} 2^{-K(Y|C)}.$$

From the Kraft inequality,[g]

$$\sum_{Y \in \beta_\alpha(Y)} 2^{-K(Y|C)} \leq 1$$

and we have proved the proposition in Equation (7.5).

7.4 Examples of ASC

Now that the math is out of the way, we can illustrate ASC with some examples.

7.4.1 *Extended alphanumerics*

Here's an example of ACS and conditional KCS using extended alphanumeric characters using different types of context. Each example uses a codebook for context. The codebook tells us how we encode and decode the bits for compression and decompression. The thickness of the codebook does not enter into the calculation of the conditional KCS complexity. It is known context. In the series of examples to follow, the context becomes more useful and the conditional KCS becomes smaller.

Assume we are tasked with finding the ACS complexity of 5 million extended alphanumeric characters. We assume we have access to an

---

[g]The Kraft inequality is discussed in Chapter 2.2.1.2.

extended ASCII[h] codebook. Extended ASCII assigns an 8 bit binary number (one byte) to each of 256 different letters, symbols, numbers and instructions. For example, the ASCII codebook assigns "H" the binary string 01001000, "q" 01110001, "§" is represented by 10100111, and "?" by 00111111. A space has the number 00100000. If we have four million extended characters randomly drawn from the 256 available in the ASCII codebook, the resulting string has an intrinsic information of

$$I = 5,000,000 \text{ characters} \times 8 \text{ bits per character} = 40 \text{ million bits.}$$

1. **Extended ASCII context.** Using the extended ASCII codebook C_{ASCII} almost assuredly generates a sequence that is not compressible when the characters are drawn at random. The shortest program is something like

```
Print the 40 million bits: 0100 ... 1100. Stop.
```

The observed KCS conditional complexity in this case is

$$\tilde{K}(Y|C_{ASCII}) \underset{c}{=} 40,000,000,$$

where c is a constant. There is therefore no ASC since.

$$A_{ASCII} \geq I - \tilde{K}(Y|C_{ASCII}) \underset{-c}{=} 0.$$

2. **Frequency of occurrence[6] context.** Knowledge of the percentage of times a character is used can reduce the complexity. The letter "z" is the least used letter in the English language and the letter "e" is the most commonly used. The space is used even more. The percentage of the total of each character's occurrence is the letter's *frequency of occurrence* (FOO).

   Coding in communication uses the FOO to write a codebook which assigns short binary strings to frequently used characters and longer strings to less frequently used ones.[i,7] We'll call the context available

---

[h]ASCII = *American Standard Code for Information Interchange.*

[i]† For a known frequency of occurrence, Huffman Codes are optimal. The average transmitted binary string in bits is bounded by the entropy of the describing probability density and the entropy plus one bit.

from this codebook C_{FOO}. For FOO context, we know that

$$K(Y|C_{FOO}) \leq K(Y)$$

A classic example is the Morse code first used in telegraphy in the mid-19th century. A short tone, a *dot*, and a longer tone, a *dash*, serve as the binary alphabet. If we assign a "1" to a dot and a "0" to a dash, then the commonly used letter "e" in Morse code is assigned the one bit symbol "1". The less frequently used letter "z" is assigned the longer code 0011. Some intermediately used letters include "a" = 11 and "r" = 101. Using the context of a Morse code codebook, messages require fewer bits to characterize than when using the same number of bits for each letter using ASCII.[j]

3. **Dictionary.** A dictionary codebook can allow even greater compression. If we assume there are about five letters per word, including spaces, commas, periods, etc., there are about a million words in the 5 million character document. Consider, then, a codebook C_{DICT} containing all of the words used in the document. To illustrate, let's assume the dictionary codebook contains

$$2^{14} = 16,384 \text{ words.}$$

We number each of the words in the dictionary starting with the 14 bit string

$$00,000,000,000,000$$

for the first word in the dictionary and

$$11,111,111,111,111$$

for the last. Using 14 bits for each of the million words in the document then requires

$$\tilde{K}(Y|C_{DICT}) = 14 \text{ bits per word} \times 1,000,000 \text{ words} = 14,000,000 \text{ bits.}$$

---

[j]† Although the difference between of using the FOO applied to Morse code versus ASCII coding is clear, there are unaddressed issues in this comparison. Morse code requires a pause between groups of bits (It is not a prefix-free code). Morse code does not distinguish between upper and lower case letters, etc. Discussing these issues in detail will unnecessarily bog the presentation down in petty details, so is not addressed.

This is roughly a third of the 40 million bits required when using the extended ASCII codebook.

$$\tilde{K}(Y|C_{DICT}) = \tilde{K}(Y|C_{FOO}) + 26 \text{ million bits.}$$

The context provided by the dictionary has reduced the size of the elegant program[k] and the corresponding ASC is

$$A_{DICT} = I - \tilde{K}(Y|C_{DICT}) \underset{-c}{=} 26,000,000 \text{ bits.}$$

4. **Word FOO Dictionary.** Just as knowledge of characters, FOO results in lower conditional KCS complexity, so can knowledge of word FOO decrease the conditional KCS information. We can then tag commonly used words with short binary strings and rarely used words with longer strings. Commonly used words assigned short strings of bits include "the," "and," "a," "that," "an" and "of." Less commonly used words assigned longer binary strings include "xu," "aby," "adit" and "erinaceous."[l]

5. **Book ID.** The numbers in the previous examples are rough approximations of statistics of the King James translation of the Bible. If you have, as context, the contents of King James Bible along with 1,027 other books in your library on your computer, the only required information is specifying and opening the correct file. Since $2^{10} = 1,028$, each of the 1,028 books can be tagged with a 10 bit ID number. One of the indices

---

[k]† The astute reader will note that if there are too many words in the dictionary there will be no reduction in the bit count. If there are $2^{40} \approx 1$ trillion words in the dictionary, coding from the dictionary would require about $40 \times 1,000,000 = 40$ million bits, the same as the value for $K(Y)$. If there are more, say 2^{45} dictionary words in the dictionary, more than 40 million bits are required when the dictionary is used. Recall that $K(Y|C_{DICT})$ is the shortest representation and if using C_{DICT} makes the maximum compression smaller, then C_{DICT} is abandoned as a resource and, when the dictionary is too long, we revert to $K(Y|C_{DICT}) = K(Y) \approx 40$ million bits.

[l] "xu" = a monetary unit of Vietnam, equal to one hundredth of a dong. "aby" = expiate: make amends for. "adit" = a horizontal passage leading into a mine for the purposes of access or drainage. "erinaceous" = of, pertaining to, or resembling a hedgehog.

specifies the KJV of the Bible. If we call this context C_{LIB}, then

$$K(Y|C_{LIB}) \underset{c}{=} 10 \text{ bits},$$

$$\leq \underset{c}{\tilde{K}}(Y|C_{FOO}) \approx 40 \text{ million bits}.$$

C_{LIB} provides rich context and reduces the conditional KCS complexity to a handful of bits. The corresponding ASC is large.

$$ASC_{books} = I - K(Y|C_{LIB}) \approx 40 \text{ million bits}.$$

The more useful context brought to an interpretation of Y, the smaller the conditional KCS complexity.

The ACS results for the 5 million characters using different contexts are summarized in Table 7.1.

7.4.2 *Poker*

Here's an example of ASC using a standard deck of playing cards. In the game of poker, there are 2,569,682, possible five-card hands.[m] Any of these hands occurs with one chance in 2,569,682, corresponding to a self-information of $I = 21.3$ bits.

Table 7.1. A summary of the different observed conditional KCS information and ASC for 5 million ASCII characters. The intrinsic information for all cases is $I = 40$ million bits. The observed conditional KCS decreases as we go down the table and the ASC bound increases. This indicates that available context is becoming more and more useful in identifying the string.

Context		Codebook		$A \underset{c}{\geq}$
Extended ASCII	C_{ASCII}	Extended ASCII	40 million bits	0
Character FOO	C_{FOO}	Character FOO		
Dictionary	C_{Dict}	Dictionary	14 million bits	26 million bits
Word FOO	C_{WFOO}	Word FOO		
Library	C_{LIB}	Library	10 bits	40 million bits

---

[m]$\dagger \begin{pmatrix} 52 \\ 5 \end{pmatrix} = \frac{52!}{5!47!} = 2,869,682.$

Table 7.2. Poker hands and their algorithmic specified complexity (ASC).

Poker hand	Frequency	ASC
Royal Flush	4	16.0
Straight Flush	36	12.8
Four of a Kind	624	8.7
Full House	3,744	6.1
Flush	5,108	5.7
Straight	10,200	4.7
Three of a Kind	54,912	2.2
Two Pair	123,552	1.1
One Pair	1,098,240	0.0
High Card	1,302,540	0.0

To place the five cards in the context of poker, we will use the 10 categories of hands listed in Table 7.2. Specifying a category takes $\log_2 10 = 3.3$ bits.

Some hands in the 10 categories have more meaning than others. There are only four royal flushes and, in the context of poker, a royal flush is uniquely identified by specifying a suit: ♣ ♦ ♥ ♠. Since there are four suits, this requires only two bits of information. The conditional KCS complexity for a royal flush is thus $K(X|C) = 3.3 + 2 = 5.3$ bits and, for the royal flush. Thus $ASC = 21.3 - 5.3 = 16$ bits.

Uniquely identifying an element of the straight flush category requires more information, i.e. (1) specifying the suit and (2) identifying the highest card in the hand. There are 36 straight flushes so that $K(X|C) = 3.3 + \log_2 36 = 8.5$ bits and, for the straight flush, $ASC = 21.3 - 8.5 = 12.8$ bits.

We can continue and calculate the result of all of the ten categories. The resulting frequency and ASC is shown in Table 7.2. As expected, the weaker the hand, the lower the ASC.

7.4.3 *Snowflakes*

Using the same available context, strings can display different levels of ASC when, within the same context, a rare event occurs. We illustrate this using snowflakes.

"No two snowflakes are alike" is a common claim. In 1988, though, Nancy Knight was looking at snowflakes for the *National Center for Atmospheric Research* and found what appeared to be two identical snowflakes.[8] This is remarkable since an estimate for the number of visually indistinguishable distinct snowflakes[9] is 10^{18}. Snowflake shapes, however, are a function of temperature, humidity and other environmental conditions. Two snowflakes have a greater chance of being identical when formed in the same place at the same time.

Although Nancy Knight's two snowflakes were identical in appearance, Caltech physics professor Kenneth Libbrecht stresses that the two snowflakes were assuredly different at the atomic level.[10] The claim that "No two snowflakes are alike" therefore requires carefully defining the word "alike". A one-third milligram snowflake contains about 10^{19} water molecules[11,n] and the combinatorics of their possible arrangements into snowflakes at the molecular level is astronomical. This is further complicated by the occurrence of snowflakes forming around a speck of dust.[12] There can thus be molecules other than H_2O in the snowflake.

- **One Snowflake.** If we estimate that there are 10^{1000} possible snowflake types, then the corresponding intrinsic information is

$$I = \log_2 10^{1000} = 3322 \text{ bits.}$$

We can then have an astronomically thick codebook label where each of the snowflakes is indexed by a 3322 bit number. If all of the snowflakes are equally likely, the best we can do is print out the 3322 bit index of the snowflake. Then the observed conditional KCS information, in bits, is

$$\tilde{K}(Y|C) \underset{c}{=} 3322.$$

The corresponding ASC of the snowflake[o] is

$$A \geq I - \tilde{K}(Y|C) \underset{-c}{=} 0. \tag{7.6}$$

---

[n]Laboratory snowflakes have been created with only 275 water molecules.
[o]Using Equation (7.4).

Even though the snowflake is improbable, its low ASC bound indicates it has little specified complexity.[p]

- **Two Different Snowflakes.** Two arbitrarily chosen non-identical snowflakes will have twice the intrinsic information as one. The intrinsic information for two snowflakes (let's call it I_2) is thus[q]

$$I_2 = 2 \times I = 6644 \text{ bits.} \tag{7.7}$$

This is a case of the information additivity property of Shannon information.[r] The conditional KCS information for 2 snowflakes, let's call it $K_2(Y_2|C)$ where Y_2 is the bit string indexing the two snowflakes, is

$$\tilde{K}_2(Y_2|C) \underset{c}{=} 6644.$$

The same codebook, C, we used for one snowflake is used for the two different snowflakes. The corresponding ACS is

$$A_2 \geq I_2 - \tilde{K}_2(Y|C) \underset{-c}{=} 0.$$

The ACS for two different snowflakes is thus the same as the ASC calculated for one snowflake.[s] The same ASC of 0 will be calculated when calculating the ACS of 10 or a thousand non-identical snowflakes.

- **Two Identical Snowflakes.** The intrinsic information for two snowflakes is the same, whether or not they are the same, i.e. $I_2 = 6644$ bits. If the two snowflakes are the same, however, the KCS complexity is much less. We simply write out 3322 bits for the first snowflake and enter a REPEAT command. The observed conditional

---

[p]† The probability of an individual snowflake under our assumptions is $p = 10^{-1000}$. Thus

$$\Pr[\Pr(\text{snowflake}) \leq 10^{-1000}] = 1.$$

This expression is an example of the claim that "Improbable events happen all the time."

[q]† If there are 10^{1000} snowflakes, then the number of distinct snowflakes pairs with regard to order is $(10^{1000})(10^{1000} - 1) \approx (10^{1000})^2$. The corresponding two snowflake intrinsic information, consistent with Equation (7.7), is then

$$I_2 = \log_2(10^{1000})^2 = 2\log_2(10^{1000}) = 2 \times 3322 = 6644 \text{ bits.}$$

[r]As discussed in Chapter 2.2.2.
[s]The ASC for one snowflake is in Equation (7.6). It is essentially zero.

KCS complexity of the two snowflakes is about the same as it is for one snowflake: $\tilde{K}(X|C) = 3322$. The ACS for two identical snowflakes, let's call it A_{same}, is

$$A_{same} \geq I_2 - \tilde{K}(Y|C) = 3322 \text{ bits.} \tag{7.8}$$

This is a significant amount of ASC according to our model! Two identical snowflakes therefore have an *enormous* amount of specified complexity.

- **Probability of Occurrence.** For the two identical snowflake example, $\alpha + c \geq 3322$ and the probability an ASC exceeds this value is a very small number:

$$\Pr[A \geq \alpha + c \geq 3322 \text{ bits}] \leq 2^{-3322} = 0.$$

```
0000000000 0000000000 0000000000 0000000000 0000000000 0000000000 0000000000
0000000000 0000000000 0000000000 0000000000 0000000000 0000000000 0000000000
0000000000 0000000000 0000000000 0000000000 0000000000 0000000000 0000000000
0000000000 0000000000 0000000000 0000000000 0000000000 0000000000 0000000000
0000000000 0000000000 0000000000 0000000000 0000000000 0000000000 0000000000
0000000000 0000000000 0000000000 0000000000 0000000000 0000000000 0000000000
0000000000 0000000000 0000000000 0000000000 0000000000 0000000000 0000000000
0000000000 0000000000 0000000000 0000000000 0000000000 0000000000 0000000000
0000000000 0000000000 0000000000 0000000000 0000000000 0000000000 0000000000
0000000000 0000000000 0000000000 0000000000 0000000000 0000000000 0000000000
0000000000 0000000000 0000000000 0000000000 0000000000 0000000000 0000000000
0000000000 0000000000 0000000000 0000000000 0000000000 0000000000 0000000000
0000000000 0000000000 0000000000 0000000000 0000000000 0000000000 0000000000
0000000000 0000000000 9513808474 5598544585 6525238905 9987188429 1599954...
```

7.4.4 ACS in the Game of Life

ASC can be nicely illustrated using various functional patterns in Conway's celebrated *Game of Life*.[13]

7.4.4.1 The Game of Life

The *Game of Life* and similar systems allow a variety of fascinating behaviors in simple cellular automata.[14] The *Game of Life* is played on a grid of square cells. A cell is either alive (a one) or dead (a zero). A cell's status is determined by the other cells around it. Only four rules are followed.

1. *Under-Population.* A living cell with fewer than two live neighbors dies.
2. *Overcrowding.* A living cell with more than three living neighbors dies.

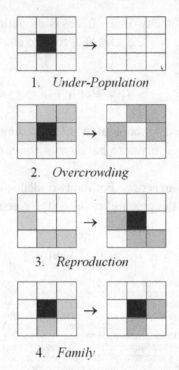

1. *Under-Population*

2. *Overcrowding*

3. *Reproduction*

4. *Family*

Fig. 7.4. Illustration of the four rules used in the *Game of Life*.

3. *Reproduction.* A dead cell with exactly three living neighbors becomes a living cell.
4. *Family.* A living cell with two or three live neighbor lives on to the next generation.

The four rules are illustrated in Fig. 7.4.

There are many object classes of *Game of Life* patterns. Here are the most elementary examples:

1. A *still life* is a pattern that doesn't change. Two examples are shown in Fig. 7.5. Many interesting patterns are given names. The patterns here are named *block* and *beehive.* Inspection of the four laws reveals that these patterns are, indeed, still lifes.
2. *Oscillators* change into another pattern in accordance to the rules of the Game of Life. For an oscillator of period two, this second pattern

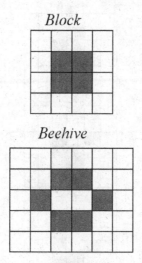

Block

Beehive

Fig. 7.5. Two examples of still lifes.

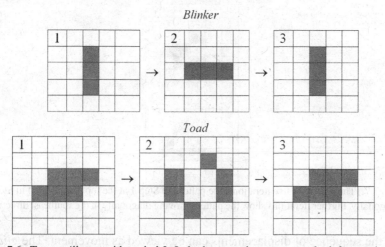

Blinker

Toad

Fig. 7.6. Two *oscillators* with period 2. In both cases, the pattern on the left turns into a different pattern shown in the middle. This second pattern then becomes the first pattern. The process continues and the pattern is seen to oscillate.

changes back to the original image. Two examples, the *blinker* and the *toad*, are shown in Fig. 7.6.

3. *Spaceships* are like oscillators except that when the original pattern is repeated, it is centered at a different position. As iterations continue,

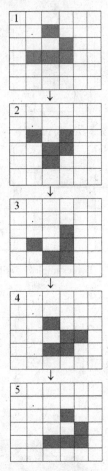

Fig. 7.7. The *glider*. In five iterations, the pattern in Step 1 at the top is replicated in Step 5 diagonally. Further iterations show the pattern moving diagonally in the southeast direction.

the sequence of displacements can be viewed as movement. The *glider* shown in Fig. 7.7 is an example. The pattern on the bottom after five steps is the same as the pattern in step one except that it has moved one cell over and one cell down.

Simpler *Game of Life* objects can appear as components in more complex objects as is the case with the *glider gun* shown in Fig. 7.8. On the top, patterns close in on each other, separate, and close in on each other again. Every time this happens, a *glider* is born. Immediately after birth,

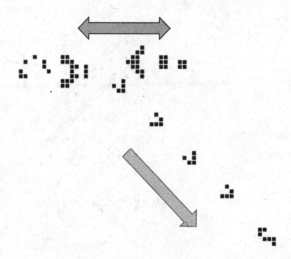

Fig. 7.8. The *glider gun*.

the glider begins its never-ending southeast trek. We have a glider gun that creates gliders. Can we go one step further and create a *breeder* that manufactures *glider guns* that then manufacture *gliders*? Remarkably, as illustrated in Fig. 7.9, the answer is yes. The cell configuration is dubbed a *puffer-type breeder.*

The *Game of Life* features an equivalent of the primordial soup in which, we are told, life first arose. Ash objects are life forms surviving when random pixels are chosen on a grid. There is a separate list for oscillators. As one expects, *Game of Life* life forms created by chance have low ASC.[15]

As witnessed by videos on YouTube, astonishing functionality can be achieved with the *Game of Life's* four simple rules.[16] If the reader is unfamiliar with the diversity achievable with these operations, we encourage them to view these and other short videos demonstrating the *Game of Life*. Static pictures not do justice to the remarkable underlying dynamics. There is also an active users group.[17]

7.4.4.2 *Cataloging context*

We should not go too far before tying the discussion back to the model of ASC complexity.[18] The context that allows us to make classes like *still lifes*, *oscillators* and *spaceships* is so familiar that it might escape our attention. We are familiar with *still life* objects that don't move, *oscillator*

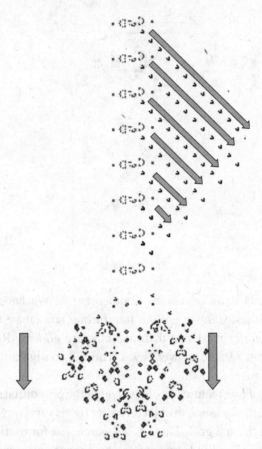

Fig. 7.9. A puffer-type *breeder* moves downward leaving *glider guns* in its wake. Each glider gun spews out *gliders* as shown in Fig. 7.8.

objects that periodically repeat themselves and objects moving at a constant velocity like *spaceships*. In such cases, we need not describe the *Game of Life* object with a sequence of bits denoting whether a cell is on or off. We can simply say "it's an oscillator" and, using this context, fill in additional details to specify the object. There are other descriptive attributes of the objects, such as the number of living cells in the initialization, the period of oscillation for oscillators and spaceships, and the speed and direction of spaceships. Using this and other context, the conditional KCS complexity can be reduced significantly.

Let's start a codebook for the *Game of Life* based on simple experiential context.

7.4.4.2.1 Still lifes and oscillators

Let Y denote an object in the *Game of Life* and $\oplus$ a single time step. If an object is a still life, it does not change after an iteration. Using our notation, we can denote a still life as obeying

$$Y = \oplus Y.$$

An example is the *block*, $Y = \blacksquare$ for which $\blacksquare = \oplus \blacksquare$.

Still lifes are a degenerate case of oscillators, one that repeats itself every cycle. An oscillator that repeats itself every two cycles has the property

$$Y = \oplus \oplus Y$$

which we can more concisely write as

$$Y = \oplus^2 Y.$$

But we must be careful. Still lifes' iterated twice also obey this property and our aim is to represent single cycle oscillators while excluding still lifes. So we will implicitly restrict the notation $Y = \oplus^2 Y$ to exclude objects obeying $Y = \oplus Y$. An example is the blinker, $Y = \blacksquare$, which we can characterize as

$$\blacksquare = \oplus^2 \blacksquare$$

The generalization is now obvious. The notation

$$Y = \oplus^i Y$$

indicates an object that repeats itself in i time steps without repeating itself in fewer time steps.

The membership of an object in the class of oscillators is now represented by the single number i that specifies the period of oscillation.[t]

---

[t]† The period of oscillation is $i - 1$.

We can now make a codebook for all oscillators. We'll start by ordering the still lifes ($i = 1$) by how simple they are by figuring out rules placing them in lexicographical order, i.e. a method to unambiguously number each still life starting at zero. Here are the rules we will use:

(1) **Cells:** Order objects from the smallest to the largest number of living cells

(2) **BB:** If the number of living cells is the same, order from smallest to largest bounding box area. In Fig. 7.5, for example, the area of the bounding box for the *block* is $4 \times 4 = 16$ and the area of the bounding box for the *beehive* is $5 \times 6 = 30$.

(3) **W:** If both (1) and (2) are the same, order from smallest to largest bounding box width.

(4) **N:** If all three of the previous criteria are the same, assign a base 2 number to the bounding box across rows and down columns, the same way we read English. Assign a 0 to a living cell and 1 to a dead cell. For the *block* in Fig. 7.5, the number is $(1111\ 1001\ 1001\ 1111)_2 = 63{,}903$ while the *beehive* is assigned the number $(111111\ 110011\ 101101\ 110011\ 111111)_2 = 1{,}070{,}521{,}599$.

(5) When there is more than a single frame, as is the case in oscillators and gliders, a score can be applied to every frame and the minimum value chosen.

Using these ordering rules, a list can be made of all still lifes as is shown in Fig. 7.11. The jth pattern in the codebook page is $Y = \oplus^1 Y, \#j$. Instead of describing all of the ones and zeros comprising the 5×5 array needed for the pattern called Ship #1, we simply need to say "$Y = \oplus^1 Y, \#11$." Using the context catalog in Fig. 7.10, this uniquely specifies Ship #1.

A similar codebook page can be made for single period oscillators. These would be denoted by $Y = \oplus^2 Y, \#j$. The first two of the single period oscillators are shown in Fig. 7.6. The first two entries of the codebook page for single period oscillators are

$$Y = \oplus^2 Y, \#1 \quad \text{blinker,} \tag{7.9}$$

$$Y = \oplus^2 Y, \#2 \quad \text{toad.}$$

Similar codebook pages can be constructed for $\oplus^3$, $\oplus^4$, etc.

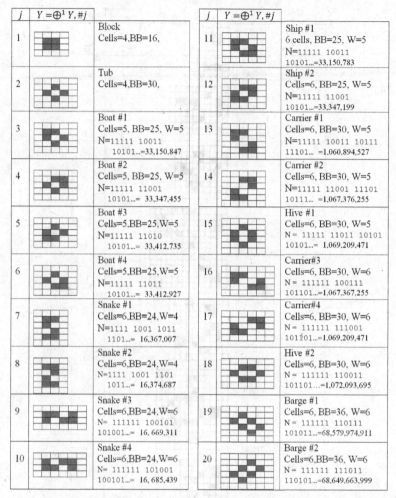

j	$Y = \oplus^1 Y, \#j$	
1		Block Cells=4,BB=16,
2		Tub Cells=4,BB=30,
3		Boat #1 Cells=5, BB=25, W=5 N=11111 10011 10101...=33,150,847
4		Boat #2 Cells=5, BB=25, W=5 N=11111 11001 10101...= 33,347,455
5		Boat #3 Cells=5,BB=25,W=5 N=11111 11010 10101...= 33,412,735
6		Boat #4 Cells=5,BB=25,W=5 N=11111 11011 10101...= 33,412,927
7		Snake #1 Cells=6,BB=24,W=4 N=1111 1001 1011 1101...= 16,367,007
8		Snake #2 Cells=6,BB=24,W=4 N=1111 1001 1101 1011...= 16,374,687
9		Snake #3 Cells=6,BB=24,W=6 N= 111111 100101 101001...= 16,669,311
10		Snake #4 Cells=6,BB=24,W=6 N= 111111 101001 100101...= 16,685,439

j	$Y = \oplus^1 Y, \#j$	
11		Ship #1 6 cells, BB=25, W=5 N=11111 10011 10101...=33,150,783
12		Ship #2 Cells=6, BB=25, W=5 N=11111 11001 10101...=33,347,199
13		Carrier #1 Cells=6, BB=30, W=5 N=11111 10011 10111 11101... =1,060,894,527
14		Carrier #2 Cells=6, BB=30, W=5 N=11111 11001 11101 10111... =1,067,376,255
15		Hive #1 Cells=6, BB=30, W=5 N= 11111 11011 10101 10101...= 1,069,209,471
16		Carrier#3 Cells=6, BB=30, W=6 N= 111111 100111 101101...=1,067,367,255
17		Carrier#4 Cells=6, BB=30, W=6 N= 111111 111001 101101...=1,069,209,471
18		Hive #2 Cells=6, BB=30, W=6 N= 111111 110011 101101...=1,072,093,695
19		Barge #1 Cells=6, BB=36, W=6 N= 111111 110111 101011...=68,579,974,911
20		Barge #2 Cells=6,BB=36,W=6 N= 111111 111011 110101...=68,649,663,999

Fig. 7.10. The beginning of a lexicographical ordering of all still lifes in the Game of Life. The *j*th entry in this list can be uniquely specified by the short index.

7.4.4.2.2 Gliders

Gliders are like moving oscillators. The pattern is repeated except that the replication occurs at a different location. In part, we recognize gliders in the context of movement. This can be used to add to our Game of Life catalog. We can denote left and right movement by horizontal arrows ($\leftarrow$ and $\rightarrow$) and up and down movement by vertical arrows ($\uparrow$ and $\downarrow$). The glider in

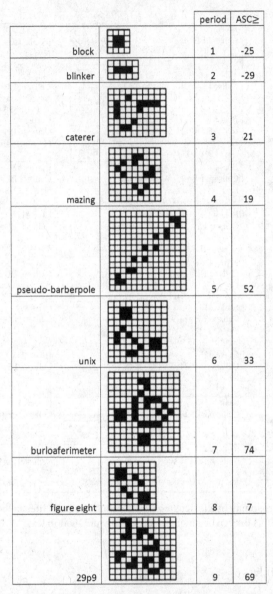

	period	ASC≥
block	1	-25
blinker	2	-29
caterer	3	21
mazing	4	19
pseudo-barberpole	5	52
unix	6	33
burloaferimeter	7	74
figure eight	8	7
29p9	9	69

Fig. 7.11. The simplest oscillators with different periods and the corresponding ASC bound. The dynamics of each oscillator can be viewed by a simple Google search of the name followed by *Conway's Game of Life*. Note the difference between the blinker's ASC bound here and Equation (7.11). The manner in which the ASC bounds were computed are similar but at variation. Note that the bounding rectangles are different.

Fig. 7.7 moves one cell down and one cell to the right in 4 cycles. Game of Life forms obeying such behavior can be characterized as

$$X \downarrow \rightarrow = \oplus^4 X.$$

This means that four cycles will reproduce the glider one unit to the right and one down. As is the case with the oscillators, we can make a page in the codebook labeled

$$X \downarrow \rightarrow = \oplus^4 X \# j.$$

The ordering of the entries would follow the same rules used for oscillators. The glider in Fig. 7.7 is the first on this list and would be designated by

$$X \downarrow \rightarrow = \oplus^4 X \# 1.$$

We can use such movement characterizations to estimate the ASC. Remember, though, there is no direct way of calculating the ASC. We can only get bounds. There are more efficient ways to catalog glider movement[19] that include variations that capture more complex movement. A higher ASC bound results.

7.4.4.2.3   Higher complexity

Let's move on to more complicated designs. Many patterns in the Game of Life can be constructed by colliding generalized gliders.[20] The *glider gun* in Fig. 7.8 is an example. In the description of the glider gun, we can make reference to the glider cataloged as $(X \downarrow \rightarrow = \oplus^4 X \# 1)$. The gun, on top, can be viewed as colliding gliders each of which is able to be indexed from the glider catalog pages.

The puffer-type breeder in Fig. 7.9 is even more complex. As the breeder moves down the page, glider guns are left in its wake. So there will be repeated references to the glider gun $(X \downarrow \rightarrow = \oplus^4 X \# 1)$ in the program describing the breeder. In turn, each of the glider guns spits out gliders. Characterizing of the big puffer cloud that creates the glider guns has not yet been done. But what is familiar about the puffer cloud? It is like an enormous glider that moves and repeats its pattern while, each time, spitting out a glider gun. Using such context can allow us to construct a catalog page of such objects.

Readers may respond to our cataloging and say "I can do a more compact characterization than that!" That, of course, is great. Your catalog will result a tighter bound on the ASC than ours does.

7.4.4.3 *Measuring ASC in bits*

All our effort thus far has been focused on setting up the structure of a codebook according to context in the Game of Life. We can use this structure to measure ASC in bits.

7.4.4.3.1 Measuring $I(X)$

Let's start with computing the self-information term, $I(X)$, in the ASC formula $ASC = I(X) - K(X|C)$. We'll model the literals in the Game of Life, like ▦, inside rectangles. If the rectangle has width w and height h, then there are $w \times h$ cells to specify. So we need a binary string that specifies w and h followed by a string of $w \times h$ bits. One way to efficiently represent integers is Levinson coding.[21] Let $l(n)$ denote the number of bits to define the integer n. Levinson coding of integers supplies compact prefix free characterization of n. For our purposes, the details of Levinson coding are of secondary importance.[u]

To count the number of bits needed to characterize X, we need to specify the rectangle length, the rectangle width and the identity all of the $w \times h$ bits inside the rectangle. The total number of bits we need to encode a literal is the sum of these values.[v]

$$I(X) = l(w) + l(h) + w \times h.$$

Here's an example. For the blinker ▦, $w = h = 5$. Since $l(5) = 5$ bits,

$$I_{\text{BLINKER}}(X) = 5 + 5 + 25 = 35 \text{ bits.} \tag{7.10}$$

---

[u]† Levinson coding expresses the number n using $l(n) = \lceil \log_2(n+1) + \log_2(n) \rceil + 1$ bits.
[v]There are more efficient ways to do this that require fewer bits, e.g. when there is a preponderance of ones sprinkled with a few zeros. We will stick with the simple sum operation, though, since it is easily explainable and easy to understand.

7.4.4.3.2 Measuring the conditional KCS complexity in bits

To measure the conditional KCS information, we need bit streams assigned to numbers, variables like X and Y and symbols such as $\rightarrow$, $\uparrow$, $\odot$, $\wedge$(power), $=$, and #. For the formalism so far, 32 characterizations suffice for the variables and the symbols. Since $2^5 = 32$, each variables and symbol can be assigned a five bit code. To declare there are no more operations to be had, we'll use the five bit sequence, 11111. Simply concatenating all the equations would not be a prefix free code since the binary encoding would be a valid prefix to other codes. After the last describing bit, 11111 is appended as a suffix preventing any longer codes from being valid and making the system prefix free.

For numbers, we'll use Levinson coding. To calculate the length of the encoding we add up the following.

1. Five bits for every symbol.
2. $l(n)$ bits for each number n in the equation.
3. The length of the bit encoding of any pattern literals, like ▦.
4. Five bits for the stop and integer call symbols.

Equation (7.9) assigns the blinker's symbols. Counting the symbols and adding a stop signal gives

$$\tilde{K}_{\text{BLINKER}}(X|C) = 8 \times 6 + 3 + 2 = 42 \text{ bits.}$$

Thus

$$ASC_{\text{BLINKER}} \geq 35 - 53 = -18 \text{ bits.} \tag{7.11}$$

The low ASC is not surprising since the blinker is the most common of all ash objects — even more common than the simplest still life, the block.[22]

7.4.4.3.3 Oscillator ASC

Oscillator periods vary according to the oscillator. Figure 7.11 lists the simplest oscillators with cycles of 1,2,3 all the way up to 9. An ASC bound is listed in each case. Not surprisingly, the ASC bound roughly increases with the period. The exception is the "figure eight" with period 8 that registers an ASC bound of only 7 bits.

7.4.4.4 *Measuring meaning*

Before we thought of analyzing the Game of Life, users had assigned meaning to the objects that can be generated by Conway's four simple rules. *Gliders, still lifes* and *oscillators* are so named because they relate to context common to experience. The fascinatingly complex objects such as *puffer breeders* are more complex than a simple glider. ASC is a simple methodology for assigning numbers to the specified complexity of objects in the Game of Life.

7.5 Meaning is in the Eye of the Beholder

An episode of the television series *Twilight Zone* titled "The Eye of the Beholder"[23] tells the story of an ugly woman about to undergo an operation to make her more beautiful. The black and white program, filmed in shadows, has a surprise ending. The woman is already beautiful but the doctors and nurse are hideously ugly — at least in our eyes. In their world, the opposite was true.

Poets agree. Shakespeare wrote[24]

"Beauty is bought by judgment of the eye"

David Hume concurs.[25]

"Beauty in things exists merely in the mind which contemplates them."

Let's substitute the term "meaningful information" for "beauty" and see how these phrases read.

"*Meaningful information* is bought by judgment of the eye"

"*Meaningful information* in things exists merely in the mind which contemplates them."

As interpreted from the viewpoint of the information definition applied to specified complexity, these phrases ring true in the sense that the degree of meaningful information is determined by the context of the observer. ASC is a model that allows quantitative assessment of contextual meaning.

Notes

1. Sir James Gray, *Nature*, 173, p. 227 (1954).
2. W. Ewert, William A. Dembski, and Robert J. Marks II, "Algorithmic Specified Complexity." In *Engineering and the Ultimate: An Interdisciplinary Investigation of Order and Design in Nature and Craft*, edited by J. Bartlett, D. Halsmer, and M. Hall (Blyth Institute Press, 2014), pp. 131–149.
3. W. Ewert, William A. Dembski and Robert J. Marks II, "On the improbability of algorithmically specified complexity." *Proceedings of the 2013 IEEE 45th Southeastern Symposium on Systems Theory (SSST)*, Baylor University, March 11, 2013.
4. W.C. Stone, *The Success System that Never Fails* (Prentice Hall, 1962).
5. Winston Ewert *et al.* (2014), *op.cit.*
   Winston Ewert *et al.* (2013), *op.cit.*
6. William A. Dembski, and Robert J. Marks, "Conservation of information in search: measuring the cost of success." IEEE Transactions on Systems, *Man and Cybernetics: Systems and Humans.* 39(5), pp. 1051–1061 (2009).
7. Thomas M. Cover and Joy A. Thomas. *Elements of information theory*, 2nd edition (John Wiley & Sons, 2012).
8. Chris V. Thangham, "No two snowflakes are alike." *Digital Journal*, December 2008.
9. And others estimate 10^{36} different types of snowflakes. Wonderopolis, "Why are all snowflakes different?" http://wonderopolis.org/wonder/why-are-all-snowflakes-different/ (URL date May 2, 2016).
10. *Ibid.*
11. A. M. Helmenstine, "Avogadro's Number Example Chemistry Problem." About.com, http://chemistry.about.com/od/workedchemistryproblems/a/avogadroexampl3.htm (URL date May 2, 2016).
12. A Guide to Snowflakes, "The Old Farmer's Almanac." http://www.almanac.com/content/guide-snowflakes. (URL date May 2, 2016).
13. Martin Gardner, "Mathematical Games — The fantastic combinations of John Conway's new solitaire game life." *Scientific American 223*, Oct 1970, pp. 120–123.
14. S. Wolfram, *A New Kind of Science* (Wolfram Media, Champaign, IL, 2002).
15. A catalog of common ash objects ordered by their frequency of occurrence is available online. There is a separate list for oscillators. http://wwwhomes.uni-bielefeld.de/achim/freq_top_life.html. (URL date May 2, 2016).

16. "Amazing Game of Life Demo." http://youtu.be/XcuBvj0pw-E, "Epic Conway's Game of Life," http://youtu.be/C2vgICfQawE, "Life In Life," http://youtu.be/xP5-iIeKXE8; (URL date May 2, 2016).
17. http://www.conwaylife.com/wiki/ (URL date May 2, 2016).
18. W. Ewert, William A. Dembski, and Robert J. Marks II, "Algorithmic specified complexity in the game of life." *IEEE Transactions on Systems, Man and Cybernetics: Systems, 2014.* Much in this section, including some figures, are from this paper.
19. *Ibid.*
20. LifeWiki http://www.conwaylife.com/wiki/Main_Page (URL date May 2, 2016).
21. A. Adamatzky, ed., *Collision Based Computing* (Springer Verlag, London, UK, 2002).
22. LifeWiki, *op.cit.*
23. Douglas Heyes, "The Eye of the Beholder." The *Twilight Zone*, CBS television, first aired November 11, 1960.
24. W. Shakespeare, *Love's Labours Lost* (1588).
25. D. Hume, *Essays: Moral, Political, and Literary* (Longmans, Green, and Company, 1907).

8

INTELLIGENT DESIGN & ARTIFICIAL INTELLIGENCE

"The most erroneous stories are the ones we think we know best — and therefore never scrutinize or question."

Stephen Jay Gould[1]

"Any physical theory is always provisional, in the sense that it is only a hypothesis: you can never prove it. No matter how many times the results of experiments agree with some theory, you can never be sure that the next time the result will not contradict the theory. On the other hand, you can disprove a theory by finding even a single observation that disagrees with the predictions of the theory. As philosopher of science Karl Popper has emphasized, a good theory is characterized by the fact that it makes a number of predictions that could in principle be disproved or falsified by observation. Each time new experiments are observed to agree with the predictions the theory survives, and our confidence in it is increased; but if ever a new observation is found to disagree, we have to abandon or modify the theory."

Stephen Hawking[2]

The fields of *artificial intelligence* (AI) and *intelligent design* (ID) both address *intelligence*. Intelligent design addresses the information observed in nature beyond that explainable by undirected randomness. Artificial intelligence has historically dealt with the mimicry of human intelligence. But computer based artificial intelligence lies far from the creative ability of the human mind. The limitations of computer creativity, as dictated by the law of conservation of information and algorithmic information theory (AIT) applied to computers, places a ceiling on the creativity both in computer models of nature and of human intelligence. Computers, are able in principle to execute any algorithm. There is something more happening in observable nature and the human mind that has not, and probably cannot, be explained by algorithms and computers.

281

The first seven chapters of this monograph have addressed issues concerning ID. A primary conclusion is that there is no successful model that explains the success of undirected Darwinian evolution. The evidence against this possibility is drawn largely from the debunking of computer models that claim evolutionary processes create information. The limitations of the computer, as evidenced by Basener's ceiling and conservation of information, preclude creativity beyond that infused into the program by the computer programmer. The same limitations are also used to argue that computers will never be creative. There is a link here worth exploring.

8.1 Turing & Lovelace: One is Strong and the Other One's Dead[3]

AI is claimed to be achieved when a computer program passes the *Turing Test*. But there is Strong AI and Weak AI, and success in passing the Turing Test requires only Weak AI. Strong AI seeks a manmade machine capable of displaying the intellectual abilities associated with humans. Weak AI seeks only to mimic the human intellect. Strong AI seeks to duplicate it.

8.1.1 *Turing's failure*

Alan Turing's test[4] requires that a text chat with a computer fools us into thinking that the computer is human. The Turing test only demonstrates Weak AI. By the Church–Turing thesis, all modern computers are variations of the Turing machine. Passing the Turing test today is impressive — but not surprising. Computers are only getting faster — not smarter. Deep Blue beating Garry Kasparov at chess and the computer program Watson winning at *Jeopardy!* are examples of what computationally powerful computers can do.

Alan Turing hoped that the computer would someday display all the intellectual capabilities of humans.[a,5] He investigated the science of computation, hoping to show someday that man was nothing more than a machine. Turing's genius resonated with his motivation and he is today

---

[a]Turing lost his close friend Christopher Morcom to bovine tuberculosis while both were still in their teens. Turing lost his faith in religion, embraced atheism, and began a quest to show that human intelligence was a material phenomenon.

considered the father of modern computer science. His contributions are taught to all computer science students. But Turing's larger goal, to show a computer is capable of matching man's creative intellect, has failed. Bringsjord, Bello and Ferrucci[6] summarize the current state of the Turing Test nicely:

> "[T]hough progress toward Turing's dream is being made, it's coming only on the strength of clever but shallow trickery. For example, the human creators of artificial agents that compete in present-day versions of [the Turing test] know all too well that they have merely tried to fool those people who interact with their agents into believing that these agents really have minds."

When introducing conservation of information, we offered numerous quotes at the beginning of Chapter 5 dismissing the dismissing the computer as a creative agent. The statements are equally applicable to strong AI. French philosopher and mathematician René Descartes expressed doubts about strong AI as early as 1637:

> "[W]e can easily understand a machine's being constituted so that it can utter words, and even emit some responses to action on it of a corporeal kind, which brings about a change in its organs; for instance, if touched in a particular part it may ask what we wish to say to it; if in another part it may exclaim that it is being hurt, and so on. But it never happens that it arranges its speech in various ways, in order to reply appropriately to everything that may be said in its presence, as even the lowest type of man can do."[7]

Roger Penrose, probably best known for sharing credit with Stephen Hawking for the Penrose–Hawking Singularity Theorem governing the physics of formation of black holes, also does not believe computers will ever display Strong AI.[8] Using Gödelian arguments, Penrose argues that humans have the ability to create beyond the ability of a computer. Gödel's requirement states that consistent formal systems based on foundational axiomatic rules, like the computer and its programs, are limited as to what they can do. According to Penrose, humans surpass this limit with their ability to innovate and create. Penrose believes there must be a materialistic explanation and looks to quantum mechanics for an answer.[b]

---

[b]His conjecture does not concern so-called quantum computers. Quantum computers have the same AI limitations as Turing machines.

If Penrose is right and we find out how to make machinery akin to what is between our ears, strong AI might be possible. With current computers and current models of quantum computers, however, that is almost certainly not possible.

8.1.2 *The Lovelace test and ID*

If the Turing test doesn't demonstrate Strong AI, what test does? Bringsjord, Bello and Ferrucci[9] suggest the *Lovelace test*, named after Augusta Ada King, the Countess of Lovelace.[c] The Countess is among those who believe computers will never be creative. Her quote in Chapter 5.1 bears repeating:

> "Computers can't create anything. For creation requires, minimally, originating something. But computers originate nothing; they merely do that which we order them, via programs, to do."

The criterion to establish computer creativity is named after her.[d]

The Lovelace test: Strong AI will be demonstrated when a machine's creativity is beyond the explanation of its creator.

Creativity should not be confused with surprise or the lack of an *explanation facility*. Some of our own recent work in evolutionary development of swarm intelligence[10] displays surprising behavior but, in retrospect, the results can be explained by examination of the computer program we wrote. Layered perceptron neural networks[11] lack embedded explanation

---

[c]DOD's Ada computer program is named after Ada Lovelace. Lovelace is considered by some to be the first computer programmer.

[d]† Here's Bringsjord, Bello and Ferrucci's more formal definition of the Lovelace test (LT):

DefLT | Artificial agent A, designed by H, passes LT if and only if

- A outputs o;

- A's outputting o is not the result of a fluke hardware error, but rather the result of processes A can repeat;

- H (or someone who knows what H knows, and has H's resources — for example, the substitute for H might he a scientist who watched and assimilated what the designers and builders of A did every step along the way) cannot explain how A produced o.

facilities, but behave in the manner the programmer intended. The Lovelace test demands innovation and creativity beyond this level. In a Gödelian sense, strong AI must create beyond the developmental level allowed by its foundational axioms, e.g. writing a great novel or proving the Riemann Hypothesis without the creator of the machine setting up all the dominoes to knock down.

Gödelian computer limitations are also linked to the inability of Turing machines to ever experience consciousness or free will.

> "AIT [based on Gödel's Theorem] and free will are deeply interrelated for a very simple reason: Information is itself central to the problem of free will. The basic problem concerning the relation between AIT and free will can be stated succinctly: Since the theorems of mathematics cannot contain more information than is contained in the axioms used to derive those theorems, it follows that no formal operation in mathematics (and equivalently, no operation performed by a computer) can create new information."
>
> "AIT appears to forbid free will not just in a Newtonian universe, or in a quantum mechanical universe, but in every universe that can be modeled with any mathematical theory whatsoever. AIT forbids free will to mathematics itself, and to any process that is accurately modeled by mathematics, because AIT shows that formal mathematics lacks the ability to create new information." Douglas S. Robertson[12]

Robertson is appealing to the limitations of computers to only execute algorithms. And the existence of free will, necessary to information creation (e.g. creativity), is beyond the algorithmic capacity of the axiomatic abilities of a Turing machine.

8.1.3 *"Flash of genius"*

In *Psychology of Invention*,[13] mathematician Jacques Hadamard[e] describes his own creative mathematical thinking as wordless and sparked by mental images that reveal the entire solution to a problem. Penrose agrees.[14] He says mathematical solutions to complex problems can appear wordlessly in his mind. It may take days to work out the details even though the solution is clearly understood.

---

[e]Engineers and computer scientists will recognize the Hadamard transform.

The great mathematician Friedrich Gauss[f] describes such an experience:

> "Finally, two days ago, I succeeded not on account of my hard efforts, but by the grace of the Lord. Like a sudden flash of lightning, the riddle was solved. I am unable to say what was the conducting thread that connected what I previously knew with what made my success possible."

The Lovelace test was even imposed by the U.S. Patent Office for a while. A "flash of creative genius"[g] was required for patentability.[h] Regarding patents, the Supreme Court ruled in 1941[15]:

> "The new device [to be patented], however useful it may be, must reveal the flash of creative genius, not merely the skill of the calling. If it fails, it has not established its right to a private grant on the public domain."

A machine that exhibits the Supreme Court's "flash of creative genius" or, as Gauss called it, "a sudden flash of lightning," displays Strong AI.

The flash of genius claimed by mathematicians Penrose, Gauss, and Hadamard is also experienced by creative minds in the arts. According to the Guinness Book of World Records, among the most recorded songs of all time is *Yesterday* written by Paul McCartney and John Lennon.[16] There were over 1,600 versions of the song recorded. Paul McCartney, who wrote the melody, was concerned he had not written the song.

> "For about a month I went round to people in the music business and asked them whether they had ever heard it [the melody to *Yesterday*] before. Eventually it became like handing something in to the police. I thought if no one claimed it after a few weeks then I could have it."[17]

Songwriter extraordinaire Bob Dylan[i] similarly chronicles the flash of genius experienced by composer Hoagie Carmichael who wrote the classic

---

[f] Gauss's namesakes are legion. They include (a) the Gauss (metric unit of magnetic field); (b) Gaussian elimination (solving simultaneous linear equations); (c) Gauss's Law for magnetism (one of Maxwell's equations); (d) Gaussian noise, and many more.

[g] *Flash of Genius* is the title of a book, later made into a movie, about the patent dispute concerning the invention of the intermittent windshield wiper.

[h] The policy was eventually rejected by Congress in 1952.

[i] Bob Dylan was awarded the 2016 Nobel Prize in Literature "for having created new poetic expressions within the great American song tradition." He was given a special Pulitzer Prize in 2008 for "his profound impact on popular music and American culture, marked by lyrical

song *Stardust*. When he first heard the recording of his composition, Hoagie Carmichael said

"And then it happened. That queer sensation that this melody was bigger than me. Maybe I hadn't written it at all. The recollection of how, when and where and how it happened became vague. As the lingering streams hung in the rafters in the studio, I wanted to shout back at it 'Maybe I didn't write you. But I found you.'"[18]

Bob Dylan ends his account with agreement.

"I know just what he [Hoagie Carmichael] meant."

Innovation that is neither anticipated nor explainable by the creator of a computer program is required to pass the Lovelace test. Humans appear to pass the Lovelace test in both mathematics and music. Turing machines look to be incapable of passing the Lovelace test. Whether some other manmade machine can do so is still an open question.

8.2   ID & the Unknowable

The creativity of the human mind and the design seen in nature have something in common. Computers look as if they are incapable of displaying the creativity demanded by strong AI. And evolution can't be simulated on a computer so that new information is created. The computer only does what it is programmed to do. Attempts by Darwinian proponents to model unguided evolution in Avida, EV and Tierra have failed. Well-intentioned Tierra just didn't do what Darwinians thought it should do. Avida and EV work only because the programmers had a specific goal in mind and designed the programs to achieve the goal. In Chapter 6, we showed both Avida and EV were infused with active information that eventually guaranteed their success. And Basener's ceiling prohibits creativity in computer evolutionary models. An evolutionary program written to design an antenna will never develop the ability to play championship chess. A separate evolutionary program dedicated to chess would need to be written and the programmer would need to set the chess-playing performance goals.

---

compositions of extraordinary poetic power". In May 2012, Dylan received the Presidential Medal of Freedom from President Barack Obama. He received the Nobel Prize in Literature in 2016 for "for having created new poetic expressions within the great American song tradition".

8.2.1 *Darwinian evolutionary programs have failed the Lovelace test*

There are those, like Roger Penrose, who agree that the human mind is beyond the capability of the computer insofar as displaying strong AI, but believe a materialist solution exists. None has yet been found. If the mechanism driving the human mind is ever identified and reproduced by technology, the impact on mankind will be unimaginable. Another possibility is that the mechanism allowing creativity in the human mind exists but, like Chaitin's number, is unknowable.

In terms of computer modeling, the information product of evolution looks to be a subset of strong AI. Conservation of information does not allow the needed creativity for successful computer-modeled evolution. If this is true, then there will never be an algorithm to explain evolution without a guiding designer. All computers are Turing machines and Turing machines, by definition, are capable of executing algorithms. Could a non-algorithmic process behind evolution be unknowable?

8.3 Finis

This book started with a quotation from Gregory Chaitin.[j,19] We repeat it here:

> "The honor of mathematics requires us to come up with a mathematical theory of evolution and either prove that Darwin was wrong or right!" Gregory Chaitin

In this book, we have addressed Chaitin's challenge and have concluded mathematics shows that undirected Darwinism can't work. An intelligent designer is the most reasonable conclusion.

Thanks for listening.

Notes

1. D.E. Jelinski, "On the notions of mother nature and the balance of nature and their implications for conservation." In *Human Ecology* (Springer US, 2010), pp. 37–50.
2. S.W. Hawking and M. Jackson, *A Brief History of Time* (Bantam, 2008).

---

[j]Who, interestingly, in harmony with the topic this chapter, wrote a book titled *The Unknowable.*

3. Portions of this chapter were previously published in: Robert J. Marks II, "The Turing Test Is Dead. Long Live the Lovelace Test." *Evolution News & Views*, July 3, 2014 http://www.evolutionnews.org/2014/07/the_turing_test_1087411.html (URL date May 2, 2016).

4. A. Turing, "Computing machinery and intelligence." *Mind*, 59(236), 433460 (1950).

5. P. Gray, "Computer Scientist: Alan Turing." *Time Magazine* (March 29, 1999).

6. S. Bringsjord, P. Bello, and D. Ferrucci. "Creativity, the Turing Test, and the (better) Lovelace test." *Minds and Machines*, 11(3), pp. 3–27 (2001).

7. R. Descartes, *Discourse on Method and Meditations on First Philosophy* (Yale University Press, New Haven & London, 1996), p. 3435.

8. R. Penrose, *The Emperor's New Mind: Concerning Computers, Minds, and the Laws of Physics* (Oxford University Press, Oxford, 1999).
R. Penrose, *Shadows of the Mind* (Oxford University Press, Oxford, 1994).

9. S. Bringsjord, P. Bello, and D. Ferrucci, *op.cit*, p. 27.

10. W. Ewert, R.J. Marks II, B.B. Thompson and A. Yu, "Evolutionary inversion of swarm emergence using disjunctive combs control." *IEEE Transactions on Systems, Man & Cybernetics: Systems*, 43(5), pp. 1063–1076 (2013).
J. Roach, W. Ewert, R.J. Marks II, and B.B. Thompson, "Unexpected Emergent Behaviors From Elementary Swarms." *Proceedings of the 2013 IEEE 45th Southeastern Symposium on Systems Theory (SSST)*, Baylor University, pp. 41–50 (2013).

11. Russell D. Reed and R.J. Marks II, *Neural Smithing: Supervised Learning in Feedforward Artificial Neural Networks* (MIT Press, Cambridge, MA, 1999).

12. D.S. Robertson, "Algorithmic information theory, free will, and the Turing test." *Complexity*, 4(3), pp. 25–34 (1999).

13. J. Hadamard, *An Essay on the Psychology of Invention in the Mathematical Field* (Dover Publications, New York, 1954).

14. R. Penrose, *op.cit*.

15. United States Supreme Court, Cuno Engineering Corp. v. Automatic Devices Corp., 314 U.S. 84 (1941).

16. Yesterday: http://www.beatlesbible.com/songs/yesterday/ (URL date May 2, 2016).

17. C. Cross, *The Beatles: Day-by-Day, Song-by-Song, Record-by-Record* (Lincoln, NE: iUniverse, Inc. 2005).

18. B. Dylan on The Mystery of Creativity, YouTube, https://youtu.be/UpuQCK JIf0M (URL date May 2, 2016).

19. G.J. Chaitin, *The Unknowable* (Springer, 1999).

9

APPENDICES

9.1 Acronym List

AI   artificial intelligence
AIT   algorithmic information theory
ASC   algorithmic specified complexity
ASCII   American Standard Code for Information Interchange
COI   conservation of information
DNA   deoxyribonucleic acid
FOO   frequency of occurrence
FOOHOA   frequency of occurrence Hamming oracle algorithm
GB   gigabyte
GUI   graphical user interface
ID   intelligent design
IEEE   Institute of Electrical and Electronics Engineers
JPG   Joint Photographic Experts Group
KCS   Kolmogorov–Chaitin–Solomonov (complexity)
LMC   López–Ruiz, Mancini and Calbet (complexity)
NASA   National Aeronautics and Space Administration
NEC   Numerical Electromagnetics Code
NFLT   No Free Lunch Theorem
PNG   portable network graphics
PrOIR   (Bernoulli's) principle of insufficient reason
S4S   search for the search

SETI	Search for Terrestrial Intelligence
URL	Uniform Resource Locator
URL date	The latest date a web page was accessed
WD-40	water displacement, formulation successful in 40th attempt
XOR	exclusive or

9.2 Variables

Here are the math variables used in this monograph and the section they are first used. Usually, these variables are used in the sections marked with a dagger (†) can be skipped by those not wishing to dig into the math.

a	average	4.2.1
a	distance	4.2.1
α	real number	7.3.2
$\mathbf{A}$	pounds	5.2.2.1
A	algorithmic specified complexity	7.3
b	bet	4.1.2.2.1
b	distance	4.2.1
B	bits	2.2.1
BB	busy beaver number	6.3.3
$\mathbf{B}$	pounds	5.2.2.1
β	set	7.3.2.1
c	constant	2.2.1
C	context	7.3
d	distance	4.1.2.2.3
f	probability density function	4.1.2.2.3
F	fitness	6.2.6
G	number of logic gates	6.2.6
w	height	7.4.4.3.1
H	Shannon entropy	4.1.2.2.1
I	self information	2.2.2
I_ω	endogenous information	5.4.1
I_+	active information	5.4.2
$I_\oplus$	active information per query	5.4.2.2
$I_\boxplus$	active information per mean query	5.4.2.2

I_S	exogenous information	5.4.2
k	integer	5.6.2.2
K	KCS complexity	2.2.1
L	length of a phrase in characters	5.2.3
ℓ_p	length of a program p in bits	2.2.1.1
M	integer	4.1.2.2.3
μ	mean	4.2.1
n	integer	2.2.1
N	integer	2.2.1
N	number of characters in an alphabet	5.4.1
O	Big O notation	2.2.1
Ω	search space	5.4.1
Ω	Chaitin's constant	6.3.3
p	program index	2.2.1.1
p	probability	2.2.2
q	probability	5.4.2
p	program index	2.2.1.1
Q	number of queries	5.4.1
r	circle radius	4.2.1
π	pi $= 3.14159\ldots$	4.2.1
π	probability	5.8.3.3
S	winnings	4.1.2.2.1
T	target	5.4.1
$\mathbf{v}$	volume random variable	4.1.2.2.3
w	width	7.4.4.3.1
W	doubling rate parameter	4.1.2.2.1
X	string of characters, object	2.2.1
Y	string of characters, object	2.2.1

9.3 Notation

Here is a list of notation and the section in which it is first used.

$\lvert \cdot \rvert$	absolute value	2.2.1
$\lvert \cdot \rvert$	number of elements in a set	5.4.1
$\langle \cdot \rangle$	average	5.4.2.2.1
$\underset{c}{=}$	equality to within constant c	2.2.1

$\sum\limits_{p}$	sum over all p	2.2.1.1
$\vec{p}$	vector	4.1.2.2.1
$\oplus$	XOR operation	5.2.2.1
$\oplus$	single time step	7.4.4.2.1
$\downarrow$	shift down	7.4.4.2.2
$\rightarrow$	shift right	7.4.4.2.2

INDEX

A

abductive inference, 3
Abraham, 21–24
absorbing states, 93
aby, 260
academia, 230
ACLU, 206
ACS, 255
active information, 1–2, 31, 42–43, 47,
  49–50, 55–56, 72, 76–77, 86, 91, 100,
  117, 120, 125, 130–150, 154–157,
  163–164, 166, 171–174, 176, 178, 181,
  184, 188, 190, 192, 195, 197–198,
  202–203, 209, 211, 217, 219–221,
  226–227, 229–230, 232, 235–236,
  241–243, 248–250, 252, 287, 292
active set method, 58
adaptive coordinate descent, 58
adit, 260
algorithmic information theory (*see also*
  AIT), 18, 105, 231, 281, 285, 289, 291
algorithmic specified complexity (*see also*
  ASC), 9, 18, 251, 255–258, 260–265,
  269, 274–279, 291–292
alpha–beta pruning, 58
alphanumeric, 252, 257
alternating projections onto convex sets,
  58
ant colony optimization, 58
antenna, 31–32, 43–45, 48, 60, 94, 135,
  145, 287

B

anthropic principle, 171, 181
antibiotics, 3
appendix, 52
Aristotle, 68–69
armadillo, 48
artificial immune system optimization, 58
artificial intelligence (*see also* AI), 62,
  109, 117, 121, 245, 281–282, 291
artificial life, 96–98, 102, 244–248
ASCII, 258–261, 291
ash objects, 269, 277, 279
atheism, 282
auction algorithm, 58
average, 4, 23, 74, 76, 88–91, 107–109,
  112, 120–123, 136–137, 147, 150–155,
  161, 172, 177, 180, 198–199, 243, 254,
  258, 292–293
Avida, 95–96, 100, 155, 160, 205–207,
  209, 212–225, 227, 229–231, 241,
  243–248, 287

backgammon, 167, 186
Barricelli, Nils, 4
Basener, 94, 102
Basener ceiling, 93, 95, 97–100, 230, 282
Basener, William F., 94
basketball, 112–118
Beck, William S., 187
beehive, 266, 272

295

Printed in the United States
By Bookmasters